The Climber's Sourcebook

STEVEN SCHNEIDER organized and taught the first rock-climbing and winter mountaineering courses even to be offered for academic credit by an eastern United States college. The innovator of several new rock and ice routes in New Hampshire, he has climbed in the Cascade and Olympic ranges of the Pacific Northwest, the Rockies, as well as in his native White Mountains. His articles about technical climbing have appeared in *Climbing, Summit,* and *Viva* magazines. He is a member of the Appalachian Mountain Club.

A former editor and book reviewer, ANNE SCHNEIDER has written articles appearing in a number of publications, including *New York* magazine, *Viva,* and *New Times.* She is currently Vice President for Planning of North Country Mountaineering, Inc., which she founded with her brother, Steve, and is at work on a novel.

The Climber's Sourcebook

ANNE SCHNEIDER and
STEVEN SCHNEIDER

ANCHOR BOOKS

Anchor Press / Doubleday

Garden City, New York   1976

This book is dedicated to our
mother and father
and to Jack Handy,
who introduced us to mountaineering

The Anchor Books edition is the first publication of
THE CLIMBER'S SOURCEBOOK

Anchor Books edition: 1976

ISBN: 0-385-11081-2
Library of Congress Catalog Card Number 75–21251

Acknowledgments

We are very grateful to the following individuals for their co-operation and encouragement: our literary agent, Elaine Markson; our editor, William B. Strachan; Tim Arnstein, Precise Imports Corporation; Leonard Bauly, Freeze-Dry Foods, Ltd.; Ethan Becker, Colorado Mountain Industries; James F. Booker, E. I. Dupont Company, Philadelphia; Jeffrey Burns; Donna M. Coutu; Steve Ditlea; the staff of the Ellenville Public Library, Ellenville, New York; Chris Ellms; Randy Gainor, for compass field testing; Sarah Gallick; George A. Harris, the Silva Company; Donna Johnson; Martin M. Josephson, M.D.; Larry Horton, Rivendell Mountain Works; Mrs. Mollie Klaf; Cathy Lazaroff, Coming Attractions; Ed Leeper, Leeper Products; Helmut Lenes, Climb High, Inc.; Harmon L. Liebman, Speedy Chef Foods, Inc.; the Lowe Brothers, Lowe Alpine Systems; John R. MacDonald, Blacks Equipment; Olle Mellin, Optimus International; Bill Nichols, Stod-Nichols, Inc.; Peter Occhiogrosso; Cole Patterson, Chase Manhattan Capital Corporation; Barbara Jo Prater, Sherpa Designs, Inc.; Hal Schneider; H. G. Snowbridge, Hines-Snowbridge; Rheua S. Stakely, the Phillips Exeter Academy; Lorenzo Stein; Ed Webster; Howard P. Widmann, Primus-Sievert; Bob Williams, Frostline Kits; Robert K. Wright, Kalmar Trading Corporation; Sue Ellen York, Village Yentas; Snow; and the Summit Artichokes Steering Committee.

Special thanks are due to Frank Sweetser for providing us with the line drawings which appear throughout the book.

Contents

Introduction

Interest in technical (roped) climbing has been growing steadily over the forty-seven years since Robert Underhill introduced European belaying techniques, rappelling methods, the use of runners, and original protection priorities to this country ("Roping Down," *Appalachia* magazine, Vol. XVII, 1928). But until *Life* magazine featured its color spread on Warren Harding's twenty-eight-day ordeal on the Wall of the Morning Light, climbing remained the sport of a few; to a great extent, mountaineering ran in families, passed on from generation to generation like hemophilia.

Technical mountaineering equipment was always hard to obtain in this country: As recently as 1957, Warren Harding, Bill Dolt, and Mark Powell were using cutoff stove legs as pitons during their ascent of El Capitan in Yosemite National Park. Yvon Chouinard's mass-produced Lost Arrow piton (a copy, with his permission, of John Salathe's custom piton), one of the most important equipment advances of the past twenty years, wasn't even being manufactured until 1958—and other influential Chouinard, Forrest Mountaineering, and CMI hardware was almost impossible to find in many states, particularly in the East, before 1962. By 1965, however, climbing equipment distributors were merchandising domestic and imported hardware and UIAA-approved imported ropes across the country—and the combination of media attention and equipment accessibility melded to cause this past decade's unprecedented technical climbing boom.

No one knows for sure how many people in this country climb. Our own estimate is that up to half a million people now filter into the mountains and onto crags with some regularity—an appalling number, really, when so much of the satisfaction of climbing is the sense of suspension in time in the natural world with just a small group of friends.

For better or for worse (better for the people whose lives climbing will now enrich; worse for veteran climbers who wish they could keep the wilderness for their own enjoyment), and whatever the causes, more people are climbing now than ever before. Equipment companies and retail stores carrying technical gear abound. Climbing schools and guide services proliferate. Camps, prep schools, and colleges offer technical climbing instruction and excursions to the lands of mountaineers' dreams: Nepal, New Zealand, Patagonia, the Mountains of the Moon. A world of services has grown too: In New Mexico, a young woman customcrafts gaiters; in Seattle, another woman constructs down clothing for mountaineers too large or too small to comfortably wear standard sizes; in Arizona, a young man will perform droop modifications on a favorite ice tool.

For years we have been rather fanatically collecting drawers full of miscellaneous information about climbing-related services: the best sources of antique mountaineering books; the names of climbing cobblers who can successfully recondition even lightweight climbing boots; clubs where instruction in ice climbing, for example, is better, and less expensive, than much private instruction. Each of us has also, over the past few years, found himself or herself in strange cities or towns—and in need of a few hours of bouldering, or longing for some climbing talk; for those other climbers who travel, as well as for ourselves, we've compiled a state-by-state guide to climbing equipment retail stores. Where there's a climbing store, of course, there's rock or ice nearby, and at least a few friendly people.

When we decided to update and compile our drawers and cardboard boxes full of information into THE CLIMBER'S SOURCEBOOK we faced a peculiar moral decision. In making such information readily available, we had to consider the possibility that we might in some way be responsible for a further increase in the use of sometimes already overburdened climbing areas. But we felt compelled to continue: We've both seen young climbers showing up at cliffs totally unprepared in any way for what lies before them—and hit-or-miss methods of learning to climb can be dangerous to all of us. The problem, as we see it, is that whether we or other climbers like it or not, every temperate weekend brings more novices into our country's woodlands and onto this nation's rock. Our duty—and the duty of every other climber—must be to see that these novices receive the best instruction possible, that they use the safest equipment available, and that through peer group pressure and education they are made aware that they must not damage the rock, or leave behind them an ugly trail of beer can rings, cigarette filters, and foil packages from dehydrated foods.

We sincerely hope that other climbers—novices and hard men or women alike—will find THE CLIMBER's SOURCEBOOK a valuable reference tool. We would be delighted to receive any additional information we may inadvertently have omitted.

PART I

Where to Learn to Climb

CHAPTER 1

Climbing Schools and Guide Services

There's a good deal of mixed feeling among American climbers about the value and efficacy of climbing schools. The most commonly voiced objections are that climbing schools are too expensive —and that most prominent American climbers have never received formal instruction. It seems to us that under certain circumstances attendance at a good climbing school can be extremely beneficial for those who can afford it. Novices who have no competent climber-acquaintances willing to work with them owe it to themselves to at least learn the basics through a reputable instructor or guide. More accomplished climbers who would like to learn, for example, aid methods, can only benefit from a day spent climbing under the supervision of an expert; the occasional inadvertent error in technique an expert can point out may mean the difference between successful, pleasurable climbing and disaster. For climbers who have achieved proficiency in rock-climbing techniques but who have had no experience of roped glacier travel or ice climbing, competent instruction can be a blessing. Supervised belaying practice is recommended for everyone. What the novice climber must guard against is the overconfidence that may result from being called an "advanced intermediate" climber after, say, three or four days of instruction. A beginning climber is a beginning climber; keep in mind that mountaineering expertise is gained over a period of years through varied experience—beware of implied promises of "instant" or near-instant "expertise."

If money is a problem (as it well may be, considering the cost these days of even basic mountaineering equipment), there are still inexpensive places where one can learn to climb under expert supervision. Several of the climbing schools listed in this section are quite reasonably priced—some as low as fifteen dollars a day for group instruction. The instruction offered by the clubs included in this chapter is either free, or very reasonably priced. More clubs are listed in Chapter 2, almost all of which offer some climbing instruction at nominal cost, usually to club members or aspirant members. College outing clubs often feature climbing instruction, usually for no cost at all; if you are not a student but live in a community near one of the college outing clubs listed in Chapter 2, you might check to see if activities are open to area residents; if not, chances are there's a competent student climber willing to work with area residents for a reasonable fee.

In cases where we feel a climbing school has misrepresented what it offers, we have indicated as much under its listing. If you should be dissatisfied with services offered by one of the schools or guide services listed on the following pages, please let us know the circumstances; no climber can afford the luxury of perpetuating incompetence.

Course offerings on the following pages are quite fully detailed. Because prices keep rising, we have not listed exact prices, but in most cases give some indication of whether or not we thought prices were fair. For exact current course costs, write or call the schools and guide services listed.

CLIMBING SCHOOLS

ARIZONA

ARIZONA MOUNTAINEERING CLUB
c/o Bob Coraf
8418 East Roanoke Avenue
Scottsdale, Arizona 85257
    Offers courses in climbing.

CALIFORNIA

MOUNTAIN AFFAIR MOUNTAINEERING SCHOOL
Idyllwild Mountaineering Institute
54414 North Circle Drive
P. O. Box 369
Idyllwild, California 92349
Classes held at 10,840-foot Mount San Jacinto.

Ice Climbing—Weekends only, dependent upon ice conditions. Emphasizes technique development using latest gear: alpine hammer, ice axe, drooped pick, climax, teradactyl, twelve-point crampons, and placement of ice screws and wart hogs while on sixty-degree hard-water ice and verglas. German and French techniques taught. Moderately expensive day rate but includes equipment.

Basic Mountaineering—Six days with evening seminar instruction. Choice of six consecutive days or three weekends. Includes rock climbing and snow and ice climbing through intermediate level, snow camping, light impact wilderness travel; snowshoeing, mountain first aid, map and compass and avalanche theory and rescue. Write for yearly schedule. Course finishes with a winter ascent of Mount San Jacinto. Moderate price considering fee includes lodging and trail food.

Rock Climbing—Offered daily at reasonable price. Private instruction available.

Basic Course—Four to six hours of knot tying, belaying, rappelling, and equipment familiarization. Techniques learned during short climbs.

Intermediate Course—Four to six hours. Reinforcement of basic technique, clean climbing techniques, and an introduction to lead climbing.

Advanced Course—Big Wall technique, direct aid, severe face and fissure climbing, and rescue. Limited to three people; five to seven hours. Content of this class is flexible according to needs of climbers in group.

Advanced Free Climbing and Aid Climbing Classes—available upon request. One instructor per student.

MOUNTAIN CRAFT
P. O. Box 622
Davis, California 95616
916-758-4315; 753-7323

Mountain Craft is a year-round mountaineering school, with a young, vigorous faculty well versed in climbing, backpacking, and wilderness preservation. Guide service available to groups planning trips. Ski touring and snow camping multiday sessions are available.

Rock Climbing—Limited to four students per instructor. One-day classes in Sierra Nevadas including basic rock-climbing skills, belaying, rappelling, rope handling, protection, and leading. Classes scheduled January to March in winter. Write for complete schedule during remainder of year.

Snow- and Ice-climbing classes—By arrangement
Mountain First Aid—By arrangement
Compass Navigation—By arrangement
Mountain Leadership—By arrangement
Avalanche Hazards and Precautions—By arrangement

Mountain Craft is also interested in voluntary programs to provide outdoor opportunities for those who otherwise would not have the chance. They may soon be incorporated as a nonprofit corporation to further work on those projects. Leaders of inner-city programs wishing to introduce their charges to wilderness activities might do well to contact the school.

MOUNT WHITNEY GUIDE SERVICE AND SIERRA NEVADA SCHOOL OF
MOUNTAINEERING
P. O. Box 659
Lone Pine, California 93545

Located at eight thousand feet in the Whitney Portals of California's Inyo National Forest. Traditionally stable weather.

The school offers six climbing course options. Usually, two days of the five-day seminars and the first day of the three-day seminars are spent in practice climbing and other activities near the school's camp in order to provide some acclimatization to the altitude. A moderate climb to about twelve thousand feet is usually possible by the third day. The seminars include a summit climb and an open bivouac.

These seminars are held through the summer months; individual and group instruction available throughout the year.

East Face Seminar—Three days. Limited to six students. Designed for the serious intermediate climber who is in excellent physical condition and has a basic understanding of roped climbing technique. Difficulty is in the altitude rather than the routes. Belays, route finding, energy conservation, knots and rope handling, protection placement and removal, bivouac. Fifth class ascent of East Face of Mount Whitney.

East Face Seminar—Five days. Limited to six students. Same techniques and game plan as above, plus simulated leading experiences, introduction to direct aid techniques. Day climb on Thor Peak via fourth-class route. Descent via Pinnacle Pass rappel.

Peak Bagging Seminars—Three- and five-day sessions; third day in the McArdie region (eight major summits in the immediate area). Good geographic and topographic introduction to the Southern Sierra Nevadas. Includes instruction/review of basic techniques, second, third, and fourth class climbing on Thor Peak. Fourth day, Lone Pine Peak. Eleven-thousand-foot bivouac. Mount Irvine and Mount Mallory and possibly Mount LeConte.

General Mountaineering Seminars—Three- and five-day periods. Rope work, knots, belaying, rappelling, fifth class orientation, route finding, map reading, natural history. Third day, ascent of Thor Peak. Fourth day, start on approach to Whitney or other major summit. Open bivouac at about twelve thousand feet. Completion of climb of major summit.

Scoutmasters are invited to attend the seminars with their groups at no charge (one leader per seminar).

Mount Whitney Guide Service—Offers mountain leadership on classic and new routes on peaks throughout the Sierra Nevadas. Guide service operates throughout the year. Best snow-climbing conditions between March and May.

PALISADE SCHOOL OF MOUNTAINEERING
1398 Solano Avenue
Albany, California 94706
415-527-8100

Palisade School of Mountaineering is the oldest mountaineering school in California and still one of the best. The student/guide ratio for beginners is three to one, and in the advanced and snow and ice courses the ratio is two to one. Lower age limit is twelve; people under sixteen must be accompanied by parent. Courses are a full week, usually June through August, meals are provided, and their instructors are absolutely first-rate.

ROCKCRAFT
609 Durant Street
Modesto, California 95350
209-529-6913
Chief instructors: Royal Robbins and Dick Erb

Rockcraft is an immensely popular school—probably because its director, Royal Robbins, is one of this country's most innovative, accomplished, and well-known Big Wall climbers. Robbins' books, *Basic Rockcraft* and *Advanced Rockcraft,* are basic reading for any climber—and particularly important for novice climbers. The school has been in operation since 1969, and the ratio of students returning for further instruction is very high (in 1973, one third of the student body consisted of satisfied former Rockcrafters seeking more advanced instruction). Mornings are usually spent in instruction, afternoons in supervised climbing. On the fifth day, a longer route is undertaken. Climbing headquarters are based in a granite area of the Central Sierras called "The Hinterlands"—an area relatively free from crowds. Sessions run from June to August, five days each, and are quite reasonably priced.

Basic Course—An introduction to climbing "from A to M," conducted by top-notch climbers. Rockcraft is really a school for more advanced climbers, but a basic course taught by experts doesn't harm anyone. Minimum age is a mature thirteen.

Intermediate Course—Offers review of basics, paralleling Robbins' two books. Some aid climbing, some Big Wall techniques if time permits.

Free Climbing—Survey of all free techniques. Special emphasis on chocks, leading, minimum-impact climbing, and on elements of safety.

Students provide their own food, except on first night. Rockcraft supplies technical climbing equipment.

THE SIERRA CLUB
Rock-climbing Section, San Francisco Chapter
c/o Vern Muhr, Chairman
6500 Tremont Street
Oakland, California 94609

Sunday climbing instruction available to Sierra Club members at such convenient locations as Cragmont Rock, Grizzly Caves, Indian Rock, Miraloma, and Pinnacle Rock. The Rock-climbing Section also sponsors out-of-area trips and other climbs.

YOSEMITE MOUNTAINEERING
Yosemite, California 95389
209-372-4611, ext. 244, May 1–June 13; September 10–September 29
209-372-4505, June 15–September 8
Minimum age for climbing courses: fourteen

Yosemite Mountaineering is one of the most venerable climbing schools in the United States. Fees are reasonable. Private instruction is available, but at approximately 3½ times the cost of group instruction.

Basic Rock Climbing—Entire day spent on the rock, learning about equipment, correct use of hand- and footholds, belays, rappels. Climbs are of moderate rock up to eighty feet high.

Intermediate Rock Climbing I—Use of nuts, runners, pitons, anchoring, aimed belays, harder climbs, friction brake rappels on vertical and overhanging rock. The "Yosemite Method" taught. Classes are small, climb and rappel pitches up to 150 feet. Strong individuals may follow variations of up to 5.8 in difficulty.

Intermediate Rock Climbing II—More emphasis on party climbing, establishing belay stances, occasional aid-pin use.

Advanced Rock Climbing—Specific instruction in special techniques. Two to four students maximum. Possibilities: Big Wall technique, crack and chimney climbing, face climbing, mountain rescue, direct aid. An intensive, strenuous course. Half day.

Summer Snow and Ice Climbing—Introduction to route selection, use of ice axes and crampons, glacier walking, step kicking, step cutting, belays, self-arrest, glissading. Other techniques depending on snow conditions. Prerequisite: *Basic Rock Climbing*. Strenuous two-to-three-mile approach to the Dana or Conness Glaciers; full day's climbing at twelve thousand feet.

Guided Climbs—Available daily, by arrangement. Guide fees vary.

Cathedral Peak Climb—Moderate climb, including almost vertical final pinnacle. *Basic Rock Climbing* and good physical condition needed. Most classic of Tuolumne peaks.

Special Programs—Guides, seminars, or programs in anything from mountain rescue to leadership of Andean expeditions. For individuals and organizations.

Special Seminars

Full Alpencraft Seminar—Seven consecutive days. Includes *Alpine Survival, Basic Rock Climbing, Intermediate Rock Climbing, Snow and Ice Climbing,* and a final guided climb.

Short Alpencraft Seminar—Five days. Same as above, without the two days of *Alpine Survival* training. In both the above courses, *Advanced Free Climbing* may be substituted for *Snow and Ice.*

Advanced Free-climbing Seminar—Three five-day seminars each summer. Up to four people per seminar. Climbs in 5.7 to 5.9 range, with qualified climbers going higher. Prerequisite: ability to follow 5.6 without difficulty.

Direct-aid Seminar—Two days. Emphasis on chocks, hooks, other nondestructive placements; Jumaring at various angles, hauling techniques, hanging belays and bivouacs, pendulum. Moderately expensive but worth it.

From May 1 to June 13 and from September 10 to September 29, all climbs are in Yosemite Valley; from June 15 to September 8, all climbs are in Tuolumne Meadows.

They also feature ski touring programs.

COLORADO

HARVEY T. CARTER CLIMBING SCHOOL
Box 962
Aspen, Colorado 81611
303-925-3798

Extremely reasonable prices for rock-climbing and ice-climbing instruction. They recommend no more than two people per instructor (and they're right) but they'll take out as many as four new climbers

The Garden of the Gods. Lower finger traverse. *Photo by Ed Webster.*

at a time if coerced; the latter arrangement would bring the cost per person below even Georgia or Buffalo, New York, prices. A good long day of instruction.

Also arranged, guided climbs in the wilderness high country around Aspen. Also, reasonably priced guide service and/or instruction for large groups with rope leaders.

Reservations requested one month in advance.

BOB CULP CLIMBING SCHOOL
1329 Broadway
Boulder, Colorado 80302

The Bob Culp School does not believe in teaching rock climbing to groups. All lessons are private or semiprivate. Lessons at the Basic

Rock School are six days, four hours each day; two lessons per day can be scheduled, but they prefer the former arrangement. Reservations should be made at least two weeks in advance. Semiprivate lessons (two student climbers) are moderately priced, and private lessons are about ten dollars more per day.

Basic Rock School

Lesson I—Knots, rope handling, belaying, equipment, climbing safety, basic free-climbing techniques. Introductory climb.

Lesson II—The Rappel—Emphasis on safety, standard methods of rappelling on rocks ranging from slabs to overhangs, learning to set up the rappel, and anchor placement. Prusiking.

Lesson III—Belaying the Leader—Practice leader belays in realistic climbing situations. Student sets up belays and places own anchors. Free-climbing practice.

Lesson IV—Leading the Rope—Techniques of leading. Sling and nut placement for leader protection. Use of pitons demonstrated, but emphasis is on clean climbing.

Lesson V—Introduction to Direct Aid—Use of étriers and nuts. Student encouraged to lead but not compelled. Ethics of the use of bolts.

Lesson VI—Continuous Climb—By this point, students should be able to climb on their own.

Big Wall School—Techniques commonly employed on multiday rock climbs. An advanced course. Limited to one or two students as desired. "Fixed" pitons used during these climbs to avoid rock damage; piton placement practiced on other rocks selected for that purpose. Three four-hour lessons.

Lesson I—Advanced Direct Aid—Techniques for difficult artificial climbing. Placement of rurps, knife blades, bongs. Use of sophisticated nut placement. Demonstration of "gadgets" such as cliff hangers. Seconding with Jumars. Difficult artificial climb.

Lesson II—Big Wall Techniques—Equipment hauling, hanging belays, hammock bivouacs, etc. An introduction to the full range of modern climbing devices, with opportunity to use them.

Lesson III—Graduation Climb—Relatively long artificial and free route approximating environment of multiday climb. Full complement of hardware and bivouac equipment hauled. Emphasis on good style.

COLORADO MOUNTAIN SCHOOL
2402 Dotsero Avenue
Loveland, Colorado 80537
303-667-8840

Comprehensive wilderness experience for men, women, and children. Low student/instructor ratio. Program conducted in Colorado's Front Range.

One-week Mountaineering Seminar—Pack into base camp. Instruction includes rock climbing, snow and ice climbing, first aid, route finding, backpacking skills, equipment selection and use, and summit climbing. Backpacks and sleeping bags no longer available for rental. Slight discount if you register before June 1. Seminars usually held between July and August, but schedule varies each year.

Special Mountaineering Seminar—Same as above, but conducted for at least two students unable to meet at regularly scheduled times. Extra charge for these special arrangements.

Special Programs—Group rates available. Programs designed to fit special needs of a particular group.

FANTASY RIDGE SCHOOL OF ALPINISM
Box 2106
Estes Park, Colorado 80517
303-586-5758; 586-5391
Director: Michael Covington

The same people who teach and guide the advanced courses also handle the basic and intermediate courses. Low student/instructor ratio. Recent instructors have included such top-flight climbers as Jim Bridwell (Yosemite). Courses are held at Rocky Mountain National Park's Lumpy Ridge—an excellent practice area for beginners, with plenty of hand- and footholds and rock similar to that of Yosemite granite, only less glaciated. More advanced courses held at higher mountains in immediate vicinity (summits between 11,000 and 14,255 feet, with climbs varying in length from 300 to 2,000 vertical feet on rock composed of both granite schist and gneiss).

Favorable rock-climbing conditions in the area usually exist from about mid-April through November. Frequent afternoon showers, spring through mid-July. Nicest weather usually mid-July through

August. September and October offer extended periods of good weather and fewer tourists in the area. Fall is the best season for ice climbing as the snow fields turn to ice. There are live glaciers in the park, but no crevasses.

Daily courses are available seven days a week, with the exception of the *Snow and Ice School,* which is available every Tuesday, Thursday, and Saturday, June through September. The Mountaineering and Rock-climbing Program is also available October through May with one week's prior notice.

Fantasy Ridge will also arrange guided climbs for individuals with previous experience. Examples of possible guided climbs: East Face of Longs Peak, Spearhead, Sharkstooth, Notchtop, South Face of the Petit Grepon, North East Face of Hallets Peak. Rates are determined by difficulty of route and number of people in party.

Basic Mountaineering—Student/instructor ratio is four to one. Knots, anchoring, belaying, basic free-climbing techniques, rappelling. Discussion of historical and sporting aspects of climbing. Good as brush-up course or for beginning climbers. Cost is quite nominal.

Intermediate Rock I—Review of basics. Running belay, emphasis on free-climbing techniques on a variety of problems up to 5.6. Four-to-one student/instructor ratio. Slightly more expensive than basic course.

Intermediate Rock II—Variety of face- and crack-climbing problems from 5.7 to 5.9. Oriented almost entirely toward free-climbing techniques. Prusiking with knots and slings. Check of protection placement and removal techniques. Includes climb on Twin Owls. Student/instructor ratio is three to one.

Day of Crack Climbing; Day of Slab Climbing—Both courses for those seriously interested in developing good free-climbing techniques. Each is a full day of continuous climbing, setting up belays, placing and removing protection. Both courses available at Intermediate I or II level. Student/instructor ratio is two to one. Moderately expensive.

Advanced Fantasies for Nuts Only—Free-climbing, clean-climbing course. Student experiences supervised leading. Student/instructor ratio is two to one. Near the end of the day, instructor leads difficult climb, but course is available at all levels of experience.

Basic Direct Aid—Learning to move in stirrups, clipping in and out of protection, hanging belays, basic piton use and misuse, advanced chock theory, setting up rappels while hanging at end of rope. For those interested in mixed free and aid climbing or Big Wall techniques. Student/instructor ratio is two to one.

Big Wall Logistics—Follow-up course to *Basic Direct Aid*. Planning and preparation for Big Wall climbs. Packing and hauling a haulbag, Jumar uses, pendulums, tension traversing, setting up hanging bivouacs, advanced piton placement. Student/instructor ratio is two to one. Both of above courses moderately expensive, but not unreasonable.

Basic Snow and Ice School—Crampon and ice axe use and care, knots, belaying, anchoring, rappelling, glissading, and self-arrest. Demonstration of crevasse rescue. Involves about three to five miles of approach march. Student/instructor ratio variable to a maximum of five to one; the more students, the cheaper the course. Cost includes use of ice axe and crampons.

Private Instruction—Rather expensive, but private instruction is costly these days. Your own potential safety is involved, so if you can afford private lessons, the difference in cost seems worth it. Semiprivate lessons also available, as are family and group rates.

Seminars—Five days each, held June to September. Price includes guide, food, and technical equipment.

The Mountain Seminar—For those with little or no mountain experience. Includes variety of mountaineering and rock-climbing techniques, including some snow and ice climbing.

Rock Seminar—For climbers with previous experience of knots, belaying, anchoring, and free climbing of at least 5.5. Instruction from intermediate level through advanced levels. May include Big Wall techniques for those interested.

Fantasy Ridge Seminar—Helpful in developing climbers' leadership abilities. Guided climbs may range from mountaineering and rock-climbing problems in high mountains to more sustained rock climbs on Lumpy Ridge. Limited to six participants; three to one student/instructor ratio.

THE FORWARD SCHOOL OF MOUNTAINEERING
1432 Tweed Street
Colorado Springs, Colorado 80909
303-635-4421
Director: Lester Guidry

Our inquiry to the Forward School went unanswered, but the

school has been recommended with great enthusiasm by the moderator of the nearby Abbey School Alpine Club.

INSTITUTE OF MOUNTAIN EDUCATION
P. O. Box 336
Eldorado Springs, Colorado 80025
303-499-1164
Directors: Hunter Smith and Robert Dugan

The institute sponsors a variety of three-week climbing instruction trips, listed separately in Part I, Chapter 6. They also offer consulting services to schools or organizations interested in expanding or creating their own outdoor programs. Seminars and brief wilderness or mountain excursions can also be arranged for groups and organizations.

Eastern Rock-Climbing Course—A seven-day program, at a very reasonable price, designed for beginning and intermediate climbers. Minimum age is sixteen. Base camp is at Eldorado Canyon. Morning seminars are spent learning rope handling, knots, rappelling, belaying, holds and style, "clean" protection, lead climbing, rescue, and climbing safety. Afternoons are spent on the rock. All food, tents, and technical equipment provided by IME; boots and sleeping bags must be provided by students. This is one of the few climbing schools to feature women climbers in their literature, and the Institute takes pains to emphasize that female climbing students are welcome and encouraged. The institute may be expanding its winter programs, so write for current details.

OUTDOOR LEADERSHIP TRAINING SEMINARS
2200 Birch Street
Denver, Colorado 80207
Program Director: Rick Medrick

Sponsors of winter touring and ski mountaineering courses. Course length is seven days, with base camp in the Wet Mountains near Westcliffe. Each program is modified to meet the needs of individuals and groups involved, but usually covers basic instruction in winter equipment use, waxing, touring techniques, campcraft, map and compass use, knots and rope handling, rock climbing, rappelling, winter safety, and survival. Food and camping equipment excluding

The Grand Giraffe, popular 5.9 route in Eldorado Springs Canyon. *Photo by Ed Webster.*

personal gear provided. Participants must provide their own touring skis, boots, and poles. Sessions meet, usually, December through April, and are divided into separate sections dubbed "Winter Mountaineering Seminar," "Ski Touring Seminar and Clinic," and "Ski Mountaineering Seminar." These courses seem more a pleasant vacation undertaking than a serious ski mountaineering course for someone interested in traveling to and from climbs over crevassed glaciers where roped skiing may be a necessity. Not to be confused with the National Outdoor Leadership School.

DISTRICT OF COLUMBIA

POTOMAC VALLEY CLIMBING SCHOOL, INC.
P. O. Box 5622
Washington, D.C. 20016
202-333-3398
Director: Bob Norris

This school offers one-day climbing courses throughout the year. Arrangements made for midweek classes. Moderate cost includes ten-thousand-dollar insurance coverage for those participating in the class. All equipment is provided, with the exception of rock shoes and boots and crampons for the *Ice-climbing Class.*

Basic Climbing Class—A one-day course beginning at 10 A.M., ending at 5 P.M., for those who have never climbed or those wishing to review fundamentals. Includes rope management, belays, knots, use and care of equipment, climbing safety, rappelling, and basic free-climbing dynamics.

Intermediate Class—Piton and artificial chock-stone placements, use of runners, setting up anchors for belays and rappels, and discussion of good climbing judgment.

Advanced Climbing—Emphasis on theory and practice of climbing dynamics. Includes fundamentals of artificial climbing techniques.

Direct-aid Climbing—Includes hanging belays, pendulums, Jumaring, hauling, advanced piton placements, hook moves, and bolts—their use and misuse. Class size limited to two students. Emphasis on developing mental attitude for safer climbing with safety procedures unique to artificial climbing.

Ice-climbing Class—Step cutting, French and German techniques,

Scarecrow, very popular 5.9 at The Garden of the Gods, Colorado. *Photo by Ed Webster.*

placement and removal of ice screws and pitons, ice-climbing safety, and use and care of ice-climbing equipment.

GEORGIA

TOO DISTANT HORIZON CLIMBING SCHOOL
3401 Valley View Drive
Morietia, Georgia 33006
Director: Denny Mays

Beginners' One-day Course—Ground instruction includes explanation of gear and its uses, knot tying, instruction in belaying. A 250-foot climb of medium difficulty, stressing importance of proper belaying, rope management, and chock placement. Bouldering (hard rock moves close to the ground), and one or two short 120-foot climbs using techniques learned at the boulder. Finish day with rappel.

Day starts at 8 A.M. and generally ends between 6 and 8 P.M. The school provides all equipment except shoes. Students provide lunch. Maximum of two students per guide. Inexpensive.

WOLFCREEK WILDERNESS
P. O. Box 596
Blairsville, Georgia 30512
404-745-6460
Director: Keith W. Evans

Wolfcreek Wilderness is a nonprofit educational organization, open to both individuals and groups. Its Director, Keith W. Evans, has been business manager, logistic co-ordinator, and instructor for the North Carolina Outward Bound School. He helped organize the first cave rescue network in the East, and has worked for the Cave Research Foundation. He was also the organizer of the Mountain Rescue Network, and currently serves as its chairman.

The school sponsors numerous workshops in canoeing, caving, and back-country travel, as well as mountaineering, and to the best of our knowledge is the only organization in the Southeast sponsoring programs of this scope. Their outdoor programs as a means of character building owe an obvious conceptual debt to Outward Bound, but while many schools have hopped on the survival-training-as-character-building bandwagon, Wolfcreek Wilderness seems heads above the local competition in the quality of its leadership, seriousness of intent, and excellence of facilities and guidance provided. They provide scholarship aid to qualified individuals, and offer special group rates where warranted. They appear to be very sophisticated about group dynamics.

Consultant Services—Wolfcreek Wilderness will provide a home base and staff members (called "facilitators") to supply logistical backup (food, transportation, etc.) and to work out appropriate routes and programs for schools wishing to enhance or complement existing academic programs with a period of wilderness activity-oriented seminars "in the field." Their group interaction and rope courses have been successfully integrated into physical education programs, summer camp programs, and mental health therapy. The school plant itself is also available as a demonstration facility prior to construction at other sites.

Located on 50 acres of woodlands in northern Georgia, basic accommodations are available at the school. An extensive outdoor library is maintained for use by participants. Group sites are limited, and there are no age restrictions.

The school holds an Open House at Wolf Creek Lodge on several dates from October through March. Inquiries about Open House are invited.

Mountaineering Rockcraft—Weekend rockcraft courses are held through the early fall. Courses limited to six students. Basic climbing skills are taught; most importantly, an integrated approach to rock climbing as an aspect of mountaineering is stressed.

Individual Instruction—Available upon completion of usual fall-to-winter schedule. Courses conducted in western North Carolina on a one-to-one or two-to-one student/instructor basis, with classes tailored to interests and abilities of students.

Rockclimbing Emergency Seminars, Wilderness Leadership Seminars, and Wilderness Emergency Medical Aid Seminars are also available.

IDAHO

EE-DA-HOW MOUNTAINEERING AND GUIDE SERVICE
P. O. Box 207
Ucon, Idaho 83454
208-523-9276
Director: Lyman C. Dye

One-day courses held in the Stanley area Monday through Saturday, June through August.

Basic Mountain Climbing—Mountain pace, knots, friction climbing, balance, belaying, and rappelling. Quite expensive.

Intermediate Climbing—Piton-craft, difficult terrain, boulder hopping, holds, belay, and rappel technology.

Advanced Climbing—By arrangement only. Direct aid, expedition planning, and leadership.

One-day basic and intermediate rock courses are also held in the Idaho Falls area on Saturdays during May and June. Minimum of three students.

Twenty-one-day Mountain Leadership Course—Usually, three sessions between June and August. A fairly undemanding course lacking in depth, at least on the evidence of information supplied by Mr. Dye. Includes instruction in snow and rock climbing, conservation, compass and map reading, equipment, expedition planning, and weather. Their statement "We do not claim we can make our students expert in all of these areas in this length of time, but we can produce safe and capable leaders" seems to us questionable; there are no safe "90-day wonders" in mountaineering.

SAWTOOTH MOUNTAINEERING, INC.
5200 Fairview Avenue Mini Mall
Boise, Idaho 83704
208-376-3731
Director: Louis A. Florence

Sawtooth Mountaineering's winter schedule includes several interesting cross-country skiing programs. Cross-country ski night is held regularly during the winter months every Thursday from eight to ten. They also offer winter mountaineering programs and winter camping weekends, the latter at pretty reasonable prices, as they include the use of quite a bit of equipment considered "personal gear" by most schools. Their summer courses of instruction, beginning each June, consist of wilderness backpacking and mountaineering expeditions combined with treks into the Sawtooth Mountain region and the adjacent White Cloud and Salmon River Mountain Ranges. Trips are conducted by certified instructors licensed by the state of Idaho. Rock-climbing courses are also offered in the Boise area; four students per instructor. Fees for the basic and intermediate rock-climbing courses are unusually inexpensive. Their equipment rental fees are also quite reasonable, so this seems an excellent place for novices who might wish to see if they're really committed to climbing and mountaineering before making expensive equipment purchases.

IOWA

IOWA MOUNTAINEERS
P. O. Box 163
Iowa City, Iowa 52240
Director of Climbing Courses: Jim Ebert

Learning to climb under the watchful eye of a reputable mountaineering club, with well-supervised, excellent instruction may well be one of the most pleasant and safe ways to learn. The director of the Iowa Mountaineers' Climbing Course is Jim Ebert—who while in the Army helped train over fifteen hundred men in mountaineering and cross-country skiing. Ebert has also led several major mountaineering expeditions for the Iowa Mountaineers, and has taught many one-week-long rock-climbing seminars for the University of Iowa, where he is chief climbing instructor for the university's weekend rock-climbing courses. What distinguishes Ebert is a rare combination of mountaineering expertise and experience and a long, successful history as a teacher of climbing and mountaineering. He is reputed to be thorough, patient, and nice—qualities that can only help the Iowa mountaineer.

Devil's Lake Climbing Course—The course is offered to members (membership is inexpensive) and is a basic climbing and mountaineering course limited to ten people. Courses are usually held during late May and early June, but interested applicants should, as always, verify course dates by writing to the Iowa Mountaineers.

Course cost for seven days is extremely reasonable, and does not include transportation or food. Courses are held at Devil's Lake State Park, with a charge of $.50 per person per night for campsite use.

First Day—Mountain walk, rope management. Lecture on equipment care and selection.

Second Day—Balance climbing, friction techniques, opposition techniques, jam techniques. Lecture on weather and hypothermia.

Third Day—Piton and piton hammer use and practice, belays and practice falls, face-climbing techniques, down climbing. Lecture on route selection, leadership, judgment, objective dangers.

Fourth Day—Anchor placement instruction and practice: slings, nuts, and pitons. Two- and three-person-party climbs. Rappelling (hasty, body, carabiner, and army wrap). Lecture on philosophy of mountaineering.

Fifth Day—Tension climbing, setting up belays. Dynamic belaying. Lecture on party makeup and party control.

Sixth Day—Instruction and practice in increasingly difficult situations. Suspension traverse. Balance techniques. Covering lecture consists of open discussion.

Seventh Day—Advanced rappelling. Dynamic belaying. Climbing using various climbing techniques. Technique review.

Minimum age is seventeen, but exceptions will be made on basis of maturity and conditioning.

MASSACHUSETTS

APPALACHIAN MOUNTAIN CLUB
5 Joy Street
Boston, Massachusetts 02108

The Appalachian Mountain Club runs a phenomenal number of activities for its members, including basic and intermediate instruction in such mountaineering prerequisites as snowshoeing, cross-country skiing, and rock and ice climbing. Activity announcements appear in the Bulletin issues of *Appalachia,* which you receive directly as a member of the club, or indirectly from a co-operative librarian. Some chapters, such as New York's, generally do not allow participation by nonmembers. The Boston and New Hampshire chapters seem more receptive to nonmember participation. Enrollment in their Basic Rock Climbing Course is limited and involves

Thin Line, at Crow Hill, Massachusetts. Sam Streibert on an early ascent. *Photo by Ed Webster.*

carefully timed reservations—but there is little or no charge, and they produce excellent, safety-conscious climbers. The New Hampshire chapter offers excellent beginner workshops in ice climbing. If you're not a dues-paying member and manage to take advantage of their instruction, send a donation to the club anyway: They're doing a fine job.

NEW HAMPSHIRE

DARTMOUTH OUTWARD BOUND CENTER
Box 50
Hanover, New Hampshire 03755

Dartmouth Outward Bound offers an eighteen-day Outward Bound-designed program for the college student between terms or as an off-campus study term. Held in the New England area during the roughest part of the winter, the program includes instruction in ski touring, expeditioning on skis, winter camping, construction of snow caves, wilderness first aid, map and compass work, and a solo survival day. Minimum age for participants is eighteen. In accordance with the Outward Bound philosophy, cigarettes and alcoholic beverages are not allowed, and the development of leadership through personal interaction with other participants in the program is stressed. College credit may be earned through the student's own college. An excellent program in the beautiful White Mountains—with one severe fault: Local New Hampshirites who would benefit enormously from the program and who are seriously interested in wilderness activities have been denied access to the program because of low parental income. This is not in accordance with the Outward Bound philosophy.

EASTERN MOUNTAIN SPORTS CLIMBING SCHOOL
Main Street
North Conway, New Hampshire 03860
603-356-5433
Director: Rick Wilcox

Offers one-day climbing courses. Basic climbing courses may include up to five students per instructor. Intermediate and more advanced instruction, two students per instructor.

Beginner and Intermediate Rock Climbing—Knots, rappels, belaying, elementary use of pitons, and general safety rules of technical

Recompense, Cathedral Ledge, North Conway, New Hampshire. *Photo by Ed Webster.*

rock climbing. The intermediate session is an extension of the basic course, including suitable multipitch rock climbs.

Beginner and Intermediate Ice Climbing; Winter Mountaineering— Training in winter camping and navigation as well as technical snow and ice climbing.

INTERNATIONAL MOUNTAIN EQUIPMENT, INC.
Main Street
Box 494
North Conway, New Hampshire 03860
603-356-5287

One of the partners at International Mountain Equipment is Paul Ross, former instructor in technical mountaineering at Hurricane Island Outward Bound and former director of the Eastern Mountain Sports Climbing School. Ross has climbed extensively in Britain and the Alps and brings a wealth of technical information and climbing expertise to the climbing staff at IME. Most contracted climbs are on an individual guide level, but IME also offers program formation and group instruction for outing clubs, college mountaineering seminars, and prep schools interested in establishing Outward Bound-type programs. Within recent years, Paul Ross has been the single most dominant and motivating climber on the northeastern climbing scene. His dowel and bolt routes have created a training ground for aid climbing in New England.

NORTH COUNTRY MOUNTAINEERING, INC.
P. O. Box 951
Hanover, New Hampshire 03755
President: Steve Schneider

Individual and small-group instruction in rock climbing, snow and ice climbing.

Basic Rock Climbing—Introduction to equipment and balance climbing, rope handling, belaying technique, knots, slings, fixing anchors for rappels and top rope anchors. Introduction to clean climbing using artificial chockstones—one-day course.

Intermediate Rock Climbing—Multipitch continual climbing for students showing beginning command of belaying and basic climbing techniques. Running belays and advanced nut placement for the leader will be demonstrated. Seconding responsibility and climbing common sense will be put to field use. Demonstration of equipment use for emergency situations. More advanced rappelling techniques using various descending devices demonstrated and tried. Explanation and demonstration of protection priorities.

Aid Climbing—For the intermediate climber wishing to move on to Big Wall technique. Use of Jumars demonstrated and tried. Advanced nut placement and pin use. Cleaning and hauling techniques. Aider work and rope handling in hanging belays. Supervised practice during long aid climbs for those with a command of at least intermediate aid climbing.

Snow- and Ice-climbing Techniques (Novice and Intermediate)— All snow- and ice-climbing instruction held at Crawford Notch and Huntington Ravine. Includes proper movement with crampons, use of the ice axe for balance and support during ice climbs, self-arrest methods and practice, use of belaying anchors (i.e., snow pickets, ice screws). Ice axe belay and other protection priorities for the winter climber. Demonstration and practice of anchors for the lead climber, and removal procedures for the second. Front-pointing technique and demonstration of the classic step-cutting technique included. The day ends with a continual climb.

Family Program—NCMI will arrange family climbing weekends or week-long seminars for your clan, including individualized instruction and lodging at one of New England's most charming inns. Supplemental activities can include sailplaning, horseback riding, and Appalachian Trail walks.

Senior Weekends—Moderate but interesting climbing excursions to the Mount Washington Valley area for adults over forty. Discounts to members of the American Association of Retired Persons. Activities can include technical roped climbing, leisurely hiking, an overnight camping excursion in Pinkham Notch, swimming, and sailplaning. Accommodations can range from quaint to deluxe.

NEW YORK

THE BLAZED/TRAIL CLIMBING SCHOOL
Abercrombie & Fitch
360 Madison Avenue
New York, New York 10017
212-682-3600

Abercrombie & Fitch may have an excellent reputation as an out-

door equipment supplier, but any store running full-page ads in the
New York *Times* featuring Dunham "climbing" boots can't be all
good. The Blazed/Trail Climbing School is their entry into this
growing field, with classes based at Sewanee Academy in Sewanee,
Tennessee. Courses are held June through August, seven days each
session. On-site classes are conducted from 9 A.M. to 5 P.M., with
additional lectures after dinner. Accommodations are campus resi-
dences, two students per room. Breakfast served at 7:30 A.M. and
dinner between six-thirty and seven-thirty each evening, with "a final
banquet on the evening prior to departure, at which certificates will
be presented." Minimum age is sixteen; students under twenty-one
must have a release form signed by parent or guardian, and prices
are very high. Student/instructor ratio is three to one.

Level I—Begins with easy scrambles, then on to easy roped climbing. Instruction includes rope coiling and handling, knots, belays,
rappelling, and such climbing movements as edging, friction, opposition, mantle shelfing, and laybacks.

Level II—Technical climbing from the first day, first with top
ropes. More difficult climbs than attempted during *Level I,* with corresponding technical belays. At the end of the course there will be
some multipitch climbs and vertical rescue drills. Evening lectures
deal with anchor placement, roping up, and group dynamics.

Seminars and Individual Programs—Seminars in mountain medicine and rescue techniques, orienteering, expeditionary planning, and
logistics.

HIGH ADVENTURE TECHNIQUES
62 Livingston Avenue
Dobbs Ferry, New York 10522
914-693-6427
Director: Ray Crawford

Rock- and ice-climbing instruction, by arrangement, by a former
Green Beret who has instructed jungle survival in Panama, winter
survival in Alaska, and skydiving with the U. S. Army Sport
Parachuting Team.

The Diagonal, Wallface Mountain, Adirondack Mountains, New York. *Photo by Ed Webster.*

NORD ALP, INC.
3260 Main Street
Buffalo, New York 14214
716-837-3300
Manager: David E. Thompson

Basic Rock Climbing—Two weekend sessions held in April, May, and the beginning of September. One day of classroom, one day on rocks at the Niagara Gorge. Second weekend is a trip to Mount Jo in the Adirondacks, with climbing both mornings. Applicants need no previous experience but must be in reasonably good physical condition, with no history of heart disease or severe allergic reactions to black fly bites. Reasonable price includes food, lodging, transportation, and technical climbing equipment and instruction.
Intermediate Rock Climbing—Held in June, five consecutive weekdays. Four students maximum enrollment. Conducted at Chapel Pond climbing area in the Adirondacks. Reasonable prices. Students responsible for own meals. Transportation worked out among students. School provides tents, climbing equipment, and instruction.
Ice Climbing—Somewhat informal, as classes depend upon weather conditions. Usually a one-day session on local ice.

NORTH CAROLINA

APPALACHIAN CLIMBING SCHOOL
Mountaineering South, Inc.
344 Tunnel Road
Asheville, North Carolina 28805
Director: Brad Shaver

This school operates during the warmer months. Individual instruction during winter available by contacting Brad Shaver. During season, basic and intermediate classes are available in rock climbing; reasonably priced. School's aim is stated as "perfection of style and a sense of harmony with the vertical world," rather than a constant striving toward bigger and harder ascents.

The school's instructors—Keith Evans, Bob Gillespie, and Brad Shaver—will climb wherever students wish to go, but emphases and usual practice areas are in western North Carolina, including Looking Glass Rock near Brevard, North Carolina, and the Linville Gorge Wilderness Area, north of Morgantown, North Carolina.

Basic Course—One-day seminar at Looking Glass Rock. Fundamentals of balance climbing, rope techniques, belaying, and rappelling. Up to five students per instructor.

Intermediate Course—One-day class at Tablerock, in the Linville Gorge Wilderness Area. Up to five students per instructor. Development of good "second man" habits.

Advanced Seminar—Limited to one or two students per instructor. Course tailored to needs of students, but can include crack climbing, friction slabbing, nut placement, or whatever other skills need sharpening.

Guided Ascents—Maximum of two or three climbers per guide. Rock area of your choice (usually in North Carolina). Guides available any day of week. Will share as much of leadership as climbers wish. Exploratory and first ascent (new route) climbs can be planned. Sliding rates based on number of climbers in group.

Special sessions arranged for climbers sixteen years of age.

School also sponsors summer climbing expeditions. (See Chapter 6.)

All equipment except shoes and clothing provided.

OREGON

MAZAMAS
909 Northwest 19th Street
Portland, Oregon 97209

The club has a basic mountaineering course open to nonmembers. Applications for enrollment normally available in February.

"Acquaintance climbs" of Mount Hood are also held each Saturday and Sunday during the summer season. No previous climbing experience required. Open to the general public. Five-dollar fee for nonmembers. Limited to twenty per group.

PENNSYLVANIA

BASE CAMP CLIMBING SCHOOL
121 North Mole Street
Philadelphia, Pennsylvania 19102
215-567-1876
Director: Edward F. Pilsitz, Jr.

One-day courses, quite inexpensive

Basic Rock Climbing—For those with no previous climbing experience; knots, technical climbing, rappelling, ethics, and safety.

Intermediate Rock Climbing—Technical climbing, rappelling, overhangs, belaying, and choosing equipment.

TENNESSEE

CAMPER'S CORNER
2050 Elvis Presley Boulevard
Memphis, Tennessee 38106
901-946-2566
Director: Bill Westbrook, Jr.

Bill Westbrook has taught basic mountaineering and backpacking at Memphis State University, and has worked as a mountaineering instructor for the Memphis city schools' twenty-seven-day Operation Wilderness Program.

Basic Mountaineering Course—Limited to twenty people. Covers rock climbing from the beginning through intermediate levels. Includes lectures, slide shows and movies on glacier travel, and high-altitude snow climbs. Two field trips will be taken by students at a nominal cost.

VERMONT

CLIMB HIGH, INC., MOUNTAINEERING SCHOOL
227 Main Street
Burlington, Vermont 05401
802-864-4122
Director: Helmut Lenes, Certified Austrian Mountain Guide

Climb High's Mountaineering School brochure is singularly unimpressive, but don't let that fool you. Helmut Lenes is one of the most experienced mountaineers living on the East Coast, and, if we had to recommend one private climbing school in the area, this would probably be the one. Lenes himself has climbed the north wall of the Eiger, and was a Certified Austrian Mountain Guide by the time he was seventeen—an unprecedented age. We've seen him do 5.8 rock climbs in heavy mountaineering boots, working at a standard rarely equaled by most self-appointed domestic "guides." Obviously, Lenes is not teaching the beginning courses, but if you can

Consolation Prize, Cannon Cliff, New Hampshire. *Photo by Ed Webster.*

talk him into doing some advanced rock and ice work with you, it's worth whatever he charges. In any case, his instructors are first-rate, and are people with whom he himself climbs.

Beginners' Course—Limited to five students per instructor. The emphasis is on climbing safely, and no student is pushed beyond his or her capacity. Includes balance and movement on rocks, as well as elemental ingredients of climbing protection: rope handling, knots, belaying, rappelling, and anchors.

Intermediate Course—Expands fundamentals used in basic climbing, on more difficult terrain. Includes more advanced methods of protection, belaying, nut placement, rappelling, prusiking. Final part of the day spent on a short climb.

Advanced Course—For the intermediate or advanced climber wishing to increase his or her Alpine abilities. Includes Big Wall techniques, direct aid, advanced crack work, and mountain rescue techniques. Climbs can be arranged in New Hampshire or the Adirondacks. Cost determined by the schedule of work included and location of climbs.

Snow- and Ice-climbing School—December through March. Introduction to techniques and equipment used on snow and ice. Route finding, use of ice axe and crampons, and self-arrest, with other techniques depending upon snow and ice conditions. Good heavy mountain boots required.

Senior Weekend—An excellent program for people over forty, including a relaxing climb on easy terrain.

WASHINGTON

MOUNT ADAMS WILDERNESS INSTITUTE, INC.
Flying L. Ranch
Glenwood, Washington 98619
509-364-3511 or 364-3488
Codirectors: Darvel and Darryl Lloyd

Mount Adams Wilderness Institute offers top programs in both rock and ice work. Both ten-day and two-week sessions are held June through August, and college course credit is available for either through Central Washington State College. The two sessions differ only in terms of backpacking distance and actual time spent on Mount Adams, an exquisite, hulking mountain with twelve active glaciers. Sessions are limited to ten participants. Hiking pace rarely exceeds six miles a day, so this is a fine introduction to mountaineering for people at least fifteen years of age with no experienced mountaineers in the family. Cost includes all food and equipment and is, as far as these things go, reasonable. Reservations must be paid in full one month before sessions begin.

Curriculum includes expedition planning, including food and equipment preparation, map reading, use of compass, cross-country navigation, mountain emergency preparation (hypothermia, accidents, altitude, frostbite), wilderness protection and preservation practices, wilderness survival skills, equipment, attitude, and backpacking. Mountaineering techniques include use of ice axe, arrests, belays, steep ice technique, care and use of rope, crevasse rescue techniques (prusik, bilgeri, and pulley), use of protection devices on snow and ice, belaying practice, glacier route-finding, cramponing techniques, glissading, and discussions and practice of climbing rules, judgment, and leadership. Mountain science and environmental topics include glacier processes, ice movement, crevasse formation, advances and retreats, glacial geology, and volcanic processes, including lava flows, cinder cones, and lava caves.

THE MOUNTAINEERS
719 Pike Street
Seattle, Washington 98107

Courses in Alpine Travel, Basic Climbing, Intermediate Climbing, Ski Mountaineering, and Winter Travel. Open only to members of the Mountaineers.

THE MOUNTAIN SCHOOL
P. O. Box 728
Renton, Washington 98055
206-BA6-2613
Directors: Ray Smutek and Bill Anderson

Ray Smutek is also editor and publisher of *Off Belay* magazine (see Part V in this book). The course is held annually during the summer, usually during July. A fairly new school, but Smutek is knowledgeable and competent, but *putzevahteh*.

A two-week program closely paralleling the traditional Northwest Mountaineering courses. First week of program is based at their mountain cabin, permitting daytime practice sessions and training climbs plus evening workshops, lectures, and demonstrations. In the second week, the program moves into the high meadows and onto glaciers; living is in tents.

Program emphasizes snow techniques. One practice session devoted to ice axe self-arrests. Another, special rope techniques for snow climbing, team arrests, bollards, and boot axe belays. Several-thousand-foot snow climb included.

Included in rock-climbing section of course are fundamentals of rope handling, belaying, balance and counterforce climbing at basic levels. Several practice sessions on belaying and fundamental techniques.

For glacier climbing, course covers route finding, cramponing, hidden crevasses, long glacier tours, and a climb of Mount Baker, a major glaciated volcano. Methods of extricating climber from crevasse; methods of stopping falls into crevasse. Two glacier climbs are planned, one night camping on glacier ice.

Weather permitting, up to six peaks are ascended. Three are in Snoqulamie Pass near their cabin: Chair Peak (6,300 feet), the Tooth (5,600 feet), and Guye Peak (5,200 feet). During second week, climbs (weather permitting) include Mount Baker (10,778 feet), Colonial Peak (7,600 feet), and Snowfield Peak (8,350 feet) in the North Cascades National Park.

Each group of twelve participants is assigned to three instructors. Over eighty miles of foot travel are involved, so reasonable preconditioning is asked of students.

Students are accepted only on a preregistration basis. Minimum age is eighteen. Attempts are made to divide the group according to age and interests.

What makes the school particularly attractive is that it is not an "adventure program," and they do not believe in the dangerous "test yourself" philosophy of some other outdoor programs. What they offer—at a fairly hefty price—is a comprehensive course of instruction that will provide a solid foundation for future self-sufficient mountaineering in any range.

RAINIER MOUNTAINEERING INCORPORATED
201 St. Helens
Tacoma, Washington 98402
206-627-1105
Summer address: May 15–September 15
Mount Rainier National Park
Paradise, Washington 98397
206-569-2227

Rainier Mountaineering Incorporated is one of the best mountaineering schools in the United States, specializing in snow- and ice-climbing techniques. Its prices are extremely fair, and personnel are excellent. Some seminar sizes are rather large (the *Five-Day Snow and Ice Seminar* may include up to twenty-five people). Co-owner of RMI is Lou Whittaker, member of the '75 K-2 Expedition, and one of the record holders for annual and lifetime ascents of Mount Rainier. RMI is an excellent place for anyone who wants supervised glacier experience in a crevasse environment with a legitimate remove from civilization. Mount Rainier itself, 14,410 feet, has served as training ground for the '63 American Everest Expedition, the '73 Dhaulagiri Expedition, and the '75 K-2 Expedition, and is an excellent place to find out whether you can handle expedition climbing. The school's season is May 15 through September 15.

Mount Rainier Summit Climb—Three two-day summit climbs per week during season. Maximum group is twenty. No experience necessary. The *One-day Climbing School* is a prerequisite.

One-day Climbing School—Conducted Wednesday through Sunday during the climbing season. Covers rope travel, knots, self- and team arrest, and cramponing. Cost is comparable to a day at a decent downhill ski slope.

Five-day Snow- and Ice-climbing Seminars—Emphasis on snow, glacier, and ice techniques. Sessions oriented to needs of beginning, intermediate, and advanced climbers. Includes arrests and belays, rope management, basic snow travel, technical ice climbing, and crevasse rescue. Evening lectures, practice, discussion at ten-thousand-foot Camp Muir. One night devoted to snow camping, tent usage, and the building of snow caves and igloos. Meals served, bunk space at school's mountain hut. Up to twenty-five students per seminar. One summit climb included.

Special Seminars

Winter Seminars—Development of regular mountaineering procedures. Skills of travel and survival in Arctic conditions. Snowshoeing, igloos, snow caves, summit attempt.

Expedition Seminars—Minimum requirements, two years' serious backpacking, and good conditioning. All phases of mountaineering. Special training in trip planning, cooking, establishing camps at different elevations on Mount Rainier. Overnight stay at the summit.

Medical Seminar—Physical fitness and altitude acclimatization. Conducted by Lou Whittaker and Kenneth Cooper, M.D. (former clinical director of the Aerospace Medical Laboratories at Lackland Air Force Base). Summit climb included.

Special Climbs and Climbing Instruction—Available upon request.

WYOMING

EXUM MOUNTAIN GUIDE SERVICE AND SCHOOL OF AMERICAN
MOUNTAINEERING
Moose, Wyoming 83012
307-733-2297
Season is usually June to September

The minimum age for participation in Exum's courses is fourteen. Their climbing school is situated across Jenny Lake, and boat fare is included in the price of courses. There is a public campground nearby, and cabins are available at Jackson Lake Lodge, Moran, Wyoming 83018, as well as several other nearby cabin facilities. The school furnishes sleeping bags, cooking facilities, and eating utensils at their high camp for two-day Grand Teton climbs. Write for personal equipment and clothing list. Excellent, interesting personnel.

Basic School—Meets daily 9 A.M. to 5 P.M. Quite inexpensive, and not overly strenuous. Introduction to fundamentals of rock-climbing technique on moderate-angle rock, with limited practice in the use of the rope for belaying and rappelling.

Intermediate School—High-angle climbing of moderate difficulty, techniques for anchoring and protection, plus more extensive instruction in rappelling. Exum feels that a combination of two days' work in their Basic and Intermediate Schools is sufficient preparation for a one- or two-day guided climb. Meets daily from 8:30 A.M. to 5 P.M. and costs slightly more than the Basic School.

Advanced School—More sophisticated use of protective equipment including nuts and runners. Oriented toward the more subtle climbing techniques needed on hard climbs. Classes scheduled on request, with class sizes kept small. Will cover any other special aspect of climbing the student wishes.

Snow School—Scheduled on request, with a minimum of three students. Teaches how to climb and descend steep snow slopes comfortably and safely.

Snow and Ice School—Two days in the higher mountains learning and practicing use of the ice axe, crampons, and other snow and ice equipment. The course functions as an introduction to technical ice climbing, and a chance to refine snow techniques for those experiencing moderate difficulties on snow slopes.

Special Seminars—Three-day courses in advanced rock climbing. Low guide/client ratio. Schedule on request.

Guided Climbs—The Guide Service will guide for all peaks in the Teton Range, with routes including an easy Cube Point ascent, to a very difficult Snaz ascent. During July and August they'll also lead a choice of many two-day ascents.

JACKSON HOLE MOUNTAIN GUIDES
Teton Village, Wyoming 83025

Jackson Hole Mountain Guides has a small student/teacher ratio —no more that four students per instructor, frequently fewer than that.

Camp I Seminar—Fundamental techniques in Alpine climbing. Four days of instruction, one day rest. Two-day climbs within the Teton Range, including bivouac at base of the climb. The first four days spent in basic, intermediate, advanced intermediate, and snow schools. Students are free to choose own Teton climb. Limit, four students per seminar. June to August. For first five days, students provide own lodging and food.

Camp II Seminar—Seven days roaming, climbing, and learning in the Tetons or Wind rivers. Participants must be able to do a reasonable amount of backpacking. Daily instruction among rock walls and snow fields en route. Level of instruction depends upon previous climbing ability of student and commitment to learn. Several one- and two-day ascents can be included. A more flexible, personalized program than Camp I. This one includes all food and technical climbing equipment. June to August.

Camp III—Limited to two students and a guide. Can be in form of a course in general mountaineering, or basic to advanced climbing. Can range into glacier systems of Wyoming, Idaho Wilderness, or the Tetons. It's possible to concentrate on a specific area of climbing such as technical ice climbing in high glacial regions. Rather expensive, but includes food and technical equipment. Dates of *Camp III* arranged to fit schedule of students.

Camp IV—Five-day camp combining mountain travel and mountain photography.

Ice Seminar—First two-day seminar incorporates one day of intensive snow school and a second day of ice-climbing instruction.

Second seminar involves two days of ice climbing. Sessions present an overview of all various methods in terms of body positions and movement as well as technical equipment. Ice axe and crampons not included in fairly reasonable seminar price. Seminars conducted by arrangement or generally during August.

Basic School—Foundations for good climbing technique. Balance and movement on the rocks. Elemental ingredients of climbing protection: knots, rope handling, belaying, rappelling, and anchors. Climb a variety of short pitches, repeating each one until student's body is accustomed to the problem involved.

Intermediate School—More difficult situations and problems than Basic School. Nut placement, use of runners, hardware handling, belay placement taught and practiced. In second half of day, do a three-pitch climb.

Advanced Intermediate—Leading under careful supervision. Methods of descent and multiple rappels. Flow of session determined by progress of individuals in class.

Advanced School—Classic Teton wall climb of five hundred feet. Requires good background in climbing. Climbing habits during multipitch session are closely watched and criticized. Sessions covering aid climbing, jumaring, and free climbing available. Maximum, two students. Individual *Advanced School* available, slightly less than twice cost of shared session.

Snow School—Starts from basics. Long working day, with safest methods in snow climbing and equipment. Self-arrest, climbing, descending, anchoring in steep snow conditions. Held on Four Shadows Peak above Teton Village. This ought to be a basic prerequisite for anyone who wishes to go on to ice climbing, deservedly their most popular course.

Guided Climbs—Prices steep for one person, but decrease with one or two others on rope. Prices vary with difficulty of climb.

NATIONAL OUTDOOR LEADERSHIP SCHOOL
P. O. Box AA
Lander, Wyoming 82520
307-332-4381 or 332-4389
Director: Paul Petzoldt

National Outdoor Leadership School has been operating with enormous success since 1965 and now has branch schools in the

Pacific Northwest, Alaska, Utah, Colorado, New England, and Baja California. Most of their expeditions last about five weeks, during which "expedition members are engaged in a serious study of the basic techniques involved in conserving and enjoying wilderness regions." One of their courses, the Biology Expedition, can be taken for six hours of university credit. Prices are pretty high, averaging $125 to $150 per week, not including personal equipment, fishing licenses, and land use permits. Since the school is a nonprofit organization, there is some financial aid available, toward which NOLS accepts tax-deductable donations. The school has received tremendous media coverage and is one of the few programs of its type where one can be sure of competent instruction. All of its courses involve some instruction in mountaineering. Any courses they offer would be fine experience for a young person pursuing an interest in this field. Most interesting perhaps to the young mountaineer are:

Wind River Mountaineering Expedition—Minimum age, sixteen. Approximately thirty-five days in the Wind River Range learning all aspects of wilderness expeditioning, but with special emphasis on technical climbing: cliff evacuation, accident prevention, route selection, leading and following, direct aid climbing, high wall technique, snow and ice techniques, camping above timberline, and the use and care of climbing equipment.

Teton Winter Mountaineering Expedition—Approximately fifteen days in Teton National Park. For this course, one must be a NOLS graduate or a seasoned winter mountaineer. Provides experience on difficult climbs under demanding winter conditions. Students carry packs on skis, live in tents and snow caves, and technical routes are attempted. Expeditions are limited to eight to twelve members. Skiing experience is a definite plus for applicants. Instruction covers cross-country skiing and equipment selection, winter camping, cooking and rationing, snow caving, use of crampons and ice axes, pacing and rhythmic breathing, and avalanche safety. Discussions emphasize clothing and winter dress, map reading with a compass, first aid and rescue, snow formations, and geology.

Advanced Leadership Expedition NOLS Instructors' Course—A thirty-five-day course for qualified NOLS graduates who expect to work in outdoor recreation. Teaching methods, wilderness techniques, cultivating own judgment, and outdoor leadership. One of the few legitimate training grounds for outdoor leadership instructors.

44 WHERE TO LEARN TO CLIMB

Advanced Mountaineering and Climbing—A four-week course for NOLS graduates and seasoned expeditioners. Emphasis on developing technical climbing and mountaineering skills. Technically difficult climbs.

The school has many other courses available, during both winter and summer, and is expanding into foreign expeditions, at least one of which will be for university credit in biology and ecology. As NOLS is a nonprofit organization, it would be nice to see them doing more to recruit and involve inner-city and young people of less than upper-middle-class incomes into their fine but expensive programs.

CANADA

ALPINE CRAFTS LTD.
Box 85697
North Vancouver, British Columbia
Canada
604-879-7431

Offers one-week courses in general mountaineering, June through early September. Minimum age, sixteen.

Basic Course—Includes basic rock climbing, belaying, rappelling, placement of pitons and chockstones. For snow and ice climbing, use of snow flukes, ice axe, crampons, and glacier travel. Course also includes work in mountain navigation, planning, accomplishment and return, and route finding. Part of course will be ascents of Rex's Pillar and Mount Matier. Three students per instructor. Maximum ten students weekly.

Intermediate—Instruction in intermediate rock climbing, further use of chockstones, use of short axe, front points, advanced ice craft, advanced snowcraft. Bivouac at end of week. Course limited to six persons per week; two students per instructor.

Advanced—This course usually held the last week of August. Alpine climbing for those wishing to learn the skills of multiday climbs and Big Wall techniques. Limited to four persons; two students per instructor.

Guides—Available for private instruction, guiding, and winter mountaineering on a day or a weekly basis.

CANADIAN SCHOOL OF MOUNTAINEERING LTD.
P. O. Box 1552
Banff, Alberta T0L 0C0
Canada
403-678-5714
Director: Ottmar Setzer

Rock climbing weeks are usually held during June, at Mount Rundle, Lac Des Arcs, and Mount Yamnuska. Ski touring and ski mountaineering weeks and weekends, April through June. Good programs, for the most part reasonably priced.

RUDI GERTSCH MOUNTAINEERING SCHOOL
Box 543
Banff, Alberta T0L 0C0
Canada
403-762-2114

Member of the Association of Canadian Mountain Guides.
Daily climbs for parties of up to four persons with one guide. These are guided climbs of technically difficult standard. Instruction is also offered in rock climbing, snow climbing, and ice climbing. The beginners' rock course, maximum six people, is quite inexpensive. Classes are usually held June 15 through September 30.

SWITZERLAND

INTERNATIONAL SCHOOL OF MOUNTAINEERING
P. O. Box 25
Leysin, Switzerland
Director: Dougal Haston

International School of Mountaineering has to be one of the most chi-chi places to go for formal climbing instruction (the only other instruction that might carry as much *caché* right now would be private lessons from Reinhold Messner, Dougal himself, or Chris Bonington). ISM was founded by John Harlin, who until his death in 1966 on the Eiger Direct, was regarded as America's foremost Alpine climber—the "climbing machine." Directing the school now is Dougal Haston—Annapurna South Face, Everest Southwest Face, Eiger Direct, Everest South Face. Haston was recently equipment and technical adviser during the filming of *The Eiger Sanction,* and is easily international climbing's "most glamorous young man." Quite moderate course costs include board, lodging, instruction, and transport throughout the course. Usual sessions held between June and August.

Standard Course—Alpine rock and ice for those with little or no experience. Long rock climbs, artificial climbing, mountain rescue, ice climbing in Chamonix. "If you can't climb after six days," they state, "it's not our fault."

Intermediate Course—Six days. One instructor to two students. Course aimed at the experienced climber who wants to get into the high Alps. Assessment of student's ability during long rock climbs in Leysin on first day. Rest of time spent in Mont Blanc Range or the Swiss Valaisian Alps. Slightly more expensive than the *Standard Course,* but well worth it.

Alpine Advanced Course—A chance to do major Alpine climbs in company of leading Alpinists. One instructor per student; six days. Course available to only highly qualified climbers. Quite expensive (approximately three times the cost of *Standard Course,* not including room and board).

Ice-climbing Course—Introduction to Alpine ice climbing, including advanced techniques. Weather permitting, includes an ascent of an Alpine ice face. Two students per instructor; four days. Extremely popular course.

Artificial or Aid Climbing—Intensive course in placing nails and taking them out again; three days.

Group Course—For people traveling in groups, a chance to sample a few days' gentle introduction to climbing. Time and costs vary with individual groups.

Ski Mountaineering—Offered in conjunction with the Swiss Ski School in Leysin. Short day tours during the winter for beginners.

CHAPTER 2

Mountaineering Clubs and Clubs Offering Climbing Instruction

People who climb like to believe themselves rugged individualists who disdain any efforts toward organization or regulation. Nevertheless, put six or eight climbers together in one geographic location, let them put up a few new routes in various rope combinations, spend some time womanizing and/or pub crawling together, and you've got yourself a climbing club, with names ranging from the "Mad Dogs" of Southern California to the "Gay Blades" of North Woodstock, New Hampshire. Assuredly, many people who climb remain (in the language of the *American Alpine Club Journal*) "unaffiliated," but clubs seem to have become an integral part of the climbing scene in this country.

Almost all of the clubs listed in the following pages offer climbing instruction, usually open to the "extended family" of dues-paying members. Occasionally, admission policies are somewhat restrictive, with recommendations from two members needed in order to join.

In any event, climbing clubs offering instruction usually provide a less expensive way to learn to climb than enrolling in one of the private climbing schools or guide services listed in Chapter 1.

ALASKA

MOUNTAINEERING CLUB OF ALASKA
Box 2037
Anchorage, Alaska 99510

The regional focus of the Mountaineering Club of Alaska is the south-central part of that great state. The MCA organizes and spon-

Mount Dickey, Alaska Range. *Photo by Howard Peterson.*

sors day hikes, backpacking trips, ski tours, one-day climbs, and mountain expeditions led by members and open to nonaffiliated outdoor enthusiasts. The MCA has also conducted schools in winter survival, winter mountaineering, general climbing, and snow and ice climbing. Fees are nominal, as instructors are club members working on a volunteer basis. The club maintains primitive A-frame cabins in the glaciated back country, and these are open to all mountaineers. The club also has a limited amount of club-owned equipment available for rental. Monthly meetings are held on the third Wednesday of each month at 8 P.M. on the top floor of the Pioneer Schoolhouse, at Third and Barrow streets. Sign-up lists for activities are available at meetings, and further activities are announced in their monthly newsletter *Scree*. This is a good, active club with a healthy nondiscriminatory attitude. If you live near Anchorage, or will be traveling in the area, you should give them your support. Family dues are $10. Adult membership is $7.50. Junior membership (people under eighteen) is $5.00, and out-of-town membership (fifty miles or more) is also $5.00.

ARIZONA

ARIZONA MOUNTAINEERING CLUB
c/o Don Sloat
4225 South 47th Place
Phoenix, Arizona 85040

The Arizona Mountaineering Club has an extensive training program in rock climbing. The club operates on a very small budget; a $5.00 subscription to their club newsletter will bring you news of their activities, including club climbs, backpacks, river runs, and other outings. Their Annual Climbing School is usually held during October and limited to the first hundred people age sixteen or over who apply. The school usually includes four evenings and three one-day weekend sessions. The fee is around $50, and covers club membership, thirty hours of instruction, a basic climbing manual, sixteen feet of prusik line, twenty feet of nylon webbing, three carabiners, and a subscription to the *Arizona Mountaineer*.

CHALLENGE/DISCOVERY
Prescott College
Prescott, Arizona 86301
602-445-3245

CALIFORNIA

BOOT & BLISTER CLUB
HSU
c/o Mike Diggles or Steve O'Meara
Arcata, California 95521

THE OUTING CLUB
San Diego State College
San Diego, California 92115

THE SIERRA CLUB
1050 Mills Tower
220 Bush Street
San Francisco, California 94101

The Sierra Club has chapters across the United States, several of
which have regional groups. The club's focus is ecology and conservation of wilderness and natural resources. Several chapters sponsor
technical mountaineering activities and instruction on a regular basis.
The most active climbing programs are offered by the San Diego and
San Francisco Bay chapters. For a copy of the current activities
schedule, enclose a check for $1.00.

Sierra Club
San Diego Chapter
1549 El Prado
San Diego, California 92101

Sierra Club
San Francisco Bay Chapter
5608 College Avenue
Oakland, California 94618

Many fine activities, everything from river running to bird feeding, are offered by all Sierra Club chapters. Annual dues for regular membership are $15 (with spouse, $22.50). Reduced dues for students and people age sixty or over. An excellent organization.

STANFORD ALPINE CLUB
Stanford University
Stanford, California 94305

WEST VALLEY HIKING CLUB
c/o Leon Berthiaume
Grant Avenue
Campbell, California 95008

COLORADO

COLORADO STATE UNIVERSITY MOUNTAINEERS
Colorado State University
Fort Collins, Colorado 80521

DENVER UNIVERSITY ALPINE CLUB
2050 East Evans
Denver, Colorado 80210

THE COLORADO MOUNTAIN CLUB
1723 East 16th Avenue
Denver, Colorado 80218

The Colorado Mountain Club has many active chapters throughout Colorado. Regular membership is $17, plus a $1.00 admission fee. Full-time students, or people under twenty-one may join for $9.00 annual dues, plus $1.00 admission fee. Family rates are available. Their fiscal year begins November 1, so dues will be paid only

Karin on a 5.8, Colorado. *Photo by Steve Hong.*

until the following October 31. New members must be endorsed by two people already members. Mountaineering schools are conducted by most groups, both winter and spring, for instruction in mountain safety and elementary rock-climbing techniques. Instruction for intermediate climbers is also available.

   They also run hiking activities for the handicapped, and their hikes for the blind with CMC member guides have been enormously successful. Membership dues include a subscription to the vigorous magazine *Trail and Timberline*.

THE OUTING CLUB
University of Colorado
Boulder, Colorado 80302

THE OUTING CLUB
University of Northern Colorado
Greeley, Colorado 80631

CONNECTICUT

YALE MOUNTAINEERING CLUB
Yale University
New Haven, Connecticut 06520
Founded in 1928.

IDAHO

IDAHO ALPINE CLUB
Idaho Falls, Idaho 83401

ILLINOIS

CHICAGO MOUNTAINEERING CLUB
2801 South Parkway
Chicago, Illinois 60616

SIMIAN OUTING SOCIETY
University of Illinois
Urbana, Illinois 61801

IOWA

THE IOWA MOUNTAINEERS
P. O. Box 163
Iowa City, Iowa 52240
319-337-7163

The Iowa Mountaineers sponsors climbing courses, cross-country skiing, and winter survival courses as well as two eleven-day mountain camps each July and/or August, usually in the western United States or Canada. Their annual summer expedition abroad has had extremely enthusiastic response. Weekend outings and films and lectures are also sponsored. For those interested only in the Mountaineers' trips, an inexpensive expedition membership is suggested. Those living in the area can become either associate or active mem-

54 WHERE TO LEARN TO CLIMB

bers. Some of the lecture programs are a bit on the hokey side, but this is a fine organization, with excellent climbing instruction and leadership.

KANSAS

GREAT PLAINS MOUNTAINEERING
Wichita State University
c/o Richard Lapted
Wichita, Kansas 67208

Ted Mize
Mountain Explorers
Topeka, Kansas

MARYLAND

MOUNTAIN CLUB OF MARYLAND
c/o H. H. Camper Haven
424 N. Eutaw Street
Baltimore, Maryland 21201

MASSACHUSETTS

APPALACHIAN MOUNTAIN CLUB
5 Joy Street
Boston, Massachusetts 02108

The oldest mountaineering club in the United States, with many branches throughout the Northeast. The AMC maintains hundreds of miles of hiking trails throughout the white Mountains, with staffed huts open to members and nonmembers alike. Their Boston branch, particularly, sponsors many interesting and worthwhile activities, as does the New Hampshire section. The AMC headquarters in Pinkham Notch, New Hampshire, serves the winter mountaineer and cross-country skier with a fabulous range of activities. The club publishes a fine annual journal, supplemented by a monthly newsletter describing activities of all chapters. Anyone in the Northeast seriously interested in mountaineering should apply for membership. Adult membership is $15, plus $5.00 initiation fee; junior membership (under age twenty-three) with publications is $7.00 and no initiation fee. Two sponsoring members must recommend new applicants, but if you don't know anyone, they may be able to provide the necessary signatures.

HARVARD UNIVERSITY MOUNTAINEERING CLUB
Harvard University
Cambridge, Massachusetts 02135

Harvard Mountaineering Club has produced some of the eastern United States' finest mountaineers. All aspects of technical mountaineering are taught by this club. They publish an annual report and journal.

MIT OUTING CLUB
Massachusetts Institute of Technology
Cambridge, Massachusetts 02139

MIT's Outing Club is the most prestigious college outing club in the United States. The Advanced Rock Climbing Committee of the MIT Outing Club has been publishing an excellent basic rock-climbing instructional manual since 1956, the most recent issue edited by Arthur Reidell (see Part V of this book for details).

TUFTS MOUNTAIN CLUB
P. O. Box 28
Tufts University Branch
Medford, Massachusetts 02153

The club consists of about three hundred members, and owns and operates a lodge-farmhouse in Woodstock, New Hampshire, which is open to members of the club and the Tufts community. Club activities in the White Mountains include canoeing, hiking, cross-country skiing, and rock and ice climbing. Rock and building climbing attempted at or around the Tufts area. Activities also include trips to Knox Caves in upper New York State. The club offers formal and informal instruction in each activity listed. Quincy Quarries is the site of most basic climbing instruction, offered to the Tufts student body almost every weekend during the fall and spring semesters. The

Physical Education Department also offers training in rock climbing
during the spring semester. Ice climbing is limited to those who can
provide their own equipment.

MINNESOTA

NORTHSTAR MOUNTAINEERS
Minneapolis, Minnesota
  Inquire at local climbing retail store.

MINNESOTA ROVERS
Minneapolis, Minnesota
  Inquire at local climbing retail store.

NEW HAMPSHIRE

DARTMOUTH OUTING CLUB
Robertson Hall
Dartmouth College
Hanover, New Hampshire 03755

  Runs an active climbing program, including instruction, open to
Dartmouth students as well as local people in surrounding communi-
ties. In past years, members of the Dartmouth Outing Club have
climbed in Alaska, Nepal, and the Patagonian Mountain Range. For-
mer members of the Outing Club were on the 1963 American
Everest Expedition, the 1969 Dhaulagiri Expedition, and the 1973
Dhaulagiri Expedition, as well as numerous private expeditions.
They publish an annual journal, ingeniously titled *The Dartmouth
Mountaineering Club Journal.*

NEW JERSEY

PRINCETON MOUNTAINEERING CLUB
Princeton University
Princeton, New Jersey 08540

NEW MEXICO

NEW MEXICO MOUNTAIN CLUB
P. O. Box 4151
Albuquerque, New Mexico
  Inquire at Mountain Chalet (retail store), Albuquerque.

THE OUTING CLUB
University of New Mexico
Albuquerque, New Mexico 87106

NEW YORK

ADIRONDACK MOUNTAIN CLUB, INC.
172 Ridge Street
Glens Falls, New York 12801
518-793-7737

The second largest mountain club in the eastern United States—
known as "ADK." It has a strong conservation bias. One of their
first projects was to build the 133-mile Northville–Placid Trail, now
maintained by the New York State Department of Environmental
Conservation.

The ADK owns two lodges, both of which are open to members
and the public. Adirondack Loj, nine miles southeast of Lake Placid,
accommodates forty-four persons and is open year-round. Johns
Brook Lodge is 3½ miles up the Johns Brook from Keene Valley,
accessible only by foot trail, and accommodates twenty-eight persons
(open only in the summer). The ADK also maintains winter shelters
there.

The club conducts a rock-climbing school in the summer and organized winter mountaineering schools in the winter. There are at
present twenty-three chapters, with a majority of members located
throughout New York and northern New Jersey.

ADK publishes some excellent books, including *Guide to Adirondack Trails-High Peak Region, A Climber's Guide to the Adirondacks* by Trudy Healy, and *Rock Scenery of the Hudson Highlands
and Palisades* by Jerome Wyckoff.

Names of chapter chairperson in your area and further membership information is available through Grant G. Cole, executive director.

THE AMERICAN ALPINE CLUB
113 East 90th Street
New York, New York 10028
212-722-1628

The American Alpine Club is American mountaineering's "status" club, with an international membership of about a thousand people. They've recently begun recruiting new young members, but two references, "preferably members of AAC or established climbers," at least one of whom has climbed with the applicant, are necessary. The right family connections help too. Applicants should have at least three years of active climbing experience, with a "variety of experience as to regions climbed in or styles of climbing done." Other factors considered are polar exploration, contributions to mountain art, photography, literature, or science, plus continued service to the mountaineering community, mountaineering organizations, or conservation. The AAC publishes a yearly journal, a newsletter, the annual *Accidents in North American Mountaineering,* and many fine books. The club sponsors large-scale expeditions to remote areas of the globe, and offers a few small grants to young climbers engaged in research and exploration of the Alpine environment. There are eight sections, the most active of which are the New York and the Sierra Nevada sections. The AAC also runs several huts and climbing camps, the most popular of which is their Teton Ranch, located within the Grand Teton National Park. The AAC's fine mountaineering library is open to the public from 10 A.M. to 4 P.M. most weekdays; they ask that anyone wishing to use the library phone ahead at least a day in advance.

CLARKSON COLLEGE OUTING CLUB
Clarkson College of Technology
c/o Frank Zupansic
Potsdam, New York 13676

OHIO

CLEVELAND MOUNTAINEERS
Cleveland, Ohio

Holds a clinic twice yearly to teach and develop safe climbing technique and rescue skills. Inquire at local climbing retail store for further particulars.

OHIO STATE MOUNTAINEERS
Ohio State University
Art Leissa, Adviser
Columbus, Ohio 43210

OREGON

EUGENE MOUNTAIN RESCUE
920 Hoover Lane
Eugene, Oregon 97404
Att: Mr. Steve Ross

MAZAMAS
909 Northwest 19th Street
Portland, Oregon 97207
503-227-2345

Membership application must be accompanied by a check for $25, of which $15 is an initiation fee and $10 are annual dues. Applicants must have climbed to the summit of a mountain peak on which there is at least one living glacier, and be sponsored by two members in good standing. Dues for "family" members are at a reduced rate after the first year. The club sponsors about two hundred climbs a year. "Acquaintance climbs" of Mount Hood are held each Saturday and Sunday during the summer climbing season, limited to twenty people per group. No previous climbing experience is required, and climbs are open to the general public. A fee of $5.00 is assessed for each nonmember participating in the climb. The club also has a winter mountaineering program, generally not open to the public. The Mazamas do sponsor an annual basic mountaineering course, with enrollment open to nonmembers. School size is limited to three hundred students. The course consists of five lectures, three field trips, and a "graduation" climb of either Mount Hood or St. Helens. Applications for enrollment in the basic mountaineering course are available in February. The club also has courses in intermediate and advanced climbing, usually limited to members. Hiking is scheduled for almost every weekend, and nonmembers may participate; there is usually a $.50 nonmember fee. Programs are held each Wednesday evening in their clubrooms, starting at 8 P.M., and are open to the general public. The Mazamas sponsor many other fine outdoor activities, making membership extremely worthwhile.

OBSIDIANS
Lane YMCA
Eugene, Oregon

OUTDOOR PROGRAMS
Erb Memorial Union—Room 23
University of Oregon
Eugene, Oregon 97403

An extremely active outing program, with rock-climbing instruction offered. These programs are open to anyone in the community, and prices are very low.

PENNSYLVANIA

EXPLORERS CLUB OF PITTSBURGH
c/o Mountain Trail Shop
5435 Walnut Street
Pittsburgh, Pennsylvania 15232

PENN STATE OUTING CLUB
c/o Dr. Smyth
Penn State University
University Park, Pennsylvania 16802

An extremely active outing club offering instruction in all phases of technical mountaineering. They've also been responsible for the development of local climbing crags.

TEXAS

THE OUTING CLUB
Texas Tech University
Lubbock, Texas 79409

UTAH

WASATCH MOUNTAIN CLUB
c/o Dr. Paul Horton
3155 Highland Drive
Salt Lake City, Utah 84106

VERMONT

GREEN MOUNTAIN CLUB
108 Merchants Row
Rutland, Vermont 05701

VIRGINIA

THE OUTING CLUB
University of Virginia
Charlottesville, Virginia 22903

THE OUTING CLUB
c/o Bob Smily
Virginia Polytechnic Institute and State University
Blacksburg, Virginia 24061

WASHINGTON

OUTING CLUB
University of Washington
Seattle, Washington 98105

THE MOUNTAINEERS
719 Pike Street
Seattle, Washington 98101

The Mountaineers have held organized climbing classes since 1935 and are presently the third largest outdoor club in the United States. Beginning each February, classes are held in Seattle, Everett, Olympia, and Tacoma. Supervised practice trips and climbs continue from March to mid-October, and the club sponsors hikes nearly every weekend. During the ski season, Mountaineer lodges can accommodate up to 270 persons who are members. Initiation fee for regular membership is $8.00, plus $12 annual dues. Spouse membership is $3.00, and junior membership (ages fourteen to eighteen) is $10, including initiation fee. Two members of at least one year's standing must sponsor the applicant. The club publishes a monthly bulletin, *The Mountaineer,* and many fine books. An excellent, active organization that was in large part responsible for the preservation of the tract of land that became Olympic National Park.

WASHINGTON STATE UNIVERSITY ALPINE CLUB
Washington State University
Pullman, Washington 99163

WEST VIRGINIA

WEST VIRGINIA UNIVERSITY OUTING CLUB
c/o C. Wamsley
336 A Stewart Street
Morgantown, West Virginia 26505

The West Virginia University Outing Club has approximately seventy-five members who backpack, climb, cave, and cycle. Instruction is provided by four or five of the more accomplished student climbers. The club provides helmets, and has other equipment available for rental. Meetings are Thursday evenings at seven-thirty at the Student Union, and weekend trips go to Seneca. One-day trips include afternoons of top-roped climbing and boulder problems at Coopers Rock.

WISCONSIN

WISCONSIN HOOFER MOUNTAINEERS
University of Wisconsin
Madison, Wisconsin 55706

WYOMING

THE OUTING CLUB
c/o Charlie Eautin
University of Wyoming
Laramie, Wyoming 82071

CANADA

ALPINE CLUB OF CANADA
Club Manager: Mr. Pat Boswell
P. O. Box 1026
Banff, Alberta T0L 0C0
Canada

Membership is open to anyone age sixteen or over who is interested in mountaineering or the mountains. Senior membership status is available for those who have climbed regularly for at least two seasons and made four ascents "of a truly alpine nature." Junior membership for those age sixteen to twenty-five is $7.50, with no entrance fee. Entrance fee for others is $10, plus $15 annual dues. Reduced rates available for married couples. This is an outstanding organization with an active membership and mountaineering program. Activities range from lectures, slide shows, and ski weeks to glacial Alpine climbing. The club maintains huts and shelters at various locations for use by members. Their mountaineering library is one of the finest in North America; inquiries about access to the library should be sent to Archives of the Canadian Rockies, Box 160, Banff, Alberta T0L 0C0, Canada. The club sponsors an excellent General Mountaineering Camp, devoted entirely to instruction, from novice to expert level. Nonmembers may participate for an additional fee of $25. Minimum attendance is one week, with fees of about $150 weekly. The Alpine Club of Canada also sponsors excursions to Switzerland, Nepal, and the Himalayas.

CHAPTER 3

Private Secondary Schools Offering Active Mountaineering Programs

We believe that people of almost any age can learn to climb, but that the person who starts early has a distinct advantage in terms of long-range development of technical skill, physical conditioning, and mountaineering judgment. Several of the schools on the list that follows have been producing an unusual number of strong, extremely promising climbers—especially within the past few years. As none of the commercially marketed prep school guidebooks has yet deemed fit to include a list of schools offering programs in technical mountaineering, we trust that the following may be of interest to young climbers and their parents. The academic excellence of some of the schools included does not necessarily coincide with the strength of the schools' mountaineering programs, but in a few cases there is a cheering correlation.

PRIVATE SECONDARY SCHOOLS

CALIFORNIA

THE ATHENIAN SCHOOL
Danville, California 94526
415-837-5375

Extensive outdoor program includes cross-country skiing and rock and snow climbing. An Outward Bound program required for graduation.

HARVARD SCHOOL
3700 Coldwater Canyon Road
North Hollywood, California 91604
213-980-6692
Director of Admissions: Elliot B. McGraw

The Harvard School has an Outward Bound-type course called Basic Wilderness Experience. This course teaches skills in map reading and compass work, shelter and fire building, edible plants, and climbing, as well as group dynamics in the wilderness. Their Basic Mountaineering course meets four days a week and is devoted to the development of skills related to rock climbing. Direct aid and protection priorities and mountaineering techniques for snow climbing are covered. Both programs are offered as an alternative to the required Physical Education program.

COLORADO

THE ABBEY SCHOOL
Canon City, Colorado 81212
Director of Admissions: Michael C. Long, Moderator, Abbey Alpine Club

In response to growing interest in technical climbing, the Abbey Alpine Club has initiated an eighteen-hour basic climbing course conducted by the Forward School of Mountaineering in Colorado Springs. The club has a good supply of top-quality backpacking equipment, but as yet limited climbing equipment.

The Abbey School owns two mountain lodges, at elevations of about nine thousand feet. One is located in the Greenhorn Range of the San Isabel National Forest, and the other is near Lake San Isabel. Both lodges give excellent access to National Forest land and peaks up to and including fourteen thousand feet.

CONNECTICUT

THE LOOMIS-CHAFFEE SCHOOL
Windsor, Connecticut 06095
Jim Wilson, Instructor

Loomis-Chaffee sponsors an excellent one-term course, called Wilderness and the Self, unfortunately restricted to only twelve seniors and qualified juniors. Integral to the course is a good deal of rock climbing, and students spend a total of about five weeks hiking, living, and climbing in the Adirondacks and the White Mountains.

Jim Wilson also runs an active rock-climbing club ($5.00 membership dues). Climbs are mostly weekends at Ragged Mountain in Southington, Connecticut—a good cliff for both beginners and experienced climbers. Occasional trips to the Shawangunks. Wilson also sponsors fall and spring trips to other climbing areas. Female climbers welcome, though in the past the male/female ratio of Wilderness and the Self has been maintained at two to one.

THE HOTCHKISS SCHOOL
Lakeville, Connecticut 06039
Director of Admissions: Peter D. Adams

There are four qualified rock-climbing instructors at Hotchkiss, all with Outward Bound training. Most extracurricular climbing is done through the Outing Club, with a relatively small core of active climbers, both male and female. Trips are held during the winter, during which basic winter technique is taught. One instructor, Mr. David Coughlin, is adept at Class 6 aid climbing, so instruction is available for all levels of student climbers. Areas at which students climb include Monument Mountain, cliffs at Limerock, Connecticut, and the Shawangunks in New York State. During the spring an Outward Bound-type course is offered, including top-roped climbing instruction.

THE OXFORD ACADEMY
Westbrook, Connecticut 06498
203-399-6247
Headmaster: Frank W. Efinger

Rock climbing is conducted by the academy as part of its athletic program in the fall and spring, with excursions to the White Mountains each term.

THE TAFT SCHOOL
Watertown, Connecticut 06795
Director of Admissions: Joseph I. Cunningham
Taft School has an outdoor training program.

Anticipation, 5.10. At Ragged Mountain, Connecticut. *Photo by Ed Webster.*

MAINE

REDINGTON POND SCHOOL
Box 567
Rangeley, Maine 04970

Redington Pond School is part of Academix, Inc. (12 Arrow Street, Cambridge, Massachusetts 02138; 617-491-6530), a year-round wilderness school. Students spend a year at the Redington Pond School—a primitive, backwoods farm and camp with "no civilized conveniences" (for example, no flush toilets, and wood heat). The community provides its own food, clothing, and shelter (tents for sleeping, wood frame camps for eating, cleaning, working). Winter mountaineering and climbing are instructed as the requirements and interest of the students progress. A group of students lived for six weeks on the Arctic Circle meeting European climbing teams. Another group has climbed in the Baffin Islands. After the Redington Pond year, students move on to the Sea School in Camden, Maine, and the V-V Ranch School in Wardlow, Alberta, Canada. This is progressive education at its most progressive—but excellent winter survival experience.

MASSACHUSETTS

ANDOVER
PHILLIPS ACADEMY
Andover, Massachusetts 01810

Mountaineering has been offered at Phillips Academy for over ten years as part of a more general outdoor program based on the Outward Bound philosophy. The winter program is available to students on a term basis. The winter program is more strictly mountaineering, with the emphasis on rock and ice climbing, backpacking, camping, and survival. Expeditions are geared to accommodate the level of skills of a particular group. The main portion of training is carried out in the White Mountains. An example of a trip would be a traverse of the Presidential Range.

Rock climbing has grown out of their regular program. Students who are exposed to the activity and are interested in pursuing this particular facet of the out-of-doors may do so under careful guid-

Henry Barber leading Fool on the Hill, 5.9+, Crow Hill, Massachusetts. *Photo by Ed Webster.*

ance. Each student must demonstrate his or her ability before being permitted to advance to a higher level of skill—for example, leading or aid-climbing. Instructors have sponsored many expeditions for students, ranging from the Mexican volcanoes to the Himalayas.

BERKSHIRE SCHOOL
Sheffield, Massachusetts 01257
413-229-8511

Most of the supervised mountaineering done at Berkshire is with the Project Lifeline students, a program adapted from Outward Bound. Emphasized is basic rockcraft and fundamental rescue work. The school is located near Mount Everett Reservation and has access to several rock faces there, primarily the "Black Rock." Other Project Lifeline programs are conducted at Monument Mountain, with faces of greater magnitude.

BROOKS SCHOOL
North Andover, Massachusetts 01845

Brooks doesn't particularly stress rock climbing, and climbing comes under the aegis of the Outing Club—an extracurricular activity rather than an activity integrated into the required athletics program. The Outing Club does, however, plan regular hiking, climbing, and skiing trips away from the school.

NORTHFIELD MOUNT HERMON SCHOOL
East Northfield, Massachusetts 01360
Director of Admissions: Frederick S. McVeigh

A number of courses entail outdoor-oriented activities: Hiking and Camping (some spelunking); Student Leadership in the Outdoors; Cross-country Skiing; Canoe and Kayak; and Rock Climbing. The latter is given in both the fall and spring terms in their trimester year. Typically, three leaders will work with twelve students for the entire term (roughly ten weeks), with concentration on the various facets of rock climbing. They meet three times during the week, with one long afternoon devoted to local rock outcrops. There are usually three or four full weekend climbing trips and three or four one-day trips. The major areas visited during the term include the Shawangunks, the Adirondacks (Chapel Pond, Pok-o-Moonshine), Cannon

Cliff, White Horse, and Cathedral Ledges in New Hampshire, and Ragged Mountain in Connecticut. In the past this has been primarily an introductory rock-climbing course, but they are planning to expand the program to include more advanced work.

MICHIGAN

THE CRANBROOK SCHOOLS
520 Lone Pine Road
P. O. Box 803
Bloomfield Hills, Michigan 48013
313-644-1600
Director, Lodestar Program: John P. H. Morris

Cranbrook has two programs involving climbing or mountaineering.

Lodestar—A course for juniors and seniors (coed) in rock climbing, offered as an alternative in both the fall and spring semesters in the athletic department. They begin with basic belaying techniques, and a student can proceed, in time, to lead climbing or multipitched faces in New York, Ontario, Pennsylvania, or West Virgina. A brief introduction to winter mountaineering takes place through scheduled trips to the Adirondacks and White Mountains.

Wilderness Expedition—An introduction to the mountain environment for sophomore boys, held in the Smokey Mountains during the January term. An eleven-day backpacking trip, including some climbing.

MINNESOTA

THE BLAKE SCHOOL
Blake Road
Hopkins, Minnesota 55343
612-938-3598
Contact: L. Mesna

Within the normal school day, beginning and intermediate rock climbing is taught at the school and at Taylor's Falls. Eligible are the seventh through the twelfth grades. The courses cover twenty to thirty hours and are an elective. Coed.

The school has also been developing an Outward Bound-type program. Write for further particulars.

NEW HAMPSHIRE

HOLDERNESS SCHOOL
Plymouth, New Hampshire 03264

No credit courses in climbing, but they do sponsor many climbing excursions in the area.

THE NEW HAMPTON SCHOOL
New Hampton, New Hampshire 03265
603-744-8157
Director of Admissions: Austin C. Stern

As part of their outdoors program, New Hampton offers instruction and experience in rock climbing, mountaineering, pathfinding, and kayaking, as well as general camping experience. Their winter outdoors program includes cross-country skiing, snowshoeing, and winter camping.

THE PHILLIPS EXETER ACADEMY
Exeter, New Hampshire 03833
Admissions Officer: Rheua S. Stakely

Exeter's curriculum is of such breadth and quality that any mountaineering supplement is simply icing on an already delicious cake. Their Outdoor Challenge is a regular option to the required athletic program during the fall and spring terms: For ten days students participate in swimming, first-aid practice, running, canoeing, rock climbing, compass study, and generally familiarize themselves with the outdoor environment. The culmination of Outdoor Challenge is an overnight at Mount Washington, combining both rock climbing and camping. In addition, for fifty years the Phillips Exeter Academy Outing Club has made weekend climbing trips to mountains in New Hampshire and Maine. Since 1939, informal rock-climbing trips have been made to local areas, especially Pawtuckaway State Park. The Mountaineering Club, formed in 1946, has helped many climbers to develop. One of the favorite climbs is the Pinnacle in Huntington Ravine on Mount Washington. The club president in

The Hanson-Echardt Route, Cannon Cliff, New Hampshire. *Photo by Bryan Delaney.*

1973–74 was the youngest member of the American Alpine Club. Adviser to the Mountaineering Club is Mr. Robert Bates, a member of several expeditions in the Himalayas.

THE WHITE MOUNTAIN SCHOOL
(St. Mary's in the Mountains)
Littleton, New Hampshire 03561
603-444-2928
Director of Admissions: Colin M. Davidson

The White Mountain School, as well as having a vigorous college preparatory program, also offers the finest mountaineering program of any private secondary school in the United States. Daily excursions to Franconia Notch include three or four days of climbing, with snowshoeing and cross-country skiing experience occupying other afternoons. Comprehensive instruction includes snow and ice climbing at Huntington Ravine, and all-season mountaineering in the Mount Washington area. Basic as well as advanced mountaineering skills are stressed. Director of the Mountaineering Program is Tom Lyman, member of the 1973 American Dhaulagiri Expedition, whose charismatic appeal to students is phenomenal.

TILTON SCHOOL
School Street
Tilton, New Hampshire 03276

Located in New Hampshire's White Mountains. Sponsors a Winter Wilderness program modeled on Outward Bound; required of junior and senior students, it includes rock climbing. Climbing instruction at Tilton is reputed to be excellent.

NEW JERSEY

THE HUN SCHOOL OF PRINCETON
Princeton, New Jersey 08540
Director of Admissions: Theodore P. McNulty

Offers weekend rock-climbing programs.

NEW YORK

ADIRONDACK MOUNTAIN SCHOOL
Long Lake, New York 12847
518-624-3845
Headmaster: Elliot K. Verner

A boarding school for boys, grades six to nine, with a summer wilderness camping program. Located near the six-million-acre Adirondack Park. Both the forest and mountains are utilized as recreational as well as educational facilities. During the wilderness summer camp, the student explores the High Peaks Wilderness area. Camping skills and generalized mountaineering are touched upon.

NORTH COUNTRY SCHOOL
P. O. Box 187
Lake Placid, New York 12946
518-523-9129
Advisers to Mountaineering Program: Mr. Harry Eldridge or Mr. Roger Loud

Offers climbing program conducted weekends throughout the Adirondack area in all seasons, including some subzero expeditions. In past seasons, climbers in their summer program have climbed in the Rockies, the White Mountains, and Scandinavia.

THE STORM KING SCHOOL
Cornwall-on-Hudson, New York 12520
Assistant Headmaster and Outing Program Supervisor: Thomas A. Donahue

Storm King has an excellent, active climbing program, designed essentially for groups of ten to fifteen students, which teaches the basics of rock-climbing technique. "The basics" mean a thorough knowledge of basic equipment, a working vocabulary, and thorough experience in rappelling, belaying, and climbing. Students trained in safety techniques. Concentration is primarily on free-form climbing rather than on use of direct aid. Program operates during the fall, winter, and spring, and generally teaches basic climbing skills to fifty to sixty students during that time.

Storm King Mountain provides an excellent climbing area (some

Son of Easy O, Shawangunks, New York. *Photo courtesy of Ed Webster.*

of the earliest routes on the mountain were developed by Miriam and Robert Underhill). The southeastern face has a series of relatively easy climbs offering the student different kinds of climbing experiences, from chimneys to open books to overhangs, etc. There are about twenty good climbs in this area, three or four of which are for advanced climbers only.

The northeastern side of the mountain offers thirty to thirty-five climbs, which are more severe in difficulty, several of which are quite severe and for the advanced climber.

Storm King School's program is about three years old. They have compiled a guidebook describing the area climbs and best technique and equipment for each.

NORTH CAROLINA

THE ASHEVILLE SCHOOL
Asheville, North Carolina 28806
704-254-6345
Director of Mountaineering Program: James G. Hollandsworth

Successful completion of a Mountaineering Experience requirement is a prerequisite for graduation from the Asheville School. The Mountaineering Course is conducted weekday afternoons, with weekend camping trips. An alternative is to enroll in the Project Mountaineering Course, which is an integral part of the Study Project Program of the school, meeting one evening and the following half day each week. The course meeting is usually in the form of an overnight practical exercise. Each of the courses includes basic campcraft and backpacking training, skill training in rock climbing, canoeing, white-water kayaking, caving, and cross-country skiing, as well as first aid and winter survival.

OHIO

THE MIAMI VALLEY SCHOOL
5151 Denise Drive
Dayton, Ohio 45429

Winter Expedition Program, led by Lou Awoday of the National Outdoor Leadership School, a naturalist with the Michigan Audubon Society.

OREGON

THE CATLIN GABEL SCHOOL
8825 Southwest Barnes Road
Portland, Oregon 97225
503-297-1894
Director of Hiking, Backpacking, and Climbing: Edward W. Feather

The program is run during weekend time from the first weekend in April and culminating in a climb to the summit of Mount Hood during the first two weeks of June. Students range in age from fifth to twelfth grades, and the majority are fifth- and sixth-graders. High school students may take the program for Physical Education credit. Hikes range from eight miles to thirty miles over very steep terrain in the Columbia River Gorge. Students are taught ice axe arrest, a variety of camping and survival skills, use of rope, and glacier camping. An elementary climbing program.

VERMONT

THE STOWE SCHOOL
R. R. No. 1
Stowe, Vermont 05672
Director of Admissions: Miles T. Bryant

Under the directorship of former headmaster John L. Handy, Jr., the Stowe School was one of the first private secondary schools in this country to incorporate the Outward Bound Program into its academic lifestyle. The new headmaster, Hubert F. O'Brien, Jr., is presently senior instructor and course director at the Hurricane Island Outward Bound School, and much of Stowe's faculty has considerable Outward Bound experience. Each academic year begins with a three-to-four-week Resource Program involving from 150 to 200 miles of hiking, during which time basic mountaineering skills are taught. During the winter, snowshoe mountaineering, winter camping, and ski mountaineering are taught by extremely competent instructors. Stowe offers one of the strongest mountaineering programs of any American private secondary school.

TRAILSIDE COUNTRY SCHOOL
Killington, Vermont 05751
802-422-3532
Directors: Mike and Diana Cohen

Trailside Country School is a fully accredited one-year high school program sponsored by Outdoor Travel Camps, Inc., in consultation with the Walden School. It's one of the most interesting approaches to progressive education we've seen. Base is a winterized farmhouse on a two-hundred-acre wildlife sanctuary in Killington, Vermont, but one usually hears it referred to as "that traveling high school." In a way the school is one of the last great indulgences of adolescence. Almost all studies are conducted in the field, from Sioux, Hopi, and Navajo reservations to Glacier and Olympic parks, with stops dictated by group feelings and interests and staff experience. Both students and staff seem extraordinarily bright, dynamic, and receptive to new ideas. Complete wilderness experience program offered, with fairly good climbing instruction and many opportunities to climb throughout the United States.

VIRGINIA

BLUE RIDGE SCHOOL
St. George, Dyke, Virginia 22935
Outdoor Program Director: The Reverend John M. Kettlewell

This school is located in the heart of the Blue Ridge Mountains on a thousand-acre campus that includes a small rock mountain. Rev. Kettlewell has directed an outdoor program for several years, with strong emphasis on rock climbing. Interested students become part of an "Explorer's" group and learn the various techniques of mountaineering through experience. There is some training given in the basics and rappelling before the students are taken out on the cliffs. In recent years the students have also shown an interest in cave exploration as a result of rock climbing. Since caving does require rock-climbing skills, the school has also instituted a caving program that has become a major experience for many, and upon which the school seems to concentrate, since the areas of Virginia and West Virginia offer many "wild" caves for exploration.

WASHINGTON

ST. GEORGE'S SCHOOL
West 2929 Waikiki Road
Spokane, Washington 99208
Headmaster: Walter R. Hoesel

"Largely because we have several academic instructors with background ability in the areas, we have for the past two years offered a variety of rock climbing, mountaineering, and cross-country skiing expeditions to our students. Included are weekly practice climbs during fall and spring, on campus cross-country skiing, weekend wilderness expeditions, and last summer two fifteen-day treks through the Canadian Rockies. One third of our student body of 245 have participated in at least one of these activities."

Practice climbs are held primarily at Minnehaha Rocks, just outside Spokane, Washington, a bouldering area with one 5.7 climb. School groups have also climbed on Mount Stephens and Chimney Rock in Idaho.

CHAPTER 4

Summer Camps Featuring Strong Programs in Technical Mountaineering

We've sifted through material from over 150 summer camps to compile the following brief list. Apparently, in the vernacular of camp directors, "mountain climbing" does not necessarily mean technical climbing; in most cases, "mountain climbing" in camp advertisements and listings indicates trekking, backpacking, and easy, unroped scrambling in mountainous terrain.

Many summer camps offer just a bit of technical climbing—not enough, in our opinion, to warrant their being listed in this section. In a few cases, exaggerated claims are made about a camp's technical climbing program; we've included a few of these, with appropriate words of caution.

If you wish to send yourself or your child to a camp with a strong technical climbing program, be sure that you ask very specific questions about climbing activities there first: Who teaches climbing; how often instruction is given, and for how many hours; what is the camper/climbing instructor ratio; approximately how much of a camper's time can be spent weekly in supervised practice climbing. Be sure, when you ask about climbing activities, that you specify technical (roped) climbing.

It's entirely possible that we've missed some camps with strong technical climbing programs; should you be associated with a summer camp offering such a program, we'd appreciate hearing from you.

CALIFORNIA

COLVIG SILVER CAMPS
Route 3, Box 248
Durango, California 81301
Director: Craig Colvig

Their twenty-eight-day Pathfinding program for people fourteen to seventeen consists of one week's study of such huge areas of concentration as survival, mountaineering, woodsmanship, outdoor cooking, backpacking, technical climbing, orienteering, archaeology, geology, botany, ecology, and first aid—supplemented by riding, swimming, and riflery, followed by three six-day trips to various areas of the Southwest. "Between trips, a day of relaxation and preparation is spent at base camp with meals taken in the permanent Silver Camps Lodge." It certainly couldn't be boring with all that activity. Obviously, limited technical climbing.

NAVAJO TRAILS
Winter Address: Don Sampson, Camp Director
  Box 886
  Los Altos, California 94022
  408-245-6789
Summer Address: Box 11
  Bickneu, Utah 84715
  801-425-3469

For boys nine to seventeen. Integrated into the general camp program of horseback riding, kayaking, and riverwork, hiking and wilderness training is a smattering of technical mountaineering that includes rock climbing. Mountaineering is, of course, prominently featured in their literature. Navajo Trails' motto is "Adventure into Manhood." Mountaineering "manhood" does not come through this camp.

PONDEROSA LODGE
11256 Homedale Street
Los Angeles, California 90049
213-472-0344
Directors: Alan Desser and Wes Armand

The lodge offers two separate programs of interest to teen-age climbers, one in Rock Climbing, the other in Mountaineering. Age range is twelve to seventeen; coeducational.

Rock Climbing—Seven-day sessions. Instruction in bouldering for refinement of technique and climbing movements. Fundamentals of face and crack climbing. Continual roped climbing during multipitch climbs. Techniques of rappelling, belaying, and equipment use are taught. Direct aid taught upon request.

Mountaineering—Seven-day sessions, including the latest snow- and ice-climbing techniques, with limited emphasis on rock work. Problems of living and traveling in Alpine environment. Other topics covered include cross-country travel and route finding, weather, bivouacking, mountain medicine, and geology of the mountain area. A valuable, enjoyable period of instruction for the rock climber with limited access to winter mountaineering areas.

EARTH CAMP ONE
Montgomery Creek, California 96065
916-337-6535
Director: Steve Kubby

Earth Camp One doesn't have as dynamic a technical mountaineering program as one might wish, but we're including it because it is nonregimented, liberal, and modern in approach. Age range is nine to eighteen, coeducational. Location is the Mount Shasta Wilderness Area of northern California. Their philosophy seems a bit like a latter-day Bucks Rock Work Camp, with more emphasis on ecological awareness. Facilities include a library, eight-inch-diameter telescope, photo lab, and natural-foods kitchen, with all the salads and most of the vegetables organically grown on their own grounds and tended by campers.

Their wilderness program offers training in wilderness skills, advanced backpacking, snow mountaineering, and an ascent of

14,192-foot Mount Shasta. The program is best suited to the moderately athletic young person seeking a very general yet positive introduction to backpacking, mountaineering, and related wilderness skills.

COLORADO

THE TELLURIDE MOUNTAINEERING SCHOOL
Box 4
Aspen, Colorado 81611
Director: Dave Farny

The Telluride Mountaineering School offers separate outdoor programs for boys and girls. The Telluride School is "for the young man who desires to taste the satisfaction of helping others through new and demanding situations, who welcomes the knowledge of doing a tough job well while discovering the beauty and excitement of nature along the way"—to give you a taste of their rhetoric. Basic mountaineering skills are taught within groups of six students and a guide during three-to-ten-day backpack trips. Ages thirteen to eighteen; two five-week sessions. Rafting, survival training, and hiking are also included.

Their advanced *Guide School* stresses technical mountaineering for boys fifteen and over with a basic knowledge of mountaineering. "Guide School," of course, is a pretty catchy title for a climbing camp.

The Telluride Mountaineering School for Girls is for fifteen girls, age fourteen to eighteen, for a six-week session. "In Base Camp two old romantic buildings serve as the girls' headquarters where they live and cook. When in camp the boys are on the trail so that the girls may enjoy full use of the many Skyline Ranch facilities" without their parents worrying about the implicit dangers of hanky-panky where boys and girls mix, as they do through most of life.

We find this an extremely strange setup. The mountaineering instruction seems good, but we find the sexist under- and overtones an abomination. If you're looking for a false life interaction, look no farther.

CHELEY COLORADO CAMPS
Winter: P. O. Box 6525
   601 Steel Street
   Denver, Colorado 80206
   303-377-3616
Summer: Estes Park, Colorado 80517
   303-586-4244
Director of Hiking and Mountaineering Programs: Jon L. Olsen

The camp borders on Rocky Mountain National Park, an excellent training ground for mountaineering. Snow climbing, cold-weather hiking, and general mountain-trekking techniques are taught, but the camp program totally lacks technical rock or ice work.

BEAR POLE RANCH
Star Route 1
Steamboat Springs, Colorado 80477
Directors: Dr. and Mrs. Glenn Poulter

This is a former dude ranch now seeking a clientele of young people eager for a trendy "outdoor experience." Their Adventure Bound Bear Pole's "Wilderness Survival, Mountaineering, Kayaking, Outdoor Leadership Skills" course for people fifteen to eighteen is one of the worst of its type we've seen.

PERRY-MANSFIELD BOYS CAMP EXPEDITION SCHOOL OF
MOUNTAINEERING
Box 328
Steamboat Springs, Colorado 80477
303-879-4152
Director: Robert G. Weiss

Coeducational. Minimum age, fifteen. Features a mountaineering training camp located in the Colorado Rocky Mountains. The camp experience is conducted under Alpine conditions and includes training in rock climbing, survival, snow climbing, backpacking, wilderness camping, orienteering, and river rafting skills. Those who successfully complete the base camp period are eligible to participate in their mountaineering tour going to Teton National Park. Members will backpack to the lower saddle of the Grand Teton and from there climb to the summit of the Grand Teton. Other peaks will be attempted as well, giving the participants in this program legitimate mountaineering experience. An exciting program run by able and competent instructors.

CONNECTICUT

INSTITUTE OF WILDERNESS EDUCATION
Diamond Glen Road
Farmington, Connecticut 06032
203-677-0780
Summer Headquarters near Missoula, Montana
Director: John M. Prutzman, Jr.

The director of the Institute of Wilderness Education has attended the Colorado Outward Bound School, the National Outdoor Leadership School, and the International School of Mountaineering in Switzerland. He has instructed climbing and mountaineering at NOLS and the International Ranger Camp in Switzerland. Unfortunately, for all of Mr. Prutzman's excellent credentials, the programs offered by the Institute of Wilderness Education lack the dynamics that make any of the above-mentioned schools and camps as attractive as they are.

The institute instructs basic and intermediate climbing, mixed in with mountain hiking. Several less than major climbs are undertaken by students. Rope handling, rappelling, and other basic skills are touched upon during the course. Their catalog states that "the student with sufficient ability is capable of starting to lead climbs and of planning and leading climbing expeditions." Leadership and the ability to lead expeditions are derived from a variety of experiences and a long apprenticeship in the mountain environment—not taught during a few-weeks' course.

OUTWARD BOUND, INC.
National Headquarters
165 West Putnam Avenue
Greenwich, Connecticut 06830

For the suburban children of successful America who provide the financial backbone of its outstanding programs, Outward Bound offers what may be the first opportunity such young people have had to rely upon their own instincts and personal strengths.

Outward Bound now has six schools in the United States, with over five thousand people participating each year. Programs include short courses for educators and others involved in wilderness education. The locations of the schools are Colorado, Maine, Minnesota, North Carolina, Oregon, and Texas. There is also an Outward Bound program operating out of Dartmouth College, Hanover, New Hampshire.

Early stages of the Outward Bound course include fitness training and conditioning through daily activities such as running, hiking, swimming, and the rope obstacle course. Participants receive instruction in safety, first aid, map and compass reading, and group interaction, as well as in technical climbing. Part of the psychological experience is the solo survival period of about three days, during which participants find themselves out in the woods, in the desert, or on an unpopulated island, with problems of having to find enough material to build a primitive shelter, enough water to drink, and food and fuel. For many people, the program provides a first experience of success—the overweight adolescent who completes the six-mile marathon, the overprotected or poorly co-ordinated person who completes a feared rappel, or one of the 10 per cent of scholarship participants who find that they've discovered an outlet for suppressed rage—and a supportive peer group.

The Outward Bound program is widely copied because it increases the psychological and physiological adaptability of almost every participant. Invariably, one leaves Outward Bound with the feeling of being capable of more than almost anyone could have thought possible. It teaches that if one finds oneself in a stressful situation, by keeping a cool head and planning a course of action, even limited knowledge can suffice.

Each of the Outward Bound schools has a special emphasis, indicated below next to the address. The Standard Course is twenty-eight days and costs up to six hundred dollars.

Colorado O. B. School
P. O. Box 9038
South Denver Station
Denver, Colorado 80209
303-825-0880

backpacking, light
mountaineering

Minnesota O. B. School   mountaineering, canoeing
1055 East Wayzata Boulevard
Wayzata, Minnesota 55391
612-473-5476

Hurricane Island O. B. School   sailing
P. O. Box 429
Rockland, Maine 04841
207-594-5548

Northwest O. B. School   mountaineering
3200 Judkins Road
Eugene, Oregon 97403
503-342-6044

North Carolina O. B. School   hiking and backpacking
P. O. Box 817
Morgantown, North Carolina 28655
704-437-6112

Texas O. B. School   desert travel and survival
4603 W. Lovers Lane
Dallas, Texas 75209
214-352-3931

Dartmouth Center   winter mountaineering,
Robinson Hall   cross-country skiing,
Dartmouth College   expedition planning
Hanover, New Hampshire 03755

VAGABOND RANCH
P. O. Box 414
South Kent, Connecticut 06785
203-927-3814
Summer: Granby, Colorado
Director: Mark Mankin

Coeducational; eleven to seventeen years. A full-length camp session with instruction in backpacking, skiing, riflery, fishing, riding, and, because of their proximity to the Rocky Mountains, a rock-climbing program. While campers receive a basic amount of climbing instruction, Vagabond Ranch's complete program lacks the dynamics of the true wilderness camp. Activities, however, are on an elective basis, and the confirmed climber can probably get in three or four days of practice climbing per week.

LOUISIANA

CAMP SEQUOYAH-TSALI
Winter: P. O. Drawer 580
  New Roads, Louisiana 70760
  504-638-8417
Summer: P. O. Box 8
  Weaverville, North Carolina 28787
  704-645-6250
Director: Bruce Capps

Rock climbing is a major camp activity. They offer three-, five-, and seven-week sessions. They also have special young or older adult climbing seminars and courses in the winter by special arrangement.

NEW MEXICO

PHILMONT SCOUT RANCH AND EXPLORER BASE
Cimarron, New Mexico 87714

Technical climbing is one of the many activities in which Scouts and Explorers participate at Philmont. Instruction includes basic rope work, rappelling, safe climbing procedures, and easy technical climbs. The program runs the entire summer, but each unit participates for only one or two days of intensive instruction, since each unit's stay at Philmont is usually about fourteen days. The climbing program is taught by well-trained, qualified individuals, and is the most complete introduction to the sport offered at any Boy Scout camp. Scouts and Explorers with previous training in technical climbing may join their instructors and trip leaders on more demanding climbs.

NORTH CAROLINA

THE ASHEVILLE SCHOOL
Asheville, North Carolina 28806
704-254-6345
Director of Mountaineering Programs: James G. Hollandsworth

In association with the Asheville School, a variety of summer mountaineering programs are offered.

Southern Appalachians Mountaineering Camp—A three-week session featuring white-water kayaking, cave exploration, and rock climbing in the mountains of North Carolina, Georgia, and South Carolina. Held in June and July for high-school-age students. Coeducational.

Western Mountain Climbing Expedition—To Wyoming and Montana. Intensive mountaineering instruction during visit to the Grand Teton and the Beartooth Mountain area.

Adult Student Expedition to the Wind River Range—This two-week trip includes students and family groups. A good way for the whole family to get instruction in wilderness backpacking and rock and mountain climbing.

MONDAMIN
Tuxedo, North Carolina 28782
704-693-7446
Director: Frank D. Bell, Jr.

There are two camps run by the same people, Mondamin for boys, and Green Cove for girls. Both are eight-week programs and include rock climbing and mountaineering in the local area for ages eight to seventeen, beginner to advanced levels. These are not climbing camps per se, but include climbing as part of their "Woodsmanship" program.

In the spring and fall, they operate Mondamin Wilderness Adventures, an outdoor educational program for all ages, including families. Expeditions have traveled to Mount Asineboine National

Park in British Columbia, and to the White Mountains. Excursions to Alaska and Mexico are planned. These are combined sight-seeing and mountaineering expeditions that do not get into highly technical climbing.

OHIO

KOOCH-I-CHING
Box 271
International Falls, Minnesota 56649
Winter: Camping and Education Foundation
7390 Indian Hill Road
Cincinnati, Ohio 45243

This camp has an exceptional outdoor program, well integrated within the complete camp living experience. Sports include tennis, sailing, water skiing, and orienteering, as well as technical rock climbing. Extremely well-qualified instructors, most of whom have attended excellent, liberal colleges. The climbing program is not particularly stressed, but the camp is fine.

TEXAS

TIMBERLINE TRAILS, INC.
Summer: Tin Cup (Via Altmont), Colorado 81210
Winter: Box 9701
Fort Worth, Texas 76107
Director: Robert Balch

Their Alpentrek program is an interesting, well-rounded program in general mountaineering. It includes hiking with large backpacks, wilderness camping instruction, outdoor cooking, orienteering, rope handling, and other technical climbing skills. Ages fifteen to twenty-one. Coeducational. Usually three sessions per summer season, with shorter sessions in bouldering, technical climbing, backpacking, and Alpine camping and climbs of specific peaks.

They have custom programming for any group of twelve or more wishing to use the camp facilities for special workshop programs, retreats, etc.

VERMONT

SWISS CHALLENGE
c/o European Camp Association
P. O. Box 1047
Stowe, Vermont 05672
802-253-8550
Director: John Morton

The program is offered in two summer sessions of just under a month each. Age range is fourteen to eighteen; coeducational. Their cover letter was a bit ridiculous: "Approximately sixty members of Swiss Challenge have conquered the majestic Matterhorn, both students and staff"—but the program comes well recommended and seems good. Camp base is Zermatt, Switzerland, and summer skiing instruction is available for novices and more advanced skiers. Ski racing instruction for the aspiring Olympics competitor is conducted by the Swiss National A and B Racing teams. Alpine hiking through the mountains surrounding Zermatt is a standard feature of the camp.

In conjunction with the Zermatt Guide Association, basic climbing instruction is offered for the novice and learning climber. After demonstration of proficiency in belaying and rappelling techniques, familiarity with crampons, ice axes, chest harnesses, and rope work, those interested in more advanced climbing will be taught glacier travel techniques. Ice-climbing instruction will follow, and climbs of the many thirteen-thousand-foot peaks nearby are included in the session. Also featured are mini-expeditions in the Zermatt area, aimed at developing mountaineering sense and skills.

Lodging in Zermatt is in chalets near the village, with food provided by the Hotel Slalom, whose facilities the Swiss Challenge program uses.

Slides depicting a variety of activities of Swiss Challenge can be sent on loan by writing to the Stowe, Vermont, office.

WISCONSIN

CAMP BLACKHAWK
Elton, Wisconsin
2059 Atwood Avenue
Madison, Wisconsin 53704
608-249-6661
Run by the Black Hawk Council of the Girl Scouts of America. Director: Ms. Janet H. Canty

Two sessions, one of which is coeducational. Grades 9–12. Camping skills are taught, in addition to techniques of belaying, rappelling, and rock climbing. Students travel through northern Wisconsin for eight days' experience in climbing and mountaineering away from the camp base. A fairly priced program and, to our minds, a fantastic opportunity for the young women who participate.

CANADA

CANADIAN SCHOOL OF MOUNTAINEERING
P. O. Box 1552
Banff, Alberta T0L 0C0
Canada
403-678-5714
Director and Guide: Ottmar Setzer

A nine-day course for teen-agers in Wilderness Mountaineering. Covered are wilderness travel and survival techniques as well as instruction by professional guides in rock, snow, and ice climbing. Canadian School of Mountaineering guides also accompany students as they ski on glaciers and swim in glacier-fed streams and lakes.

Small groups can participate as a unit, if they wish, and customized wilderness outings can be arranged for them.

HIGH HORIZONS
Box 1166
Banff, Alberta T0L 0C0
Canada
403-762-3292 or 762-2868
Directors: Bernie Schiesser and John Gow, both members of the Association of Canadian Mountain Guides

High Horizons offers one of the most attractive mountaineering programs for young men and women thirteen to eighteen we've yet seen. They don't pretend to be running an Outward Bound session, a "survival" program, or an encounter group—simply a camp located thirty miles south of Banff in an Alpine valley of seldom-used or -traveled Forest Preserve, where young people learn to live and travel peacefully and safely in the high mountains. The rock on most of the mountains in the area offers excellent climbing, and some of the smaller peaks close to camp have limestone "practice areas" for training. They use the glaciers behind camp as a snow- and ice-training area, and one hour's travel takes campers onto the ice, where safe glacier-traveling techniques, ice climbing, crevasse rescue procedures, and basic avalanche problems are taught by the professional mountain guides who staff the camp. The women guides, of course, get to do the cooking as well as the supervision of the girls' section.

Program I—Twenty days. Not prohibitively expensive. Ten days training at base camp, ten days traversing glaciers, climbing peaks, and camping beside small mountain lakes and streams. Distance traveled each day is minimal, just enough to reach another prime climbing area.

Program II—Twenty days. Similar to *Program I,* but run at a more aggressive level for campers who have attended one of the mountaineering schools previously, or who have mountaineering background. After a training session, they set out to do climbs of a higher caliber. The group works together to plan trips, prepare supplies and equipment, and participate in leading. Usually conducted between late July and mid-August.

Junior Mountain Camps—for children eight to twelve. A first introduction to mountains. Six to eight campers per leader. The children learn hiking, basic climbing, explore a glacier, and make easy climbs and trips. Campers are made aware of "wilderness manners," how to camp in the mountains without damaging them, and are assigned evening chores such as firewood carrying and dishwashing on a rotating basis. Ten-day sessions, with possibility of registering campers in two ten-day sessions.

Adult Beginning Mountaineering Week—Usually held in late August, in Burstall Lakes regions. The week includes rock- and ice-climbing schools, with ascents planned to the ability of the group. Covered during the week are introduction to route finding, map and compass work, and trip planning. Stay during the week is at comfortable base camp. Less expensive than a week at a resort hotel and certainly healthier and more fun.

High Horizons has other ski, backpacking, and cycling programs as well as a guiding service. They'll also arrange custom programs for groups.

SWITZERLAND

INTERNATIONAL RANGER CAMPS
1854 Leysin
Switzerland
Director: Mrs. Sigrid B. Ott

This coeducational camp for boys and girls eight to fifteen provides an introduction to the sport and lifestyle of mountaineering unsurpassed by any other camp we have encountered. Instruction is given by experienced and trained mountaineers, and classwork includes rock climbing, belaying, equipment, types of rock, safety, and other elementary instruction for the novice. Staff and campers are cosmopolitan, with English the primary language used. Studies are supplemented by slide shows, mountaineering films, excursions, and lectures by whichever prominent local mountaineer Mrs. Ott can corral. Lecturers in the past have included Dougal Haston.

CHAPTER 5

Traveling Camps Featuring Strong Programs in Technical Mountaineering

Some of the traveling programs listed on the following pages were enough to make us wish we were younger. The camps combine a fine opportunity to travel in the northwestern United States and other mountainous areas of the world with unusually strong technical mountaineering instruction and opportunities.

Few traveling camps are as vague or evasive about their technical climbing programs as many stationary summer camps seem to be, but it doesn't hurt to make some of the same inquiries suggested in the introduction to Chapter 4 before sending in your deposit.

ADVENTURE BOUND, INC.
Box 278
16–18 Washington Street
Ellicottville, New York 14731
716-699-2364
Directors: Chris and Heidi Rounds

Adventure Bound is a traveling camp catering to young people ten to sixteen. The camp is the only one we have encountered to require a hair length restriction, indicating their nonliberal approach to the wilderness experience. On occasion, rock climbing and various technical mountaineering situations are encompassed in their programs. Several camp sessions per year are planned, with an occasional trip abroad.

ALBERTA BOUND
Jasper, Alberta, Canada
Winter: 40 Sherwood Road
  Ridgewood, New Jersey 07450
  201-444-8699
Directors: Mike and Gabe Holmes

Coeducational; ages fifteen to twenty-one. Seven weeks of mountaineering, backpacking, and climbing in the beautiful remote areas of the Canadian Rocky Mountains. Backpack trips are ten to fifteen days in length, with the group divided into sections of ten campers and two staff. The "rugged life" is punctuated by periodic "town days" and "tourist days." Excellent climbing instruction, with climbs determined by strength and skills of campers in each section. An ice axe is part of the required personal equipment list. Very expensive, but the cost—almost two thousand dollars—includes airfare.

COLUMBINE MOUNTAINEERING SCHOOL
116 West Cedar Street
Walsenburg, Colorado 81089
303-738-2824
Directors: Jim and Terry Aherns

A coeducational camp, ages fourteen and up. Thirty-six days. A four-to-one camper/counselor ratio. The trip goes from Rocky Mountain National Park to Lathrop State Park, Colorado, and on to Great Sand Dunes National Monument, Mesa Verde National Park, and Colorado National Monument. Other scheduled stops include Dinosaur National Monument, Utah; Hells Canyon of the Snake River, Idaho; Yellowstone National Park, Wyoming; and the Wind River Range Primitive Area. The emphasis seems to be on hiking rather than climbing, but the use of rope, ice axe, and other technical equipment is taught. People signing up for the trip before March 1 receive a one-hundred-dollar discount on the high cost.

THE INFINITE ODYSSEY
14 Union Park Street
Boston, Massachusetts 02118

Infinite Odyssey has an extremely interesting range of wilderness trips to exotic parts of the world, open to high-school- and college-age men and women. Ten to twelve participants, with two leaders. Some schools and colleges have granted academic credit for Odyssey trips. The trips are quite expensive, but The Infinite Odyssey has a few financial aid grants available, with preference given to students who work to pay part of the trip expense.

Alps Mountaineering—Extensive climbing and hiking in French and Swiss Alps, Otztaler Alps in Austria, and the Italian Dolomites. Bicycling in France, work on a Bavarian farm, and stops at cultural centers such as Zurich, Salzburg, Vienna, Zagreb, and Venice. Eight weeks.

Bolivian Andes Expedition—Extensive high mountaineering in the Cord Real region of the Andes, north of La Paz. Rigorous climbing, hiking, long ridges. Studying at Lake Titicaca and the ancient city of Machu Picchu. Visits with Bolivian families. Also a possibility of building a raft and descending an estuary of the Amazon. Six weeks. Minimum age, seventeen.

East Africa—Two-week participation in the Kenyan Outward Bound School with African students. Climbs of Mount Kilimanjaro and Mount Kenya. Bushcraft and first aid studied with the Masai and Bemba. Except when at Outward Bound schools, trip base is the bush of the Serengeti, the shores of the Indian Ocean, and Tanzanian game parks and reserves. Six weeks.

New Zealand Walking Tour—Flora, fauna, geology, climate, culture, and human settlement of New Zealand. Backpacking on the west coast of the subtropical Northland. Climbing Mounts Egmont, Ruapeho, and Ngaurahoe. Hiking through Hermitage Glacier region, Alpine fjordland, and Hawkes Bay and the Mahia Peninsula. Eight weeks.

American Northwest—From Denver to Yellowstone on bicycles. Other activities, including several days' climbing in Grand Teton National Park. Five weeks.

British Isles and Outward Bound—Available only to Outward Bound alumni and associates. An extended Outward Bound experience in the British Isles. Participation with British students and instructors at Devon, Aberdovey, and Moray. Hiking on Dartmoor, white-water canoeing, climbing in the Scottish Highlands, sailing on the North Sea. Six weeks. Minimum age, eighteen.

India, Nepal, and the Himalayas—No climbing stressed in trip outline, but this area of the world is a pilgrimage for any young mountaineer. Ten weeks of intensive study and physical activity.

NORTH AMERICAN WILDERNESS SURVIVAL SCHOOL, INC.
205 Lorraine Avenue
Upper Montclair, New Jersey 07043
201-783-7711
Director: Jay H. Reichbach

Courses and trips are held during the fall, winter, and spring. Most are conducted at the Dix Wilderness area of the Adirondack Mountains in northern New York State and last from nine to twelve days. Their *Concentrated Course* offers instruction in wilderness travel, camping, and mountain survival.

Weekend trips are run from Labor Day to Memorial Day and provide two- and three-day instruction in technical rock work and snow and ice climbing. All levels of instruction covered, from novice to very experienced for those wishing to brush up on new developments.

College credit possible through Ulster County Community College.

During the summer months, NAWSS offers a month-long High-altitude Mountaineering Expedition to the Big Horn Mountains of Wyoming. Instruction includes rock and snow climbing, extensive orienteering, travel in whiteout conditions, and search-and-rescue techniques, as well as wilderness nutrition. A very dynamic program with good technical instruction.

Also offered during the summer are Basic Survival and Advanced Survival, both of which are taught in the Adirondacks, with the first course a prerequisite for the second.

All groups limited to approximately ten persons. Coeducational.

NORTH COUNTRY MOUNTAINEERING, INC.
Box 951
Hanover, New Hampshire 03755
Chief Guide: Steve Schneider

North Country Mountaineering, Inc., is the only traveling camp devoted exclusively to mountaineering. All trips last from thirty-six to forty-two days, and are open to young people fifteen–twenty. Nine campers, three guides.

The Enchanted Valley: Olympic Mountain Range, Washington State—Technical climbing and instruction at several of the most popular and prestigious crags in the United States with enough glacier experience to complete successfully at least two major Alpine ascents.

Climbing sites visited include White Horse Ledge, New Hampshire; Clifton Gorge, Ohio; the Needles in the Black Hills of South Dakota; Enchanted Valley in the Olympics. Ascents of Mount Steel and White Mountain, Washington. Featured climbs include Weissner's route on Devil's Tower, and ascent of the Grand Teton.

Rainier: Ascent of the Second Highest Glaciated Massif in the Continental United States—Comprehensive instruction in high Alpine ascents, including glissading, snow bridge crossing, crevasse rescue procedures, use of wands, ice axe self-arrest, Prusiking, and Jumar use. Ascents include Mount Lacrosse, Diamond Peak, Mount Anderson, and Mount Rainier itself. Culminating hike of entire West Coast Trail in Vancouver, British Columbia—ocean scenery more spectacular in its way than the view from Mount Rainier.

Hard Rock: The Best Crag Climbing in the East—White Horse Ledge, New Hampshire; Cathedral Ledge, New Hampshire; Bolton Rock, Vermont; Pok-o-Moonshine, New York; Chapel Pond; Washbowl Cliff; the Shawangunks (featured climbs include Horseman's, High Exposure, Cascading Crystal Kaleidoscope, Antline—5.9+— for those able). Climbs also at Seneca Rock, West Virginia, including Gendarme, Conn Direct, and Triple S Corner. First ascents of new routes at Coopers Rock, West Virginia. Gorges and rock faces in Carolinas. While traveling from crag to crag participants will meet some of the best-known technical climbers in the East.

OUTDOOR TRAVEL CAMPS
Killington, Vermont 05751
802-422-3532
Directors: Vic and Jane Kalina

Outdoor Travel Camps run two trips that include generalized mountaineering and rock-climbing instruction, but climbing is not particularly stressed. Participants may opt to receive an accredited summer travel study expedition and encounter course, Field Studies in Natural Science, worth one Carnegie unit.

Travel Camp West—An eight-week tour limited to twenty high-school-age expeditionists. Visits South Dakota, Wyoming, Utah, Arizona, New Mexico, and Colorado, with instruction in hiking, mountaineering, and rock climbing in the Tetons and Wind River ranges. Visits to many state and national parks. Stops at pueblos to explore cliff dwellings.

Outer Circle West—Coeducational. Fifteen participants. A total of 8½ weeks spent visiting and hiking in the Wheeler Geological area of Colorado, the Chaco Canyon of New Mexico, Havasu Canyon in Arizona, the Sierra Nevadas in California and Nevada, etc., up to Glacier National Park in Washington. It includes a rock climbing school in the Grand Teton National Park and a climb up the Grand, or "snow climbing school," and climbing to the summit of Mount Rainier.

WILDERNESS ADVENTURE
P. O. Box 1259
Taos, New Mexico 87571
505-776-2943

21-Day Mountaineering Course—Backpacking and climbing in the San Juan Mountains of Southern Colorado. Instruction includes rock and snow climbing, map reading, route finding, and minimum impact camping. Food, tents, packs and sleeping bags provided. Moderately priced. Two sessions, July and August.

WILDERNESS BOUND
R. D. No. 1, Box 365
Highland, New York 12528
914-691-2377
Director: Larry Arno

Wilderness Bound's scheduled trips to the American Northwest, the Southwest, and into Canada include some climbing. The first described is a mountaineering trip.

Washington and Wyoming—Twenty-nine days, beginning in Seattle, Washington, and ending in Salt Lake City, Utah. Seven or eight days in areas providing experience in three types of climbing environments commonly found in the United States: snow, mixed snow and rock, and rock. The itinerary includes Olympic National Park, Washington, North Cascades in Washington, and Wyoming's Wind River Range. Ten campers, three guides. Minimum age, sixteen (some exceptions made for campers with much mountaineering or backpacking experience).

Colorado and Wyoming—Twenty-six days. Denver to Salt Lake City. Trip emphasizes backpacking, with excursions planned in the

San Juans and Rockies of Colorado and the Wind River Range of Wyoming. Includes a raft trip in Wyoming and hiking in the Tetons. Some snow-climbing instruction while at Rocky Mountain National Park.

Southwest and Wyoming—Twenty-six days. Grand Canyon National Park in Arizona, Zion National Park in Utah, Cedar Breaks National Monument in Utah, Bryce Canyon, Timpanogos Caves National Monument, and Grand Teton National Park, Wyoming. Primarily a hiking trail, with some untechnical caving and a very short bout of rock climbing school in the Grand Teton National Park.

WILDERNESS EXPLORATIONS
40449 Lafayette Road, R. D. No. 1
Jamesville, New York 13078
315-469-1088
Director: Dr. Richard E. Stultz

An interesting traveling program with a fine staff. Their six-week program includes travel by auto/trailer caravan through eleven states and Canada, cave exploration instruction, kayaking, canoeing, and three-day basic climbing school followed by ten days in the Uinta Mountains in Utah, during which time supervised climbs are encouraged. They're extremely safety-conscious and make no claims about imparting climbing "expertise" to their students in such a short time—to our minds a definite "plus." A good opportunity to experience diversified wilderness experience with people who care about wilderness preservation.

WILDERNESS VENTURES
8560 Concord Hills Circle
Cincinnati, Ohio 45243
513-791-3548
Directors: Mike and Helen Cottingham

Coed; ages fourteen to eighteen. The Summer Expedition this past year was a fifty-four-day Northern Rockies and Pacific Northwest Wilderness living and backpacking trip for thirteen participants and two leaders. Itinerary included Grand Teton National Park, Wyoming, for hiking; backpacking in the Three Sisters Wilderness, Oregon; rafting on the Deschutes River, Oregon; backpacking in Olympic National Park-Pacific Beach Region, Washington, and the Glacier Peak Wilderness of the state. Participants attended a climbing school at Mount Rainier National Park, then attempted a two-day guided ascent of Mount Rainier. The final section of the trip was spent backpacking in the Absaroka Wilderness-Yellowstone National Park, Wyoming. A good traveling camp, run by people truly interested in the outdoors. Not as much technical mountaineering as one might wish, but the introduction to climbing at Mount Rainier sounds just fine.

CHAPTER 6

Guided Ascents, Expeditions, and
Mountaineering Trips to Faraway Places

Expeditions are a serious undertaking, requiring more time, money, and logistical knowledge than most climbers possess. Yet there comes a point in the life of every climber when the big mountains beckon. The following trips may not provide each life's Annapurna —but they certainly sound like good, rigorous fun.

ALPINE CRAFTS, LTD.
Box 86597
North Vancouver, British Columbia
Canada
604-879-7431

One-week trips, mid-July. A week of worry-free mountaineering in the Joffre Creek Area of British Columbia. There is one guided climb per day, with an option for those who wish to relax to simply unwind for a day at base camp. Participants should have basic mountaineering skills. Course limited to ten persons, three people per instructor. Very limited instruction offered during week.

THE METROPOLITAN NEW YORK COUNCIL OF AMERICAN
YOUTH HOSTELS, INC.
132 Spring Street
New York, New York 10012

American Youth Hostels schedules only two trips including instruction in technical mountaineering. The third listed is a hiking trip to the '63 Everest base camp. All of their excursions are interesting and well run. They're now also offering at least one outing with a moderately feminist orientation for young women only—a welcome respite from the ubiquitous mating game.

Trans-Swiss Backpacker—The group spends a week at either the Centre Alpin Pour les Juenes in Arona or in the Swiss Mountain Climbing Institute in Meiringen, where novices will be instructed in rock, ice, and glacier climbing: use of ropes and knots, simple ways of belaying, ascending and descending, cutting steps in snow, firn, and ice, and the use of crampons. The week ends with an instructional climb and overnight bivouac. The rest of the time is spent backpacking through the Swiss Alps with unspecified further opportunity to climb. Thirty-five days. Minimum age, fifteen.

Colorado—Begins with seven-day trek through the Rocky Mountains. The trip leader, Dick Mitchell, is a member of the Colorado Mountain Club and the Rocky Mountain Rescue Service. Introductions included to hiking, spelunking, climbing, and white-water rafting. Rest of the trip is vigorous hiking. Thirty-five days.

Everest Trek—Not a technical mountaineering expedition, but strenuous hiking through Himalayan foothills to eighteen thousand feet. If interested, write American Youth Hostels for a preview sheet for this trip.

APPALACHIAN CLIMBING SCHOOL
Mountaineering South, Inc.
344 Tunnel Road
Asheville, North Carolina 28805
Director: Brad Shaver

Eastern One—A one-week climbing trip in the best rock climbing areas of North Carolina. Designed for climbers of intermediate skill.

Eastern Two—Advanced climbers only. More difficult routes in North Carolina.

Teton Ascents—Ten-day expedition to Grand Teton range in Wyoming. Guides meet climbers in Jackson, Wyoming, and proceed into interior on foot.

FRANK ASHLEY, ALPINE GUIDE
P. O. Box 291
Culver City, California 90230
213-870-3508

All trips are led by Frank Ashley himself. Trips are only moderately demanding, consequently fine for families, people with desk jobs, or novice hikers and climbers. Trip dates vary, so write to Ashley for current schedule.

Wind River Country, Wyoming Backpack—Departure point is Pinedale, Wyoming. Backpack about sixty miles through Bridger Wilderness Area over a twelve-day period (a leisurely pace). Most of the climbing is nontechnical, but there will be opportunity, according to group interest, for some technical climbing. Ashley also leads a *one-week trip into the Wind River Country,* with base camp and day hikes and climbs included.

Mexican Volcano Expeditions—One-week trips leaving from Mexico City. Climbs of Popocatepetl and Iztaccihuatl, the most accessible 17,000-foot peaks available to residents of the United States. Technical climbing, but not very difficult for those with lungs undamaged by smoking.

Mount Chimborazo, Ecuador Expedition—Nontechnical four-day ascent (after three days' acclimatization in Quito) of 20,566-foot Mount Chimborazo.

BASE CAMP CLIMBING SCHOOL
121 North Mole Street
Philadelphia, Pennsylvania 19102
215-567-1876
Edward F. Pilsitz, Jr.

Inexpensive trips planned to the Catskills, Adirondacks, White Mountains, West Virginia, or area of your choice. Trips can be of any length or difficulty, depending upon ability of the party. Can include backpacking, rock climbing, caving, winter camping. Fee negotiable.

CO-OPERATIVE WILDERNESS ADVENTURES
Outdoor Program, Room 23
Erb Memorial Union
University of Oregon
Eugene, Oregon 97403

This is one of the most exciting concepts in wilderness education and travel we've come across. Trips are fantastic, trip initiators work on a volunteer basis, and cost is inexpensive. Participants are of all ages and come from varied backgrounds and from all over the United States. The operational philosophy is participatory learning and co-operation—no platoon leaders, and generally very good vibes. Friends of Co-operative Wilderness Adventures publishes a seasonal trip brochure, toward which you should enclose at least fifty cents for printing and mailing. Colleges participating in the program include Adams State College, Alamosa, Colorado; Eastern Oregon State College, LaGrande, Oregon; Haskell Indian Junior College, Lawrence, Kansas; Idaho State University, Pocatello, Idaho; Mercer University, Macon, Georgia; Montana State University, Bozeman, Montana; Southern Oregon College, Ashland, Oregon; Texas Tech, Lubbock, Texas; Tulane University, New Orleans, Louisiana; University of Idaho, Moscow, Idaho; University of Minnesota, Minneapolis; University of Oregon, Eugene; Utah State University, Logan, Utah; West Texas State University, Canyon, Texas; and Western Washington State College, Bellingham, Washington. Climbing trips in the past have included Mount Hood, Oregon; Castle Crags State Park in northern California; Pok-o-Moonshine in New York State; Mount Jefferson in Oregon; and Knight Inlet, British Columbia. Trip lengths vary from a two-day outing to a month-long backpacking/climbing excursion.

EE-DA-HOW MOUNTAINEERING
P. O. Box 207
Ucon, Idaho 83454
Director: Lyman Dye

Coeducational trips in the Sawtooth Range, not limited by age or experience.
Six-day Climbing Expeditions—Late May through early September. Group makes camp in high country, with instruction and ascents from that location. Enough snow available until middle of June or

early July to allow instruction in snow climbing as well as in rock climbing. Weather permitting, five to eight climbs included in trip.

Thirteen-day Expeditions—Requires more stamina than the six-day course and some backpacking experience. Trips scheduled June through September. Some snow climbing instruction as long as snow holds out. Ten to fifteen summit climbs. An introduction to mountaineering for those with only backpacking experience.

They will also lead expeditions to other areas for specialized instruction and climbs. Available to individuals and groups.

FANTASY RIDGE SCHOOL OF ALPINISM
Box 2106
Estes Park, Colorado 80517
303-586-5758 or 586-5391
Director: Michael Covington

Will provide guides for individuals wishing to climb outside the Rocky Mountain National Park Area. Let them know what your interests are and they'll suggest possibilities.

FREE-LANCE ALPINE RESEARCH TEAM
c/o West Ridge Sports
11930 West Olympic Boulevard
Los Angeles, California 90064

They plan summer climbing expeditions to different areas of the globe. Trips change yearly, so write to them for current schedule. These are for the experienced mountaineer—no training programs.

GENET EXPEDITIONS
Talkeetna, Alaska 99676
907-733-2328
Expedition Leader and Registered Guide: Ray Genet

Ray Genet offers guide services to individuals and groups for climbing, cross-country ski touring and snowshoeing, hunting, fishing, and Alaskan river trips. Annual expeditions under excellent leadership to Mount McKinley. One follows the West Buttress route to the summit, the other following the Kahiltna-Muldrow Traverse.

Mount McKinley, West Buttress—Three or four expeditions, April through July. Approximately fifteen to twenty days each. Fly in from Talkeetna to 7,000-foot level of Kahiltna Glacier with an experienced glacier pilot. From 7,000-foot level, expedition-style climbing to 20,320-foot South Peak, also North Peak if desired. Return by same route, flying out to Talkeetna.

Kahiltna-Muldrow Traverse—Fly in from Talkeetna to 7,000-foot level of Kahiltna Glacier. Climb to 20,320-foot South Peak, also North Peak if desired. Descend by Muldrow Glacier-Wonder Lake route. Return to Talkeetna by ground transportation. Approximately twenty to twenty-five days. Trips scheduled in May and June.

Mount Hunter, altitude 14,570 feet—By West Ridge route. Fly in from Talkeetna to southeast fork of Kahiltna Glacier. Expedition-style climbing and ascent by West Ridge to summit. Descend by same route; fly out to Talkeetna. Approximately ten to fifteen days.

By now, Ray Genet must hold the record for ascents of Mount McKinley. The trips are not overly expensive (two trips, at last correspondence, were under one thousand dollars, including food and general expedition gear). In any case, McKinley remains a formidable ascent, with extremely tricky weather conditions. The mountain gets a good deal of traffic these days—but if one is new to expedition-style climbing at high altitudes under demanding conditions, this seems an excellent way to approach the mountain. McKinley, as well as providing excellent adventure, remains a status climb. All flights in were formerly with the late Don Sheldon, whose loss this past year to cancer after decades of treacherous mountain rescue work is one of American mountaineering's most ironic and deeply felt tragedies.

INSTITUTE OF MOUNTAIN EDUCATION
P. O. Box 336
Eldorado Springs, Colorado 80025
303-499-1164
Directors: Hunter Smith and Robert Dugan

During past summers, IME has sponsored three three-week sessions, including trips to Granite Mountain, Arizona; San Juan Mountains, Colorado; Eldorado Springs, Colorado; Elk Range, Colorado; and Wind River, Wyoming. Coeducational; minimum age is sixteen, and courses are limited to sixteen students on a first-come, first-served basis. Tuition is extremely reasonable.

The courses are divided into two parts. The first seven days are spent at rock crags offering easy access, standardized routes, and excellent protection. Instruction includes rope handling, belaying, knots, rappelling, equipment selection, climbing safety, holds, and style. Also included: protection techniques, "clean" climbing, free and aid climbing, and rescue and Big Wall techniques. Much time spent on basic and intermediate routes.

The second fourteen-day segment is spent in the more remote areas of the Rocky Mountains. Emphasis during this period is on fundamentals of expedition planning and mountaineering. Includes rationing, backpacking, map and compass reading, mountain navigation, ecological campcraft, cooking, accident prevention, route selection, snow and ice technique, and some bivouac training—as well as as many summit climbs as possible. Specialized equipment, including tents, stoves, ropes, etc., provided by IME.

IOWA MOUNTAINEERS
P. O. Box 163
30 Prospect Place
Iowa City, Iowa 52240

The Iowa Mountaineers sponsors an annual outing to such exotic locations as Nepal and the Quebrada Ishinka of Peru. Round-trip fare is always extremely reasonable, with concessions made by the airlines to accommodate the heavier-than-usual baggage of mountaineers. The trips are invariably suitable for hikers as well as climbers. We've heard only positive feedback about Iowa Mountaineers expeditions.

Also scheduled each year is at least one very reasonably priced domestic outing (this past summer it was a slightly less than two-week trip to the San Juan area of Colorado), suitable for both confirmed hikers and climbers.

JACKSON HOLE MOUNTAIN GUIDES
Teton Village, Wyoming 83025
307-733-4979

Available to guide climbs into far regions such as Hinda Kush or Peru. Write to them stating area that interests you, how many people in party, and time available for proposed climb.

LUTE JERSTAD ADVENTURES, INC.
P. O. Box 19527
Portland, Oregon 97219
503-244-4364

Lute Jerstad was one of the first Americans to reach the summit of Everest.

Domestic trips not listed include river running on the Deschutes and Snake rivers. For more details, write to them for the current brochure.

Domestic Climbing Trips: Ice Climbing, Mount Hood—Five days, held June though August. Trip in late June/early July is a Mountain Medicine/Rescue Seminar, which sounds quite intriguing. Price almost as steep as some ice, but one climbs with top-notch leaders.

Rock Climbing—Five days, June through August.

Advanced Ice Seminar—First week of September. Mount Baker, Washington. Ice is, to our minds, the most rewarding climbing medium—so this seminar (though expensive) sounds thrilling.

Foreign Trekking Trips

Langtang Trek—Nepal Himalayas—Sixteen days trekking, twenty-four days total from New York. Central Nepal. Highest point reached will be Ajang La (16,400 feet). Departures in October and April; less than $1,000, not including air fare.

Everest Base Camp—Eastern Nepal Himalayas—Twenty-three days trekking, thirty days total trip from New York. Highest point reached is 18,400 feet. Departures in November and March. Less than $1,300, not including air fare.

Indian Himalayas Trek—Ladakh, Lahoul, Spiti Valleys—Twenty days trekking, twenty-five days total from New York. Northern Himachal Pradesh on Ladakh, Kashmir border. Highest point reached, 16,000 feet. May departure. Less than $1,100, not including air fare.

Foreign Climbing Trips

Ultimate Trek—Hongu Basin, Nepal—Thirty-six days trekking/climbing, forty-four days total trip from New York. Eastern Nepal between Makalu and Everest. Highest point reached (depending upon conditions), 20,300 feet. For climbers and hikers in excellent condition only. March departure. Less than $2,000, not including air fare.

Himalayan Expedition to Unclimbed Peak—Approximately six weeks total from New York. Indian Himalayas, Himachal Pradesh. Highest point reached should be about 21,000 feet or more. Less than $2,000, not including air fare. For experienced climbers only. May departure.

Foreign Sightseeing/Trekking Trips—Schedule includes a *Rhododendron Tour—Nepal;* ten days trekking, four days Tiger Tops, twenty-three days total from New York. Central Nepal—Bara Pokhari near Himalchuli. Rhododendron expert accompanies trip. Just over $2,000, plus air fare. Departure in March.

JOHANN MOUNTAIN GUIDES
P. O. Box 19171
Portland, Oregon 97219
503-244-7672

Midwinter excursion to Popocatepetl, southeast of Mexico City. Eight-day trip involving technical climbing of moderate difficulty at high altitude.

MOUNTAIN CRAFT
P. O. Box 622
Davis, California 95616
916-758-4315 or 753-7323

Peru Mountain Camp—A thirty-day mountaineering trip designed for beginning and intermediate climbers. They teach all basic skills, avalanche safety, mountain medicine, practicing what is learned by climbing peaks. Participants are expected to assist in buying food, hiring burro drivers, camp chores, etc. What they are attempting to provide is an opportunity for those who dream about going on an expedition but haven't been invited to participate in an actual expedition. Mountain Craft serves as guidance and a source of expert instruction, providing all group equipment and handling all organizational responsibilities. Their camp is located on the Cordillera Blanca in the Quebrada Santa Cruz. Group size varies depending upon the number of applicants, but the group is usually kept to less than twelve participants (plus two American guides and one Peruvian Guide), allowing a small, highly mobile format. In some cases, participant group size may be as small as six, but no more than fifteen people can participate. Instruction in ice, rock, and snow climbing is included, along with glacier travel. Several peaks climbed, including one 6,000-meter peak. Any profits made during this or other Mountain Craft enterprises are used to support their volunteer programs and to promote wilderness conservation. Past volunteer programs have included work with the East Yolo Probation Department, the Sacramento YWCA, and the American Red Cross in Sacramento. All instructors are highly qualified, with ascents including the Salathe Wall and the Nose of El Capitan, the East Face of Washington Column, and the first ascent of the East Face of Huascaran. Fee is very reasonable, with discounts available for those flying from Miami.

MOUNTAIN TRAVEL, INC.
1398 Solano Avenue
Albany, California 94706
415-527-8100
Partners: Leo LeBon, Barry Bishop, Allan Steck, Alla Schmitz

Mountain Travel offers some of the most exciting trips to faraway places we've seen. Group size is small (eight to eighteen people), leadership is exceptional, and prices run high. Listed below are just some of the trips involving climbing. Many of their excursions (for example, summer in western Nepal) involve no climbing, but are well worth looking into anyway. Departure dates vary from year to year, so if you are seriously interested, write for their fine catalog. Unless otherwise indicated, approximate prices noted include air fare.

The Huggar Mountains—Camel expedition into the central Sahara. Objective is the mountainous regions of Ataror, with rock carvings and paintings, unclimbed granite domes, and the ruins of the Sahara's ancient civilizations. Twenty days. Touareg guides accompany the party, and there will be opportunities for those who wish to ascend one or more of the Hoggar peaks, such as the Tezouiaig. The cost is under $2,000.

The Mountains of East Africa—They hope to climb both Mount Kilimanjaro and Mount Kenya. Includes a five-day traverse of Mount Kenya. Mount Kilimanjaro will be climbed by the fairly easy northern side. Visits also to Lake Naivasha, Hell's Gate (Kenya's best-known rock-climbing area), and game viewing in Amboseli and Tsavo National Parks. Twenty-one days; less than $2,500.

Baltoro Glacier—This is not a climbing trip, but who could resist

Pittock Pass, Alaska Range. *Photo by Howard Peterson.*

listing it? Twenty-nine days of strenuous trekking to Concordia, the foot of K-2 in the Karakorum Range, Pakistan. Traverse of the Baltoro and Godwin Austin Glaciers to the Chogori base camp area. Return to Skardu via the Masherbrum La, a 17,000-foot pass leading south to Hushe, then following the Shyok River. At least thirty days, possibly forty; cost is less than $2,000. Basic mountaineering experience required.

Chitral Scouting Trek—Fly from Peshawan to Chitral town. Trek circular route toward Tirich Mir base camp. Some climbing planned. Twenty-two days; less than $1,500.

Fall and Winter Annapurna and Dhaulagiri Trek—Options include hike to 12,000-foot grassy bench below the Dhaulagiri Icefall, plus possible climb of 17,000-foot White Peak. Thirty-five days; just over $2,000.

The Khumbu Himal—Mountaineering trek to Mera Peak and Everest base camp. Trekking in Inuku and Hongu valleys, with possible ascent to Mera Peak (21,120 feet). Forty-four days; less than $2,500.

The Caucasus—Climbs and hikes in the Soviet Alps. Ascent on Mount Elbrus (18,481 feet) will be included. Trip begins in Leningrad, ends in Moscow. An extraordinary opportunity to climb in the Soviet Union. Twenty-three days; less than $2,000.

Transsiberia and the Far East—Mount Fugi, Lake Naikal, Samarkand, Swat, Katmandu. A six-week circle of mainland China, with optional ascent of Mount Fuji. Fifty days; just over $4,000.

Java-Bali-Borneo—Udjung Kulon Wildlife Refuge and ascent of Mount Kinabalu (13,455 feet), the highest mountain in Southeast Asia. Twenty-nine days; less than $3,000.

The Galapagos Islands—White beaches, black lava cliffs, blue lagoons. Cruising the archipelago in small vessels. Several overnight hikes and climbs to craters. Twenty-five days; less than $2,000.

Mountains of Ecuador—Climbs of Chimborazo and other peaks. Eighteen days; less than $1,500.

The Cordillera Blanca—Climbing and trekking in the Peruvian Andes. Basically moderate climbing at high altitude, but qualified climbers may attempt alternate climbs. Thirty-one days; just over $1,000.

Aconcagua Expedition—The Polish Route—Involves 1,800 feet of low-angle technical ice climbing on the highest mountain outside Asia. Difficulties are presented by weather and acclimatization. At least six years of mountaineering background required. Twenty-seven days; less than $2,000.

Other trips include climbing at Arctic National Wildlife Range; Mount McKinley; climbing in rural Mexico—and more. This is a phenomenal organization, run and staffed by some of this country's ablest mountaineers, including (besides those mentioned as partners) Smoke Blanchard, Willi Unsoeld, Norman Dhyrenfurth, and Mike Banks (British).

NORD ALP, INC.
3260 Main Street
Buffalo, New York 14214
716-837-3300
Manager: David E. Thompson

Runs unscheduled one-week mountaineering sessions to points throughout the Northeast, depending upon availability of snow, instructors, and students. Prices vary with the nature of the trip.

NORTHERN LIGHTS ALPINE RECREATION
Box 399
Invermere, British Columbia V0A 1K0
Canada
Mr. Arnor Larson

Northern Lights Alpine Recreation has a number of programs for both novice and experienced mountaineers. Most programs are either one or two weeks in duration. The usual student/guide ratio is three to one, and the level of competency of guides is very good indeed.

The Lakes Camp—One week each session, fairly priced, late June through mid-September. A camp for the beginning climber or those wishing to review basic techniques. From their camp at 7,000 feet, they climb over a dozen peaks by numerous routes of varying difficulty. They provide all technical equipment, including ice axes and crampons.

Camp Catamount—Early July to mid-September. A week of longer routes for climbers with at least one year of experience.

Camp Serena—Mid-May to mid-October. Special sessions arranged for areas such as the Bugaboos, Leaning Towers, or other areas. Occasionally, exploratory climbing expeditions are organized for various areas in the Canadian Alps. Sessions can also be arranged involving instruction in or predominant use of artificial climbing: the additional charge for this one-week aid session is nominal.

Exploratory Climbing Expedition and First Ascent Weeks—These have a three-to-one client/guide ratio and are booked months in advance, so write well ahead of the time you'd like to climb. Sessions are held during the summer months, and this past season included four 10,000-foot first ascents in an untouched area.

Their winter program is extremely strong on ski mountaineering. Of particular interest to climbers are:

Winter Mountaineering—Offered mid-November to early April. Session open to those with two or more years of summer mountaineering and a good knowledge of ski touring and/or snowshoeing. Rock climbing may be included, according to the desire of participants. Much ice axe and crampon practice, and most ascents will be first winter ascents.

Snowshoe Mountaineering—Offered mid-April to late May. Open to people with minimal climbing experience. Instruction includes rope use, ice axe, crampon, and snowshoes handling. Reasonably priced, as are most of the Northern Lights Alpine Recreation programs.

NORTHWEST ALPINE GUIDE SERVICE
P. O. Box 80345
Seattle, Washington 98108
206-762-5165
Director: Brad Bradley

Northwest Alpine Guide Service is apparently a travel agency with a "wilderness" slant. Their guided climbs cost approximately the going rate (about $30 per person per day with several people on the rope), but their wilderness school does seem a mite expensive—more for the four-week course than six weeks at NOLS or Outward Bound.

Challenge Yourself—Minimum age, sixteen; no upper age limit. A wilderness school apparently for people with almost no previous outdoor living experience; the school can last one, two, three, or four weeks. Some technical climbing instruction included. Program culminates in ascent of a glaciated summit in Washington. June and July "departures."

WHERE TO LEARN TO CLIMB
118

Mountain Climbs—June through Labor Day; several climbs scheduled each week. One-day instruction on basic rock or snow climbing offered prior to climbs requiring technical skills. Climbs are one to four days in duration and can cover Mounts Anderson, Baker, St. Helens, Shuksan, Sloan, Stuart, Tooth, etc.

POTOMAC VALLEY CLIMBING SCHOOL, INC.
P. O. Box 5622
Washington, D.C. 20016
202-333-3398
Director: Bob Norris

Offers guided ascents to more difficult rock- and ice-climbing areas on the East Coast.

RICK HORN WILDERNESS EXPEDITIONS
Box 471
Jackson Hole, Wyoming 83001
307-733-2258

Plans camping, mountaineering, and rock-climbing expeditions in Wyoming wilderness areas. All mountaineering equipment is supplied by Rick Horn Expeditions. Moderate rates, very good personnel. Trips are from July through September. The length of the programs usually varies from one to fifteen days, but some are up to thirty-four days.

CHAPTER 7

Mountaineering and Wilderness Courses for Academic Credit

Wilderness education courses can sometimes earn students academic credit in such diverse fields as biology, physical education, English, environmental studies, and recreation. Our suspicion is that we've uncovered just the surface of such available programs. Information about other wilderness education and mountaineering courses for academic credit would be greatly appreciated.

University of Colorado
Boulder, Colorado 80302
   Rock-climbing courses for credit.

The Iowa Mountaineers
P. O. Box 163
Iowa City, Iowa 52240
   The Iowa Mountaineers sponsor many courses through the University of Iowa, Iowa City, Iowa.
   January: **Cross-country Skiing and Winter Alpine Camping and Survival Course to Colorado.** Thirty to thirty-five people, mostly college-age students. Includes instruction in cross-country skiing, up to twenty hours of lectures on cold-weather survival, and instruction in winter shelters (for example, snow caves and igloos). Everyone camps out in tents at 10,000-foot elevations and helps with camp chores and cooking. One week; one hour of University of Iowa credit.

March, during spring vacation: **Grand Canyon of Arizona.** One hour of University of Iowa credit. Eight days. Hiking and backpacking skills taught and put into practice while descending either the Bright Angel or Kabab trails.

May and June: Three consecutive **One-week Rock-climbing Courses,** which can be taken for two hours of University of Iowa credit. Includes over eighty hours of instruction and lectures. Each course limited to fifteen people.

Memphis City School System
Memphis, Tennessee
   Twenty-one day Operation Wilderness program.

Memphis State University, Continuing Education Department
Memphis, Tennessee 38111
   Basic mountaineering and backpacking course. For information, contact:
   Bill Westbrook, Jr.
   Campus Corner
   2050 Elvis Presley Boulevard
   Memphis, Tennessee 38106

Mount Adams Wilderness Institute, Inc.
Flying L Ranch
Glenwood, Washington 98619
509-364-3511 or 364-3488
Codirectors: Darvel and Darryl Lloyd
   Five credits available in Education, Recreation, or Environmental Studies through the extension division of Central Washington State College for those completing the two-week program. Four credits through Central Washington State College for completing the ten-day program.

National Outdoor Leadership School
P. O. Box AA
Lander, Wyoming 82520
   Biology Wilderness Expedition—Six hours of university credit in Biology, or six hours' credit toward a master's degree. High school students may earn six hours of university credit with special permis-

sion. Thirty-five days in the Wind River and Absaroka ranges. Minimum age, sixteen. College credit expenses are $120, plus the standard $600 NOLS course charge. Course travels from the desert zone up through Alpine tundra, accompanied by college professors. Rock- and snow-climbing instruction included.

North American Wilderness Survival School, Inc.
205 Lorraine Avenue
Upper Montclair, New Jersey 07043
201-783-7711
Director: Jay H. Reichbach
 College credit earned at Ulster Community College of the State University of New York. For information, write:
 Chairman, Physical Education Department
 UCC
 Stone Ridge, New York 12484

Northern Arizona University
Flagstaff, Arizona 86001
 Climbing courses for academic credit.

Olympic College
Bremerton, Washington 98310
 Co-ordinates outdoor activities with other schools.

Outdoor Travel Camps, Inc.
Killington, Vermont 05751
802-422-3532
Directors: Vic and Jane Kalina
 One Carnegie unit credit for summer travel study expedition and encounter course "Field Studies in Natural Science." See listing in Chapter 5.

Outward Bound, Inc.
National Headquarters
165 West Putnam Avenue
Greenwich, Connecticut 06830
 Many secondary schools and colleges give credit for Outward Bound courses. See your school adviser for details.

State University College at Potsdam
Wilderness Workshop
English Department
Potsdam, New York 13676

Course No. 2224-ENG-320: The Wilderness in American Literature (three credit hours). For graduate credit, Course No. 2224-ENG-620. A five-week course. The first 3½ weeks are an independent study period spent off campus, during which student reads all the prescribed texts (rather innocuous, pleasant, easy reading). The field period covers the last ten days of the course and is spent with workshop instructors in the more remote Adirondacks, where many of the principles and techniques of the Outward Bound program are utilized. Students learn techniques in map and compass orientation, survival, campcraft, river fording, rock climbing, and rappelling.

Course held during the summer months. Over a hundred dollars per credit, but equipment, food, and lodging provided while in the field.

Also offered is **Course No. 2224-ENG-321: Western American Literature** (three credit hours). For graduate credit, Course No. 2224-ENG-621. Physical and intellectual contact with the western wilderness experience. Field period begins and ends in Durango, Colorado.

Prescott College
Challenge/Discovery
Prescott, Arizona 86301
602-445-3245

Twenty-six-day outdoor program offered during the spring for entering freshman and transfer students. Outward Bound-style activities, including river running, rock climbing, extensive hiking, and backpacking, as well as wilderness survival training. Program then continues through the year for those interested in all phases of outdoor activity. Former director of mountaineering activities was Rusty Baillie, who was on the first British ascent of the Eigerwand.

Plymouth State College
Plymouth, New Hampshire 03264

One-half credit given for technical mountaineering instruction taken through Eastern Mountain Sports Climbing School, North Conway, New Hampshire.

University of Southern California
Los Angeles, California 90007
   Frank Ashley of Frank Ashley Mountain Guides is an instructor in mountaineering here.

Washington State University
Pullman, Washington 99163
   Reported to have programs in climbing for university students, including instruction in glacial ascents, rock climbing, hiking, and wilderness activities.

PART II

Technical Mountaineering Equipment

CHAPTER 1

Manufacturers, Importers, and Distributors of
Technical Climbing Equipment

The following is a cross section of the leading manufacturers and importer/distributors of technical climbing equipment, with comments on what is, in our opinion, the best or most interesting equipment produced and handled by each. A guide such as the one that follows is by its very nature subjective. While we find, for example, that the best warm-weather rock shoe for most American climbing conditions is the EB, many other climbers find equal or better satisfaction from the PA, or the Robbins, or the Chouinard shoe (as available). We have no wish, certainly, to impose our tastes on other climbers. Certain equipment, however, is subject to considerations other than personal taste: reliability, sturdiness of construction, safety characteristics, and economy. It is our hope that the material that follows in this chapter will be of use to novice and experienced climbers alike. For the former, it provides a leisurely survey of the best of the current market; and for the experienced climber, it should serve as a fairly comprehensive update on unusual equipment innovation.

What must become apparent to any climber looking into the equipment field is the basic similarity of products offered by each company. Soon after one manufacturer introduces something particularly worthwhile—the 1968 Sierra Design 60/40 parka, for example—almost every other company modifies the design and releases its own version.

What differentiates one company's products from that of another is often its standards of quality control. Often, a small company that produced a superbly crafted piece of equipment or clothing begins to slip as its production quotas increase. If you find that a manufacturer whose line suited you perfectly four or five years ago is now producing or importing, say, a sleeping bag or climbing vest with improperly reinforced seams, take the item back to the retailer where you bought it. If no satisfaction is forthcoming, write to the company's director of marketing, describing clearly the problem and the action of the retailer. In cases of broken pack frames, most companies will replace the faulty product, providing the frame was not wantonly abused. Or should your ice axe or hammer break, check to see if the retailer or manufacturer will replace it. Great Pacific Iron Works, for example, will replace broken axes sent to them via registered mail.

There are trends in climbing equipment as there are trends in any other field in which consumption is determined by a combination of new technical developments and peer group pressure. The most important development in American climbing over the past ten years has been the refinement and popularization of "clean climbing" using artificial chockstones. Without their use, our most popular climbing areas would already have become an ugly mess of piton scars and defaced routes. With major American routes such as the Nose of El Capitan already having been done as all-nut ascents, it seems clear that the "ironmongery" stage of American climbing has come to a close. In fact, in some areas of the United States, showing up at a cliff with pitons and piton hammer is enough to get one promptly run out of the neighborhood. Before totally retiring all of your pitons, though, it might be wise to read Forrest Mountaineering's excellent "Protection Priorities" in their *Catalog and Guide to Natural Climbing.*

Not as crucial for the preservation of the climbing environment, but a development that should be an incalculable boon to climbing comfort, is the recent return to the frameless pack system. Spearheaded by the Jensen Pack, introduced here during the early 1970s, this system is a return to the European modified rucksack approach. Having the advantage of being comfortable both during the approach and ascent, this pack system has since been adapted by Kelty, Chouinard, Mountain Traders, Wilderness Experience, and many others.

Another possibly more far-reaching technical development within the past few years has been the boon in sales of Dacron Fiberfill II and Polarguard-filled products; both of these are rapidly replacing down in much cold-weather gear. Although there is a slight increase in the weight of sleeping bags and garments using these insulating materials, both retain their loft and insulating properties when wet—making them not only desirable for wet climbing conditions, but also, in some cases, a survival necessity. While individuals who have made substantial economic investments in down gear are understandably not running out to replace everything with Fiberfill II or Polarguard, the increase in popularity of the two for Alaska and extreme cold-weather-bound mountaineers has become particularly noticeable, especially within the past year.

While certain trends in climbing equipment are all for the good, others remain whose effects can only be detrimental. With the increasing number of people climbing, it is becoming more and more apparent that climbing without a safety helmet is courting unnecessary injury. Sometimes even the most competent and most experienced climbers fall; there is no reason to invite head injury—and in so doing to endanger the lives of one's climbing companions and potential rescuers (to say nothing of the aesthetic effect of having to rescue a climber who has suffered a serious, gaping head injury). Helmets seem a distasteful subject to most climbers. In the past, they were hot, ugly, restrictive of hearing, heavy, and uncomfortable. The MSR helmet is still ugly, although the other disadvantages of helmets have been largely eliminated. Wearing a helmet is *not* an admission that you climb poorly; climbing without a helmet is only an admission of poor climbing judgment.

As equipment prices continue to rise, it seems a wise investment, if you have the spare cash, to buy extra climbing ropes now. In 1971, 150-foot Interalp climbing ropes were selling in the New England area for $25 to $30; the same rope now runs between $95 to $110. If you can locate places where good ropes are selling for less (and we do indicate some of these sources in the following chapter), see if you can put a couple of ropes away now for future use; at this point, they're a better investment than blue-chip stocks. A word of caution for novices: Do not buy a used rope from anyone with whom you do not frequently climb, or who you do not completely trust; novices are too often sold ropes that look good, but on which at least one severe fall was taken.

If you are climbing with a group of people regularly, see if you can talk your cohorts into forming an equipment co-operative. Retailers will invariably offer a discount for bulk orders, especially for purchases of bulk webbing and rope.

Mountaineering equipment is designed to be used safely. Incorrect use of equipment can affect others on your rope as well as yourself. Please do not hesitate at any time to ask your retailer for complete directions for the use of technical gear before venturing near a rock wall or mountain area. Read the "Letters" and announcement sections of such magazines as *Summit, Climbing,* and *Off Belay* regularly; manufacturing defects do occasionally turn up, and should there be an equipment recall, that's where you'll be most certain of seeing the announcement.

The following manufacturers, unless indicated by the words "ORDER DIRECT," do not sell equipment directly to individuals; so don't bother to write to them for orders unless you have a Dun & Bradstreet listing.

Adventure 16 Products
656 Front Street
El Cajon, California 92020
714-444-2161

The A-16 comfort and sleep system concentrates on four of the essential items for the climber and packer.

PACKS: A telescoping frame used on the A-16 makes this a system that cannot be outgrown. One pack will extend from twenty-nine to thirty-five inches in height; if you're five-foot-six to six-foot-seven, it will fit.

PADDED BACKBAND: The padded lower backband carries all the load and reduces the effect of fatigue that comes with using hard foam belt pads.

TENTS: A 2½-man dome-shaped tent with fly is stable in the wind, and its rounded profile utilizes space better than the A-frames.

BAGS: They have a nice goose down sleeping bag with a "v" tube construction that comes in three height sizes up to six feet, ten inches.

Air Lift   ORDER DIRECT
2217 Roosevelt Avenue
Berkeley, California 94703
415-845-1195

The Air Lift mattress (Air) is a design that uses individually inflated tubes of cold-tolerant polyvinylchloride with a rip-stop or taffeta shell. It weighs a hefty 1½ pounds. In any case, air mattresses are virtually obsolete unless one is traveling with porters. A closed

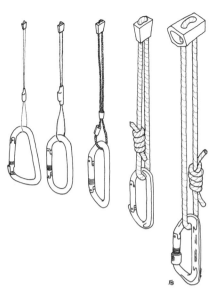

Hiphugger backpacks by
Adventure 16 Products.
*Photos courtesy of Adventure
16 Products.*

foam insulation like Ensolite does not require handling in cold weather and is much easier to use.

Alpenlite Products   ORDER DIRECT
P. O. Box 851
Claremont, California 91711

The Alpenlite Pack is very well designed. Their packbag is made of quality materials, but its suspension system is only adequate, placing unnecessary tension on the hips. They are marketing a new collapsible canteen (The Alpenlite Collapsicube) made of clear, transparent plastic that holds a full quart of liquid, but when empty reduces to a four-inch cube; excellent for warm-weather climbing use.

Alpine Designs
6581 East Arapahoe
Boulder, Colorado 80303

Alpine Designs is a well-established company that used to be known for its rigid quality control. Their Expedition Parka and Glacier Parka—both down-filled—are the standard expedition-grade parkas used by most climbers, and are excellent. For those looking for sleeping bags and clothing that retains its insulating properties in wet weather, their Polarguard (a material similar to Fiberfill II) sleeping bags and clothing are a worthwhile investment. We do not recommend their Expedition Pack; having used it during winter travel, we find it lacks the necessary capacity for large-volume winter equipment. Their Eiger Tour and Rock Climbing packs used to be fine investments, but on packs of recent manufacture we've noticed disconcerting signs of the lack of their old quality control, with things like seam stitching that comes apart. On the whole, their equipment is durable, quite good, and a wholesaler's dream, with up to an 80 per cent markup on certain items.

Alti-Wear
129 West Water Street
Santa Fe, New Mexico 87501
505-982-5065

Alti-Wear manufactures a fiber and foam combination sleeping system. The bottom layer of the sleeping bag is made of one inch of foam, which provides insulation from the ground. The covering layer

is baffled Fiberfill II. The result is a well-designed, serviceable product suited for the average technical mountaineering situation.

American Marine Products   ORDER DIRECT
240 Shore Drive
Hinsdale, Illinois 60521
312-654-3600

Primarily a distributor of ropes for marine use, this company carries braided nylon rope that is strong enough for use as runners at
about half the cost (it's known as Multifilament Polyester solid-
braided rope; either the 5/16-inch SBP 31200 can be used, or the
3/8-inch rope, catalog No. SBP 37500). Their rope is also strong
enough for fixed-rope hand rails for steep snow and moderate ice
work between base camps. For this we'd recommend the solid-
braided nylon cord, or the diamond braid; thickness of cord used as
fixed rope varies according to the circumstances of the climb or the
personal tastes of the climbers involved. Ropes can be ordered
directly from American Marine Products or can be found at many
marine equipment retailers.

Antelope Camping Equipment   ORDER DIRECT
Manufacturing Company
21740 Granada Avenue
Cupertino, California 95014

Antelope Camping is a relatively new company, producing an interesting line of packs designed for recreational use. Although lacking the computer designs of the larger companies, the equipment is
well thought out. An excellent line of packs for Scout or Explorer
hiking, or for summer camp use.

Ascente
Pacific Tent
P. O. Box 2028
Fresno, California 93718
209-233-5213

Extremely high-quality garments used by Warren Harding on
Yosemite's "Wall of the Morning Light." We have tried Ascente
parkas in the cold winter winds of Mount Washington in New
Hampshire and were very comfortable. An excellent line of products.

Eddie Bauer Expedition Outfitter   ORDER DIRECT
1926 3rd Street
Seattle, Washington
206-622-2766

Eddie Bauer is one of the most respected names in down sleeping bags, parkas, and clothing. Most other companies' products will last a few seasons; Bauer's products last years. For those not needing Fiberfill II, the Eddie Bauer Karakoram sleeping bag is one of the top down bags available on the American market. The best mountaineering down vest that we have ever used is the Snowline vest, cut extra long, with a high neck and allowing full free arm movement. This vest has been the choice of professional mountaineers for years. To extend the comfort range of your current sleeping bag, Eddie Bauer features a sixteen-ounce Mummy Inner Bag, which will increase the warmth of your bag by twenty-five degrees without a lot of extra weight or bulk.

Write for their mail-order catalog—the camper's wishbook.

Snowline vest by Eddie Bauer. *Photo courtesy of Eddie Bauer, Inc.*

Beck Outdoor Products   ORDER DIRECT
P. O. Box 1038
Crescent City, California 95530

Beck crampon bindings have become the safest, standard crampon bindings now in use. Their new neoprene nylon binding doesn't crack, stretch, freeze, or fall off during extreme technical climbs. At the time of writing, all Chouinard crampons come equipped with Beck bindings. Beck also produces snowshoe bindings of equal quality.

Bernzomatic Corporation
740 Driving Park Avenue
Rochester, New York 14613

Bernzomatic manufactures a complete line of camping stoves and camp lanterns. Though mostly geared to the family or group recreational camper, of interest to the climber is the Backpack stove and lantern. They are light in weight, function very well in cold weather, and because the fuel is in a sealed can rather than a bottle (from which it can easily spill), it is a safe little item to use. Do be sure to pack out empty gas cylinders.

Bellweather
1161 Mission Street
San Francisco, California 94103
415-861-3106

Bellweather, Inc., produces a top bicycle softwear line, including soft packs, saddle packs that convert to backpacking overnight bags, rain capes, and seat packs—all top-quality equipment that can be used on bikes or mountain trails. Their Professional Rear Touring Pack is particularly interesting; with it, you can bicycle to a backpacking area and, once there, use the same pack carried on the bicycle on your back.

Bishop's Ultimate Outdoor Equipment   ORDER DIRECT
Box 4
Oakton, Virginia 22124
703-281-4576

The Bishop's Ultimate tent is a result of design collaboration between Barry Bishop (Everest '63) and Robert Blanchard, inventor

Bellweather
Professional Rear
Touring Pack. *Photo
by Moss Photog.,
courtesy of
Bellweather, Inc.*

TENT

FITTED FLY

Standard tent with fitted rainfly. *Courtesy of Bishop's Ultimate Outdoor Equipment.*

of the Draw-Tite tent. The Blanchard concept features an exterior skeleton of tubing that is tensioned outward, the tent being set up inside this frame. Of the Blanchard-type tents, the Bishop Ultimate tent is the best designed we have seen. The quality control is superb, as the tents are produced in Bishop's small family-run workshop. The tent can be packed in and out without much difficulty, and it is easy to move while still erected. The catch, of course, is that the Ultimate tent costs over a hundred dollars more than other tents of similar design. Nevertheless, if money is not a problem, if you are looking for a domed tent to accommodate two, four, or six people comfortably—particularly for extended stays at base camp—this is the best available.

Bishop's Pack Lite II, considerably less expensive than the Ultimate and more flexible for on-mountain use, is one of the five top-quality A-frame tents on the market. A two-man tent, its construction includes a crosspole for tension and stability.

Blacks   ORDER DIRECT
225 Strathcona Avenue
Ottawa 1, Ontario, Canada

Blacks is primarily a British firm, with many outlets in England. They manufacture their own tents, which are of good quality for general mountain use. They carry a complete line of British climbing equipment, including Hiatt pitons, Viking Kernmantle climbing ropes, Karrimor and MOAC products (packs, gaiters, climbing belts), and Tiger webbing. They are wholesalers as well as running an American mail-order operation, handling, for the most part, good-quality merchandise. Their canvas anoraks are well suited for rough climbing use in wet and slimy chimneys, as well as for preventing rope burn during body rappels.

Boulder Mountaineer Designs   ORDER DIRECT
The Boulder Mountaineer
1329 Broadway
Boulder, Colorado 80302

Haulbags and climbing packs designed by the well-known Colorado climber Bob Culp and developed during use in his climbing school reflect superior design innovations for the climber. The teardrop tube shape of the haul sack, for example, is very functional, designed for rough use, and doesn't get caught on rock projections.

Bugaboo Mountaineering
170 Central and Pacific Grove
Monterey, California

Equipment adequate for most mountain situations. We would be more specific, but they failed to answer repeated inquiries—not a good sign, in any case.

Camp Trails
P. O. Box 14500
Phoenix, Arizona 85063
602-272-9401

Camp Trails produces the most consistently well-developed and fairly priced equipment on the market. They also manufacture pack systems for companies like E.M.S. of Boston, which E.M.S. then sells

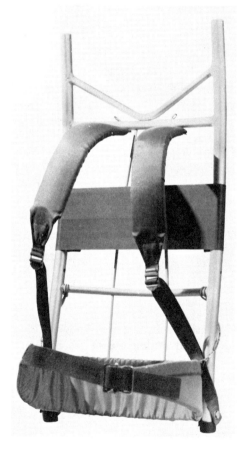

Astral Cruiser frame. *Photo courtesy of Camp Trails.*

under its own label. One of our Camp Trail frames has been in constant use for the past ten years and will undoubtedly last at least another decade.

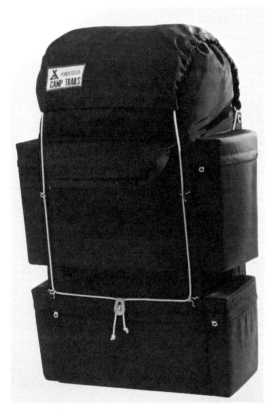

Ponderosa packbag. *Photo courtesy of Camp Trails.*

Camp 7, Inc.
3235 Prairie Avenue   802 South Sherman
Boulder, Colorado 80301   Longmont, Colorado 80501

Camp 7, Inc., carries a full line of standard-quality down products. Their "Hut Sleeper" is a full rectangular bag that unzips on one side and across the bottom to form a fairly luxurious down quilt—good for use in a camper, station wagon, or at home. It can also be zipped open and joined to another Hut Sleeper—a feature that is increasingly common these days with the rise of coeducational outdoor programs.

Cannondale Corporation   ORDER DIRECT
35 Pulaski Street
Stamford, Connecticut 06902

Cannondale produces wonderful bikepack touring systems including stands, packs, cables with security chains, and an interesting item called the "Bugger." The latter is a trailer with a load capacity of eighty pounds that doesn't affect the handling of the bike (unless, of course, you're hauling eighty pounds or pedaling up- or downhill).

Carikit Outdoor Equipment Kits   ORDER DIRECT
c/o Holubar, Box 7
Boulder, Colorado 80302

Carikit was the second company to come out with kits for making one's own equipment. Their line includes down vests, parkas, sweaters, mittens, children's parkas, rainwear, sleeping bags, tents, and for the growing child, an extendable bag that can be added to as the child grows. Prices reflect a 50 per cent savings over buying premade products. Excellent-quality materials and design.

Champion Industries   ORDER DIRECT
35 East Poplar Street
Philadelphia, Pennsylvania 19123
215-MA7-7477

The only thing of interest to technical rock climbers in Champion Industries' catalog is probably the Millet Rucksacks, all of which have been well proven in the Alps. Champion also handles Swiss-manufactured down sleeping bags, which are well constructed and fairly inexpensive. Purchases can be made directly from them or through your dealer.

Chuck Roast Equipment   ORDER DIRECT
P. O. Box 224
North Conway, New Hampshire 03818
603-447-5424

One of our favorite harnesses for climbing was made by Chuck Roast, operating out of a small shop in North Conway. Chuck Roast produces climbing harnesses, personally constructed haul sacks, Grade VI climbing packs, and day tripping bags. Their canvas gaiters are fast becoming the most popular ice-climbing gaiters in northern New England. They will custom-construct equipment for individuals, but on a limited basis.

Class 5 Mountaineering Equipment ORDER DIRECT
2010 7th Street
Berkeley, California 94710
415-548-6223

Class 5's coloring book retail catalog is one of the most interesting approaches to advertising in the industry and is well worth having. Their Ringling Brothers tent, a modified teepee design with center pole instead of external framing, weighs only six pounds, seven ounces, and is well designed for base camp work, being nice and roomy. Their mountain tent, the "Uptite," is a very good buy compared with others on the market, and their entire line of sleeping bags demonstrates Class 5's ability to provide reasonably priced, well-designed equipment for the backpacker and climber. Their 60/40 parka comes close to being almost as good as the Sierra Designs' 60/40.

Climb High, Inc. ORDER DIRECT
Ferrisburg, Vermont 05456

Climb High, Inc., is an importer and distributor of Edelweiss-Everdry ropes, harnesses, webbing, and boot laces. The Everdry rope with which we have worked has proven to have some highly desirable characteristics for wet- and freezing-weather conditions: This rope does not gain weight or freeze when wet, and resists caking and coating with ice—a familiar situation in freezing temperatures. The Everdry that we tested during the winter season of 1974–75 was, however, disappointing in its wear resistance: While a worn outer sheath does not necessarily indicate an unsafe rope, being able to see the inside fibers through the sheath after only a few climbs does not instill confidence. Also, the rope's feel was rather limp and mushy. We still think the idea of a non-water-absorbing rope for winter use is excellent, and are at present much happier with the Super-Dry Elite rope.

Jumar ascender on Everdry rope.

CMI—Colorado Mountain Industries
1896 Reading Road
Cincinnati, Ohio 45215
513-232-3398

One of the most frequent mishaps that used to befall Mummery's
Alpine guide, Alex Burgener, was having the wooden shaft of his axe
break at times when he most needed it. It was something that continued to plague mountaineers for more than the next half century. Yet
when CMI came out with a metal-shafted ice axe during the 1960s,
the reaction of most American climbers was that a wooden shaft was
"more aesthetic." More aesthetic or not, subsequent research by
Mountain Safety Research and other companies conducting their
own tests confirmed that the metal-shafted axe is safer—and it has
since become the norm, with the exception of Chouinard fanatics.

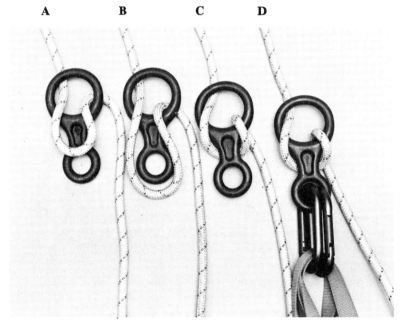

RAPPEL. (A) Take a bight in the rope and pass it through the upper
(larger) oval ring. (B) Pull the bight down below lower (smaller) ring.
(C) Pull lower ring through bight with slight tension on the rope. (D)
Attach the carabiner or carabiners to both your seat sling and lower ring.
Grasp the rope with your control hand, and rappel.

A   B   C

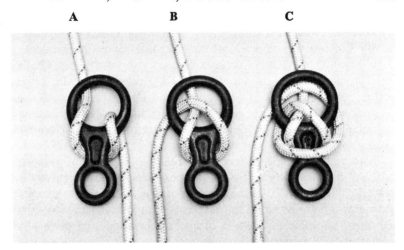

BELAY, LOAD LOWERING, RESCUE. (A) Normal configuration for applying friction. (B) Rope lock for 7/16 laid or 11 mm single or double Kernmantle, doubled 7–9 mm. (C) Double lock for more security on smaller single ropes, heavy loads, etc.

A   B   C   D

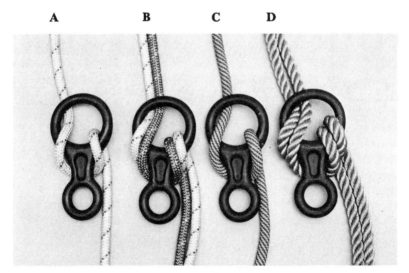

VARYING ROPE SIZES. (A) Single 9 mm Kernmantle rope. (B) Double 9 mm Kernmantle rope. (C) Single 11 mm Kernmantle rope. (D) Double 7/16 laid rope. *Photos by Robert W. Eubanks, Jr., courtesy of CMI.*

The original CMI ice axes have since become collector's items, and the company (which closed down for a while and recently reopened, based in Cincinnati) still produces that excellent, innovative product.

The Mountaineer Rock Climbing Hammer was another of CMI's better products. It has, in approximately the decade since its introduction, seen hundreds of first ascents—and to our mind is still the best rock-climbing hammer available. The company also produces a fine, reliable line of angle pitons, small-crack tacks, and offset-eye pitons.

Not to be outdone by its record as a climbing equipment pioneer, CMI has recently introduced a descending device, the Figure-of-8 (officially, the CMI "8" Ring), which is one of the most exciting new pieces of equipment we have recently seen. We've staged several falls on it, using the Figure-of-8 in a belay situation, and there was no slippage in the system other than natural rope stretch; during two nonscheduled falls, the Figure-of-8 held equally well. In the latter situation our partner was unable to get back into a comfortable stance to attempt a move sequence over a bulge; he was lowered to the belay stance, using the Figure-of-8, with the utmost ease. If the situation had been one of a leader fall, the second would have been in a better position to help than, to the best of our knowledge, with any other device or body belay setup. For rappelling, the Figure-of-8's ease of attachment to the rappel rope during potentially dangerous situations ought to make it a welcome addition to any rack. In below-

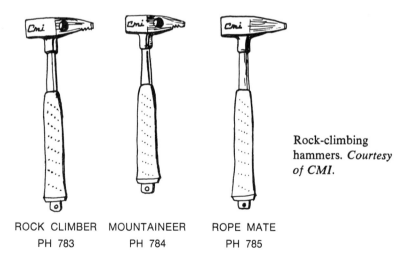

Rock-climbing hammers. *Courtesy of CMI.*

ROCK CLIMBER   MOUNTAINEER   ROPE MATE
PH 783   PH 784   PH 785

freezing situations, it is easier to use with mittens on than it would be to set up a 'biner brake.

CMI has also recently come out with a full range of common hexᵣcentric nuts similar to those manufactured by the Seattle Manufacturing Corporation. The common hexcentric design has been improved by the addition of a support beam in the internal design of the nuts, making the nuts more resistant to crushing. The one fault of these nuts is that they seem to lack the taper-bite action that make the Chouinard hexcentrics more versatile and secure in use.

CMI has also come out recently with one of the kookiest additions possible to anyone's climbing gear—earrings for pierced ears featuring their smallest-size nuts (No. 610). They are light, surprisingly attractive, and a proven conversation starter.

Coleman Outing Products
250 North St. Francis
Wichita, Kansas 67201
316-AM7-3211

Coleman distributes their own line of camping equipment, including tents, lanterns, camp stoves, heaters, propane accessories, sleeping bags, and packs. Their equipment is geared to the family camper rather than the climber. A particularly good buy is their Sportster Stove—a gas-operated dependable pump stove.

Columbia Sportswear
660 North Baltimore Street
Portland, Oregon 97203

Manufacturers and distributors of an entire range of Dupont Dacron Fiberfill II products for the climber: vests, jackets, and mixed climbing attire. They also carry camping and hiking clothing of conventional materials. Not so conventional is their "Bowser Bag," which can convert your pup into a pack horse.

Coming Attractions
6519 76th Street
Cabin John, Maryland 20731
301-320-3518

This is a T-shirt and graphics company offering two T-shirt designs for the climber. One depicts an ice climber, and the other a dirty Warren Harding-like hard man climbing on rock in EBs.

The Bowser Bag for the climbing pup. *Photo courtesy of Columbia Sportswear.*

The Columbia Sportswear Fiberfill vest. *Photo by Allan J. de Lay, courtesy of Columbia Sportswear.*

Graphic T-shirt. *Photo courtesy of Coming Attractions.*

Graphic sweat shirt. *Photo courtesy of Coming Attractions.*

They're very good graphics and these will probably be the "in" T-shirts at crags across the United States. Coming Attractions also produces sweat shirts adorned with graphics of climbers and a rugby-type shirt with an ice-axe and rope insignia for those tired of Lacoste alligators.

Comfy-Seattle Quilt
310 First Avenue South
Seattle, Washington 98104

Comfy down sleeping bags, jackets, and vests are marketed under many well-known "brand name" labels. If you can locate a retailer carrying Comfy bags under Comfy's own label (e.g., Peter Limmer in New Hampshire), you will be getting yourself a better buy.

The Donner Mountain Corporation (DMC)
2110 5th Street
Berkeley, California 94710
415-843-6705

Donner distributes Pivetta Boots, Edelweiss ropes and accessory cord, Plymouth Goldline climbing ropes, Stubai climbing hardware,

Bonaiti carabiners, stoves, tents, and a variety of other gear, including the EB climbing shoes. The EB is probably the most sought-after rock shoe in America, and it has become increasingly difficult to locate retailers with any in stock. If your local store has no EBs in stock, you might remind them that DMC is the primary distributor here and is the most likely place to have any available.

Bonaiti carabiner.

The Down Depot   ORDER DIRECT
431 Belvedere Street
San Francisco, California 94117
415-664-4313

The Down Depot will clean your best bags; their custom process preserves the natural oils of the feathers and the loft of the down. If you don't have a reliable cleaner and have much money tied up in your equipment, give them a try. They also have a full line of equipment: sleeping bags, jackets, and down accessories.

The Dry-Dan Corporation   ORDER DIRECT
Box 295
Moraga, California 94556
415-376-0289

Dry-Dan is a company known primarily for its rescue devices for military operations (one of their products is a miniaturized rappelling device to facilitate self-rescue of tree-stranded parachutists).

Their Hobbs Hook, a lowering device for rescue work (rock climbing, building evacuation, helicopter lowering, and litter lowering), is the best of its type on the market and ought to be included in the emergency equipment list of every mountain club, every school that instructs in technical mountaineering, and in the haul sack of any Big Wall climber. It's expensive, but it's worth every penny. Control requires use of only one hand, and it is an excellent device

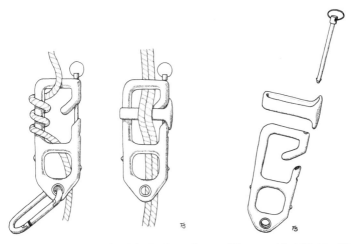

Hobbs Rescue Hook with single and double rope rappels rigged.

Disassembled Hobbs Hook.

for instilling confidence in persons being trained to climb or work aloft. Both its ease of function and safety characteristics are extremely impressive.

Dupont Fiberfill Marketing Division
308 East Lancaster Avenue
Wynnewood, Pennsylvania 19096

Dupont is the originator and manufacturer of Fiberfill II. This revolutionary innovation in insulation is fast becoming the single most used baffling material in sleeping bags, climbing parkas, climbing booties, vests, and mountaineering mittens. Unlike down garments, Fiberfill II retains over 80 per cent of its insulating value when completely saturated. Fiberfill II garments can be hand wrung when washed and returned to their full loft in a short period of time (particularly at low temperatures), compared to days for down products.

Another advantage of Fiberfill II is the reduction in cost of all products using this insulating material rather than down. The insulating qualities of down and Fiberfill II are exactly the same; the only disadvantage of Fiberfill is the slight increase in necessary weight of each product. For example, the EMS "Franconia"—a sleeping bag rated to $+20°$ F—made of Fiberfill II, weighs four pounds, twelve ounces, while the down-filled Gerry "Camper," a bag with the same design features and temperature range, weighs three pounds, eight ounces. In terms of safety, it seems logical that during unpredictable winter conditions (and winter mountaineering conditions are by their very nature to some degree unpredictable), it would be worth carrying the small additional weight to insure one's personal comfort and survival.

Eastern Mountain Sports   ORDER DIRECT
1041 Commonwealth Avenue
Boston, Massachusetts

Eastern Mountain Sports has been one of the fastest-growing manufacturers and retailers of outdoor equipment. They now carry a full line of EMS-label sleeping bags, down and Fiberfill climbing jackets, backpacks, tents, and freeze-dried foods. This equipment is generally good quality for the price charged. Most important, from our point of view, are the EMS kits. These are inexpensive and easily constructed precut kits for sleeping bags, tents, vests, packbags, and many other products used by the outdoorsman and mountaineer. In some cases there is up to a 50 per cent savings over preassembled items.

For the ice climber, the EMS Molitar Eisboot is the best single technical ice-climbing boot on the American market—the same boot that Yvon Chouinard features in his Great Pacific Iron Works catalog.

The EMS catalog is available for $1.00, refunded with purchase. A composite selection from recent catalogs appears on pages 152–59.

Elite-Bernina Ropes   INQUIRIES INVITED
Kalmar Trading Corporation
P. O. Box 77343—Department CSB
San Francisco, California 94107
415-647-6474

The Elite-Bernina rope is the first with a fluorescent color sheath —a valuable innovation that makes it easier to see against dark backgrounds and provides greater visibility in minimal light situations. This would aid in the evacuation of a climbing party in an emergency situation. Both the Elite-Bernina standard model and Super Dry model feature the fluorescent color. We have tested the handling characteristics of the Super Dry rope and found that the rope remains flexible and pliable in extreme cold, that it does not gain

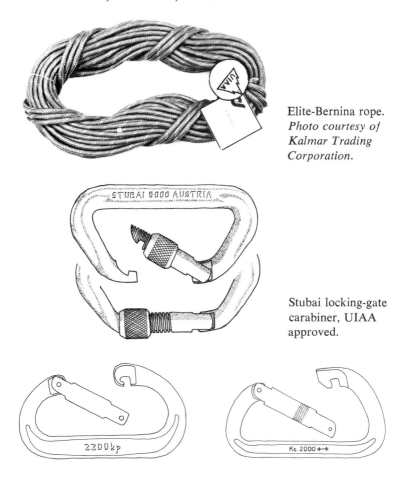

Elite-Bernina rope.
*Photo courtesy of
Kalmar Trading
Corporation.*

Stubai locking-gate
carabiner, UIAA
approved.

excess weight through water absorption, and that the outside sheath does not wear as quickly or unnervingly as some other water repellent models. In winter situations, the climber using a Super Dry rope does not have to contend with rigid, frozen climbing line, uncoilable hanks of wire, and unworkable rappel situations. While the Elite Super Dry rope is not as well known on the American market as others, it is a wise and safe investment.

Stoves

Today, stoves of one kind or another are carried by most experienced and practical walkers. There are a large number of arguments to explain this change-over from the traditional fire. Simply enough, a wood fire offers only two advantages: there's little or no weight to be carried with you and the warmth and cheer of one is way out ahead of a light-weight stove when it comes to esthetics. In fact, even the esthetic argument is open to question. Colin Fletcher offers the sensible observation that fires define a very small, well lit world around a camp. Which makes that camp feel very cozy and secure. But it limits your sense of where you are as well. It puts you in something very much like a room, drugs you with senseless calm that comes with staring at a flame and then leaves you there. Since walking seems to be intended to get you closer to the natural world rather than sealing you off from it, Mr. Fletcher suggests you avoid fires. Stick to a small stove, turn it off when you're finished cooking and concentrate on the night around you. If it comes to it, and for one reason or another you'd like a fire and the area you're in does not suffer from overuse, build one. However, that's seldom a reason for failing to pack a stove with you when you go.

All backpacking stoves burn volatile gases. The fuel they store is invariably liquid, but by the time it reaches the business end of the stove, the burner, it is in a gaseous state and mixed with air. Fuels are stored as liquids either because they come that way at normal temperatures or because they are more compact in that form, but when a stove is operating correctly, they always burn as gasses.

In the case of butane, propane or the newest LP fuels, a pressure tank holds the liquified fuel. When released through the stove burner to normal temperatures and pressure, it turns into a gas, mixes with the air and burns when ignited. Pressure for forcing the fuel out of the tank is supplied by the fuel itself as it trys to change from a liquid to a gas within the confines of the tank.

The most serious problem with fuels in pressurized tanks occurs at very low temperatures, like those found at high altitudes or in the dead of winter, when effective pressure in the tank decreases. Having lost pressure, the cooled tank doesn't force fuel to the burner as well as in a warmer environment. For this reason the older fuels are favored by some winter campers and mountaineers.

Traditional liquid fuels operate on the same principle as the newer gas stoves. Fuel is kept in a tank in liquid form. It is forced, under pressure, through a passage where it turns to a gas and then burns. The trouble is, these stoves have permanent tanks and the fuels in them must be pressurized by heating or with a hand pump to move from the tank toward the burner.

The permanent tanks on kerosene and white gas stoves are pressurized in two ways. Kerosene stoves usually have a pump and gas models rely on heat from the burning fuel to expand air in the tank and so force fuel to the burner. Both liquid fuels are vaporized in a thin walled tube leading from the tank to the burner. This tube gets hot as the stove operates. Obviously, in order to get the tube hot you have to heat it and since the stove won't work until the tube is hot you have to heat it by some method other than operating the stove.

Which is to say the problem is somewhat circular. So you have to vaporize the tube with auxiliary fuel. Most kerosene users carry a starter fuel and white gas stoves can be heated by a few drops of their own fuels. How this pressurization and priming is managed is discussed in detail below.

Kerosene
Kerosene is the least volatile of the common stove fuels. It won't explode no matter how poorly it is handled and so is favored by those who worry about this unlikely danger. It's the cheapest fuel and is available almost everywhere in the world, an important consideration for those traveling outside North America. Kerosene is slightly more dirty than gasoline as it burns and smells if it is spilled on clothing or camp gear. But, by the same token, it won't burn if you do manage to slurp some of it on your hands or clothing.

Since kerosene won't light unless vaporized these stoves require some sort of more readily volatile priming fluid. Alcohol, white gas, lighter fluid or specially manufactured flammable pastes do the trick. The fuel is stored in a tank. Between the tank and the burner nozzle there is a passage called a vaporizing tube or generator. Once the stove is primed this tube becomes hot and vaporizes the liquid fuel. In a vaporous state the kerosene will burn, continuously vaporizing fuel as it passes through the tube.

Kerosene stoves come equipped with pumps to assist the passage of fuel to the burner. This isn't necessary on white gas stoves because that fuel vaporizes much more readily than does kerosene and is driven through the vaporizing tube without additional pressure.

White Gasoline
Gasoline is considerably more volatile than kerosene. That characteristic makes it a more convenient fuel for a backpacking stove and slightly more dangerous at the same time. However, because of the greater ease of these stoves' operation and the greater efficiency of the fuel most campers opt for them.

Slurped gasoline won't smell on your clothing, but it will burn until it evaporates. It burns very cleanly, as cleanly as most kitchen stoves, and won't soot your pots. Gasoline is extremely efficient by weight.

Kerosene requires a volatile priming fuel to preheat the vaporizing tube. White gas does not. All you need do is coat the generator of the stove with an eyedropper full of fuel from the stove itself. This makes the priming business considerably less fussy, and you don't have to get the stove nearly so hot before a satisfactory flame will pick up. If the stove dies or burns yellow you can simply lower the flame and let it burn a few moments until the tube is heated. Then turn the flame back up and hope it comes on blue.

White gas' volatile nature makes the hand pumps that are standard on Kerosene stoves unnecessary except in extremely cold weather operation. White gas is most readily available in North America, and some difficulty may be experienced in obtaining this fuel in more remote areas of the world.

Butane & Propane
Butane and propane are gasses that come packaged in canisters a lot like shaving creams cans. They aren't as efficient fuels in terms of weight, they're much more expensive than kerosene or gas and aren't always as readily available. Both propane and butane burn very cleanly however. They also have the advantages of extreme convenience. If the small rituals of filling, pre-heating and priming a liquid fuel seem forbidding to you then canisters are the answer. They're as simple to use as the kitchen stove. In fact, you use them exactly as you would a stove that doesn't have a pilot. Turn them on, apply a match and cook.

Cook Kits & Utensils

Even among experienced campers, personal camp routines and procedures are as varied as the individuals themselves. Consequently, it's hard for us to recommend the most "correct" or simple method of performing any camp-cook activity. Experience, of course, does dictate certain universals. And we do talk about these; but only as methods that have been proven through experience to work well. Basically, what we've written about are common procedures used by many, but certainly not by all, experienced backpackers. Once out on the trail, you'll soon discover the methods of cooking that work best for you.

The lightweight simplicity of the foods that you choose for the wilderness trail should be reflected in your cooking and eating utensils. At the end of a day of climbing or backpacking, you may not have the desire to put together a seven course Roman feast or lug along the pots it would take to do it. Numerous mixing pans are an extravagance on the trail, particularly with today's freeze dried camping foods. You can improvise the mixing operation with a large cup or plate. In fact, many backpackers dispense with plates altogether and eat their meals from the pot they cooked in or from a large cup. An insulated cup retains the heat of your food longer than a plate, but also concentrates that retention at the rim and therefore your lips.

For cooking on stoves with small-diameter pan supports, the pots that work best have small, flat bottoms. Small diameter pans lessen the possibility of tip-overs, and their thick bottoms protect your food from sticking or scorching over the small concentration of heat from the stove's flame. In the available camp cook kits manufacturers have boiled down camping utensils and pots to the essentials. These aluminum kit pans are tough and easily cleaned because most have rounded corners. If you're in trout country, or if you happen to like pancakes or scrambled eggs, you'll find a Teflon frying pan indispensable. On the other hand, if you're a fanatic for cutting down pack weight, you may want to take just one pot. One-pot cooking is easiest when the bulk of your food intake is freeze dried foods. Most require only the addition of boiling water. A typical list of cooking equipment for two people would most likely include a pot with a lid that doubles as a plate, a hunting knife, one or two cups and two spoons or utensil kits.

Polyethylene containers are great for isolating and storing items like sugar, margarine, powdered milk, biodegradable detergents, and water (be sure the screw-on cap is leakproof). Unfortunately, those containers have one drawback. They take up a set amount of space, regardless of the quantity of food inside them. Baggies, on the other hand, don't define your space; as you use up the food packaged in the baggies, the bag volume shrinks, taking up less room in your pack. Squeezable plastic containers (sold housing honey and mustard) are refillable and good for wind-whippable foods like powdered milk. Other items you may want to carry are light salt and pepper shakers and a waterproof matchsafe of metal or plastic.

Cleaning up can be one of the drawbacks of the whole procedure of eating; but it's important to ward off wilderness bacteria. Last night's dinner may add a certain twang to your breakfast dishes, but your lower tract may feel it later. Take an abrasive scouring cloth for your sticky stuff, and boil your washing water in a pot or tea kettle. Snow or sand does the scouring job as well as a store bought pad. If you use biodegradable soap, and dump your after-effects well away from a stream, you'll be helping out the world. It's worth it.

Gasoline Stove Care and Operation

These instructions generally allude to the SVEA 123, but are applicable in principle, if not specifically, to our other gasoline and kerosene stoves.

Preventive home check-out

1. Gently bend the burner plate tabs to tighten plate onto the head.

2. On Svea 123 and Optimus 80 only — unscrew burner head and then burner tip, the latter with the hole in the key. Sight through the small hole in the tip and run the cleaning needle through it once. When visible particles are removed from both tip and inside top of vaporizing tube, blow out both areas vigorously before reassembling firmly. Remember, the only way to clean the stove is to remove the burner tip. If you don't take it apart first, you'll be pushing dirt into where it was never intended, causing more difficulty later. (The 8R and 111B stoves have built-in cleaning mechanisms.)

3. Loosen tank cap parts (it takes some force) for inspection. Inside should be a small spring; also a plunger with hollow at one end that accepts a snug-fitting rubber plug (which caps the hole of the tank over-pressure escape valve). The rubber plug should be well-seated into the hollow at all times. Reassemble firmly, so that the cap can be easily inspected at a later date. Use the small slot in the key handle for this.

4. Tighten the packing nut firmly with pliers, still allowing spindle to turn freely with the key. This and the burner plate are now field-secure.

5. On stoves with pumps only — unscrew the pump rod and make sure that the leather washer on the plunger is pliable and that it is not dried out or cracked. If it is dry and stiff, soak it in oil awhile and then gently slide it back into pump assembly.

Safety

When cooking outside, clear the area around the base of the stove to prevent a possible fire. Make sure the base of the stove is secure and will not easily tip over.

When cooking in a tent, make sure that the tent is well ventilated. The carbon monoxide from a cook stove can cause nausea and in extreme cases, even death. NEVER cook inside unless forced by the elements.

Starting: preparatory

All of these stoves need a small amount of pressure to start; a larger amount to operate and cook. The greater the pressure, the hotter the flame will be. Pressure is created by significantly raising the stove's temperature, so, insulate the stove from ground, wind, cold, etc.

When using a small amount of gasoline to start your stove, exposing this fuel to the air means you'll have to act fast to get sufficient flame for heating (to beat evaporation time).

Carefully regulate the flow of gas at all times: unless there's a specific, limited reason to have the valve on, then keep it off. Leaving it on when starting will cause premature pressure loss. Build pressure, don't lose pressure.

Have plenty of book matches on hand for use in starting.

After preheating — including lighting the priming fuel — the first of three phases of ignition has then begun. Learn the following three stages of fuel flow with corresponding combustive symptoms:

Stage 1:
The first spurt of liquid only; some collects in spirit cup below. If stove is ignited at this stage, it is premature and the resulting yellow flame may contribute to carbon clogging.

Stage 2:
The fuel flow is now between liquid and vapor. You will hear a hissing which alternates with the liquid spurt. Ignite burner head of stove here. Flaring orange flame will alternate rapidly with the desired small blue flame.

Stage 3:
If the flame were to go out at this point, you would hear a hissing noise only, representing a steady flow of vapor. Merely reignite. Combustion at this stage is blue only, with characteristic roar. Put on the pot!

Starting your stove
1. Prepare space or stable platform for the stove. Have food or water in pot nearby, ready for cooking. Unfold or take off windshield as need be for access.

2. Unscrew tank cap to release possible vacuum from previous operation. Rescrew tank cap and tighten with wrench.

3. Cap is tight; valve is off.

4. Using eyedropper or special fuel bottle spout-cap (better), pour fuel as follows:

SVEA 123 and Optimus 80, into burner head from top, allowing extra fuel to flow down the vaporizing tube, only a small amount collecting in the cup below.

8R, same, but fill cup part way.

111B, a few pumps will cause spurt, with which cup is to be filled part way.

111 and other kerosene stoves, follow instructions — for using alcohol as priming fuel — that come with stove. A kerosene stove may also be primed with gasoline or in an emergency with toilet paper soaked in kerosene. Try to learn the optimum amount of priming fuel to use.

5. With valve off, quickly ignite and wait until flame is almost out. Then, open valve and quickly ignite burner tip. Stove should now be at stage two or better. If not, shut off and try again. (If orange flame persists or burner flame shoots to side, then shut off and clean, as in part two of "preventive . . . ", above.)

6. Instantly put your food or water on for heating. By doing this, you conserve fuel, build to operating pressure most speedily and keep out excessive air movement that could blow out the flame.

7. For optimum results, cook at maximum flame: remember that the pot is cooling constantly and that to get it as hot as possible, you must heat it with the maximum flame.

Winter starting

In winter weather you should apply, especially to the SVEA 123, as persistent and sizable a flame as that which comes from a ball of ignited paper on a cleared space of ground. Fast, more massive heating is necessary because heat gained is lost so quickly. For the same reason, heat is better conserved, especially on snow, by a small square of closed-cell foam placed underneath the stove for insulation. In winter it is particularly important to keep the stove out of the wind. For winter use it is recommended that one use a stove with a pump. The pump is convenient for starting, but its primary function in winter is to build pressure in the tank thus producing a better flame. For optimum results, one should pump quite frequently.

Overheating

All stoves are made (and specially vented also) for a plateau of continuous, relatively high heat and pressure. Significantly above the plateau on all gasoline stoves, the safety valve in the tank filler cap will give way to release the overpressure. As what is released is vapor, it can be counted on to ignite and the resulting mass of shooting flame is understandable cause for concern. Leave the stove itself alone for fifteen to twenty seconds, doing nothing except to prepare yourself to lunge with key in hand to turn off the burner head flame. In this time the pressure may be sufficiently relieved for the safety valve to turn off. If not, then extinguish the burner head flame and vigorously blow out the flame coming from the safety valve. It will continue to hiss, but now, with no flame present, cooling begins instantly. The idea is to keep from overheating the rubber parts in the safety valve, which will first swell and then become truly burnt or crusty, either way rendering them for the most part useless. (Note: too much baking of the stem in efforts to start the stove will cook the cotton wick inside. Gas flow is impeded significantly through the burnt portion of the wick.) Causality for this blowing off can be found in too much heat or lack of ventilation creating too much heat, or blocking or clogging that would cause too much pressure.

It is important that large pots not be allowed to hang over the tank of the 111B and 8R. They reject heat back on the tank and this is probably the most common cause of over-heating.

Storage

Clean stove after each use. At the end of the season or when a stove will not be used for awhile, drain all fuel from the tank since the toxic residue left by evaporation can damage the stove.

One last point: unscrewing of the whole stem is usually a more involved process than you would think. We will be glad to help you with this or any other question about your stove. Think prevention though, and you'll probably get years of reliable use from your stove with little or no service.

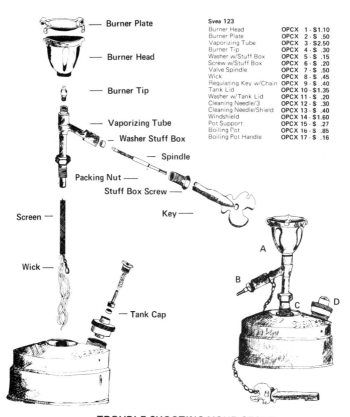

Burner Plate

Burner Head

Burner Tip

Vaporizing Tube

Washer Stuff Box

Spindle

Packing Nut

Stuff Box Screw

Screen

Key

Wick

Tank Cap

A

B

C

D

Svea 123

Burner Head	OPCX 1 -	$1.10
Burner Plate	OPCX 2 - $	.50
Vaporizing Tube	OPCX 3 -	$2.50
Burner Tip	OPCX 4 - $	.30
Washer w/Stuff Box	OPCX 5 - $	.15
Screw w/Stuff Box	OPCX 6 - $	.20
Valve Spindle	OPCX 7 - $	.50
Wick	OPCX 8 - $	.45
Regulating Key w/Chain	OPCX 9 - $	.40
Tank Lid	OPCX 10 -	$1.35
Washer w/Tank Lid	OPCX 11 - $	.20
Cleaning Needle/3	OPCX 12 - $	.30
Cleaning Needle/Shield	OPCX 13 - $	.40
Windshield	OPCX 14 -	$1.60
Pot Support	OPCX 15 - $	.27
Boiling Pot	OPCX 16 - $	.85
Boiling Pot Handle	OPCX 17 - $	.16

TROUBLE SHOOTING YOUR STOVE

Please refer to the exploded view of the SVEA 123.
All the gasoline and kerosene stoves we sell are covered by this guide in principle.

Problem	Possible Cause	Solution
Failure to start	Pre-heating insufficient, thus pressure insufficient.	Fill burner head to overflowing and reignite.
Failure to operate	Leaded gasoline	White gasoline only
	Vapor leak	Tighten at points A; B, C or D.
	Clogged burner tip	Clean tip NOTE: Remove burner tip from stove before cleaning unless stove has internal cleaning needle.
	Impacted debris from long use or carbon (caused by overheat) in cotton wick inside vaporizing tube.	Replace wick — major job, best done at home.
Gas or flame leak at point B	Packing nut loose	Tighten
	Packing worn	Replace
	Spindle worn or broken	Replace
Gas or flame leak at point C	Vaporizer tube loose at base	Tighten
Gas or flame leak at point D	Tank cap gasket missing, cracked or burned	Replace
	Internal plug in plunger askew	Unscrew top of tank cap and reseat rubber plug in plunger. NOTE: When assembling, be sure cap is firmly tightened yet can be easily loosened again.

TABLE OF SPECIFIC DETAILS FOR STOVES

Stove	Phoebus 625	Phoebus 725	Optimus 77A	Optimus 8R	Svea 123	Optimus 111B & 111	Grasshopper	Bluet S-200	Gerry Mini
Weight complete (ounces)	40	35	24	26	18	54	12	16	7
Dimensions closed (inches)	5½dia.x7½	5½dia.x4½	8dia.x4½	5x5x3	4¾x4¾x5	7x6¾x4	3¼x3¼x17	4½x3½x9½	4½dia.x1½
Fuel	Gasoline	Gasoline	Alcohol	Gasoline	Gasoline	Gasoline Kerosene	Propane	Butane	LP Gas
Fuel capacity (pints)	1.0	.63	.35	.3	.35	1.0	1.7	.8	.4
Burning time (minutes)	150	90	25	45	45	90	360	190	180
Boiling time (minutes)	3¾	4	7½	7	6	4	9½	12	6.1/6
Pressure pump	Yes	No	—	No	No	Yes	No	No	No
Built in cleaner	Yes	Yes	—	Yes	No	Yes	No	No	No
Very cold weather usage	Yes	Yes	Yes	Maybe	Maybe	Yes	Maybe	No	Maybe
Simplicity and convenience	Average	Average	High	Average	Low	Average	High	High	High
Needs priming fuel	No	No	No	No	No	No Yes	No	No	No

1 Dimensions are to tips of all extremities (handles, etc.)

2 Burning time was measured under continuous full flame; "normal" operation would add a few minutes to these times.

3 Boiling time is the time it took to boil one quart of tap water; the stove was operated in a nice warm room. These times are given for comparison purposes; again, "normal" operation would give somewhat longer times, depending on the circumstances.

Ellis Industries, Inc.
16640 Oakmont Avenue
Gaithersburg, Maryland 20760
301-977-9090

Ellis Industries will be releasing an American-made Perlon climbing rope during the spring of 1976 or soon thereafter. The ropes will
meet all safety standards delineated by the UIAA and will be considerably cheaper than any European import. If Ellis succeeds in
fulfilling the product description he gave us, this could turn out to be
one of the most popular ropes on the American market.

Forrest Mountaineering Ltd.   ORDER DIRECT
1517 Platte Street
Denver, Colorado 80202
303-222-6164

For safety's sake as well as for your personal library, send $2.00
for Forrest Mountaineering's *Catalog and Guide to Natural Climbing.* This catalog explains the use of the full line of Forrest gear. The
probability is that if you get your equipment from Forrest, you'll
never have to look for another source; it's all excellent. A selection
from their catalog appears on pages 162–69.
    The Tetons are their most versatile nuts; they provide both cam
and jamming placements in a wide variety of cracks. In a vertical
crack system, rotating the Teton lodges it in place. In a horizontal
crack system, sideways placement results in an extremely secure running belay. In narrowing cracks, the Teton can successfully be slotted. These features make the Teton one of the best nuts for severe
free climbing.
    Forrest's Copperheads, a copper swag fixed on the end of a metal
cable, can be jammed into a variety of vertical or diagonal cracks,
enabling safe passage across shallow crack systems. The Arrowhead,
similar to the Copperhead but having a six-degree tapered profile,
aids in the placement of surface protection.

The best and most comfortable single anchor bivouac hammock available in the United States is the Forrest Hammock. It has an expander pole that eliminates the crushed-in feeling of overnight bivouacs, and a separate detachable rainfly that will keep one dry in the most severe rainstorms. The shoulder-and-leg-support system of the hammock causes no strain on any part of the body.

Frostline Kits   ORDER DIRECT
452 Burbank Street
Broomfield, Colorado 80020

Frostline was the first company in the United States to manufacture and market camping equipment kits. Their line is still more comprehensive than that of any other kit manufacturer. Through their Educational Service Department, Frostline is now offering a series of teaching aids, instructional pamphlets, and lesson plans developed for classroom use—providing students with worthwhile sewing projects as well as some sophisticated information about insulation, fabrics, outdoor garments, and sleeping bag construction. They offer discounts for class orders and seem to have come up with a remedy for one of our public educational system's duller areas of concentration.

Gerry Division of Outdoor Sports Industries, Inc.
5450 North Valley Highway
Denver, Colorado 80216

Gerry has been producing equipment for many years, and their quality control has never faltered. Their ski jackets, parkas, packs, and light backpacking stoves are functional, if perhaps not as aesthetically pleasing as some other lines of equipment. Their mountaineering tents are excellent.

Chocks

Experience in the use and manufacture of climbing nuts is our forte as we have been making them longer than any current American manufacturer. Forrest chocks are carefully sized to fit the entire range of crack widths and are well known for their unique shapes that make maximum use of even the most subtle placements. In addition, the uniform taper of Arrowheads, Foxheads, and Titons makes them excellent for stacking. Forrest chocks feature high strength to weight ratios and size for size are unmatched for performance and reliability.

Hopefully, the development of chocks will reach the point that hammered anchors become entirely unnecessary. In the smaller sizes, our Arrowheads and stainless steel Titons make a significant stride in this direction.

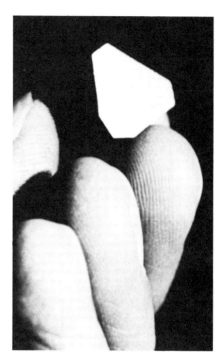

**Cammed —
Vertical Crack**

**Cammed —
Horizontal Crack**

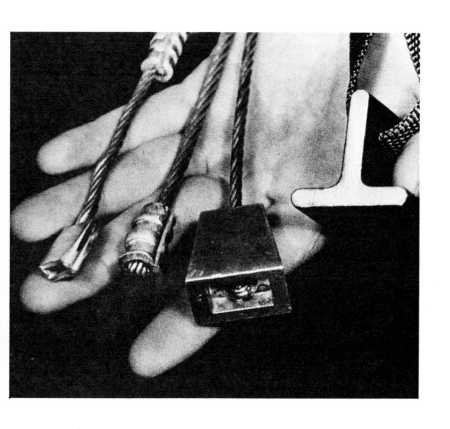

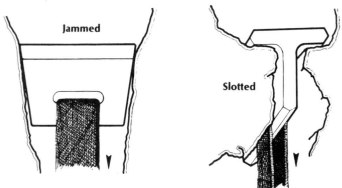

Jammed

Slotted

Chocks

COPPERHEADS™

SINGLE CABLE JAM NUTS

In the late sixties we offered five sizes of COPPERHEADS ™. They were uniquely mounted on a single cable — a system that has enjoyed wide acceptance because it works. We now offer single cable nuts that will fit cracks ranging in size from 3/16" to 1-1/4" wide. The distinct advantages of the single cable system are:

- *Control of the head of the nut during placement and removal — you get it where you want it.*
- *Additional reach.*
- *The flexible nature of the single cable reduces the possibility of dislodgement by rope drag and serves well in opposition placements.*
- *The slender, single cable sling threads neatly behind flakes and through holes that are too narrow to accept nylon web and double wires.*
- *The strength of the swaged head and eye loop in this assembly exceeds that of the aircraft quality wire rope.*

We offer three styles of single cable nuts: Copperheads, Arrowheads, and Foxheads. Since some climbers prefer a short wire sling for easier carrying and direct-aid we make single cable nuts in two lengths; the shorter nuts are indicated with the letter "S". Tying nylon web directly to the wire loop or eye is not a good practice; a carabiner provides a much stronger attachment. Both the head and eye swages are made of copper that is zinc plated to prevent corrosion.

Copperheads were solid the first time we placed them; they grabbed well in narrow cracks, and we knew they were good. Since then they have become essential equipment, and a great many climbers have added them to their hardware selections. They have a proven record of safety and usefulness and have gained international acceptance.

Copperheads number 3, 4, and 5 have been instrumental in enabling climbers to get good tree climbing protection in the smaller cracks. Their relatively soft heads "bite" well and resist the rotation problem that can cause dislodgement of harder metals. Placement and removal are simplified with the unique Forrest single cable system. Although they have stopped short falls, number 1 and 2 Copperheads should be used primarily for direct-aid due to their small wire diameter.

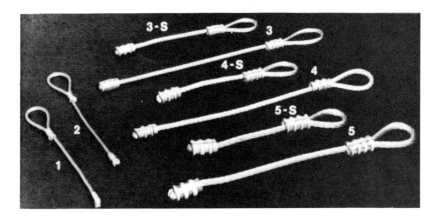

Copperhead Statistics

Nut #	Nut Length	Nut Diameter	Overall Length	Cable Diam.	Approximate Strength in lbs.	Weight in oz.
1	1/2″	3/16″	5-3/4″	3/32″	920	.5
2	1/2″	1/4″	5-3/4″	3/32″	920	.5
3	3/4″	5/16″	9-1/2″	1/8″	2,000	1.0
3-S	3/4″	5/16″	5-3/4″	1/8″	2,000	1.0
4	7/8″	7/16″	9-1/2″	5/32″	2,800	1.5
4-S	7/8″	7/16″	5-3/4″	5/32″	2,800	1.5
5	1″	1/2″	9-1/2″	3/16″	3,500	2.5
5-S	1″	1/2″	5-3/4″	3/16″	3,500	2.5

Chocks

TITONS

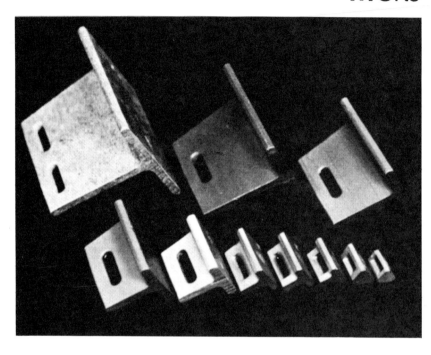

Titons (pronounced like the Teton Mountains) are our most versatile nuts as they provide both cam and jam placements in a wide variety of crack sizes. Titons exhibit the characteristics that we strive for in all our products — optimum performance achieved with a minimum of material.

In a vertical crack, Titon cam action is achieved by inserting the nut lengthwise at a slightly tilted angle so that the edges of the flange engage the sides of the crack. As pressure is applied to the stem (with a firm tug), the flange is forced to rotate which causes it to wedge

Titon Statistics

Number	Material	Flange Width	Length	Weight	Color	Recommended Web Size	Approximate Strength of Nut-Web Unit
1	Stainless Steel	1/2″	11/16″	1/2 oz.	white	1/2″ Tub.	2,300 lbs.
2	Stainless Steel	5/8″	7/8″	3/4 oz.	yellow	1/2″ Tub.	2,300 lbs.
3	Stainless Steel	3/4″	1″	1 oz.	green	5/8″ Tub.	2,500 lbs.
4	Stainless Steel	7/8″	1-1/4″	1-1/2 oz.	orange	3/4″ Flat	4,000 lbs.
5	Stainless Steel	1″	1-3/8″	2 oz.	purple	3/4″ Flat	4,000 lbs.
6	Aluminum	1-1/4″	1-3/4″	1 oz.	Gold	1″ Tub.	4,000 lbs.
7	Aluminum	1-1/2″	2-1/4″	2 oz.	Green	1″ Tub.	4,000 lbs.
8	Aluminum	2″	2-3/4″	3 oz.	Red	1″ Tub.	4,000 lbs.
9	Aluminum	2-1/2″	3-1/4″	5 oz.	Blue	1″ Tub.	4,000 lbs.
10	Aluminum	3″	4″	8 oz.	Alum.	1″ Tub.	4,000 lbs.

Note: When threading web through #1 and #2 Titons it is helpful to angle-cut the threading end.

tightly. This same cam effect is achieved in a horizontal crack by placing the flange towards the back of the crack with the stem pointing slightly upward. Any downward pressure on the stem will cause the flange to rotate into a more tightly wedged position. This cam action permits secure placements in horizontal, shallow, flared, and parallel sided cracks.

Titon edges are beveled to increase stability in the cammed position, and their ends are uniformly tapered to provide a snug wedge fit in endwise or stacked placements. They may also be effectively slotted in bottleneck cracks and behind cracked blocks and boulders. Titon sizes are graduated to fit cracks from 7/16″ to 4″ in width. Each Titon web slot is carefully finished to prevent sling damage.

Titon numbers one through five are made of stainless steel to achieve superior strength in smaller cracks. These tough little dudes are the strongest nuts available in their size range. Titons six through ten are made of wrought aluminum and are anodized for color coding.

Chocks

These nuts were developed to give reliable protection where horizontal pitons were formerly the only reasonable solution. **Arrowheads** are similar to Copperheads but are more narrow and have a six degree tapered profile. This taper is formed in a shaping die that produces a slim wafer which slots and holds with authority in thin cracks. Because Arrowheads provide the leader with high strength nut protection that was heretofore unavailable, we expect they will make a significant contribution to the feasibility of all-nut ascents.

Arrowhead Statistics

Nut Number	Top Width of Head	Head Height	Overall Length	Weight in oz.	Cable Diameter	Approximate Strength in lbs.
1	.238″	.663″	9-1/2″	1	1/8″	1,800
1-S	.238″	.663″	5-3/4″	1	1/8″	1,800
2	.295″	.732″	9-1/2″	1.5	5/32″	2,300
2-S	.295″	.732″	5-3/4″	1.5	5/32″	2,300
3	.400″	.875″	9-1/2″	2.5	3/16″	3,000
3-S	.400″	.875″	5-3/4″	2.5	3/16″	3,000

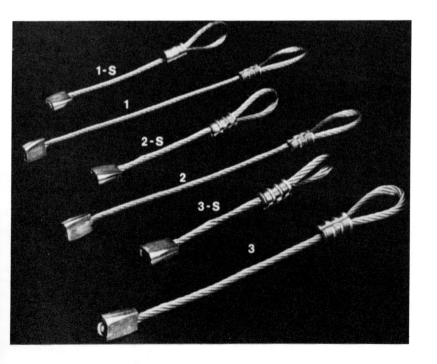

Gibbs Products 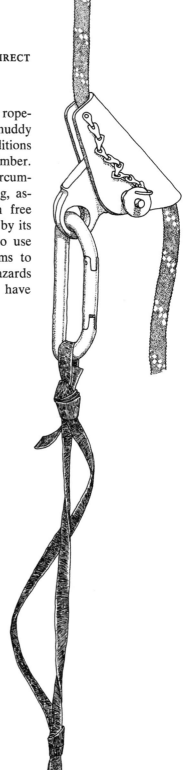ORDER DIRECT
854 Padley Street
Salt Lake City, Utah 84108

The Gibbs ascender is a marvelous rope-ascending device that works well on muddy ropes and ice-laced nylon lines—conditions familiar to every caver and winter climber. It's safe, almost foolproof, and in circumstances when we've used it for hauling, ascending, and as a safety backup on free rappels, we've been extremely pleased by its performance. Many people still opt to use Jumars, but while Jumar failure seems to be accepted as one of the expected hazards of mountaineering, no Gibbs failures have yet to our knowledge been recorded.

Gibbs ascender.

Gibbs ascender in use.

Great Pacific Iron Works   ORDER DIRECT
Chouinard Equipment for Alpinists
P. O. Box 150
Ventura, California 93001

Yvon Chouinard has probably done more to popularize climbing
in this country than any other person. Before 1965, almost all climbing hardware was imported or made by one climbing friend for
another—and was relatively difficult to obtain. Basic technical information was hard to come by unless one climbed and traveled
regularly in Italy, France, Britain, or Switzerland. Today, with
Chouinard-inspired American mass production of climbing hardware,
retail stores carrying the more advanced technical climbing gear are
found throughout the United States, and technical information is
readily accessible.

Chouinard equipment "firsts" include:

The Chouinard carabiner, introduced in 1957, an improved version of the old standard Pierre Allain 'biner. The Chouinard version
featured the ability to stack side by side two other carabiners, aiding
in the development of the Yosemite system of artificial climbing.

The Ringless hand-forged Lost Arrow piton, introduced in 1958,
the first American-made, commercially available piton of its type,
with a thick horizontal body construction with vertical eye.

The Horizontal Knifeblade, 1959, as well as the Lost Arrow piton
of the previous year, were made from a superhard metal that resisted
deformation caused by repeated pin placement common to European
pitons available at that time.

With the Aluminum Bong, 1961, protection became possible in
those superlarge jam cracks that refused the smaller pitons
previously available. The Bong provided much more security than
the European wooden wedges that used to fill the gap.

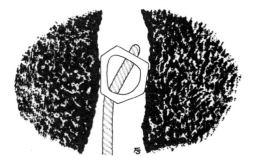

Chouinard
Hexcentric chock.

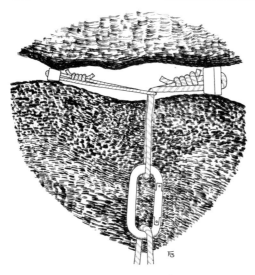

Chocks in opposition use.

In 1968, Chouinard introduced the rigid crampon—an innovation that revolutionized ice climbing the world over. This crampon is still pushing the standards of ice work up beyond the wildest expectations of its manufacturer.

venture where he had never dared before—onto ninety-degree ice climbing hammer. Combined with the Chouinard Frost ice axe, which features a drooped pick, these ice tools enabled the climber to venture where he had never dared before—onto ninety-degree ice walls.

In 1974, both the Chouinard Alpine Hammer and the Chouinard ice axe received major design improvements. The Alpine Hammer was lightened, and additional teeth the entire length of the curved pick were added. These changes have produced the perfect ice-climbing tool. Additional teeth have been added to the Chouinard ice axe to improve its holding qualities in the common hollow ice waterfalls of the United States.

An original Chouinard invention is the Climbaxe. This tool, a miniaturized ice axe the size of an Alpine Hammer, is another contributing factor to the newly advanced standards of ice climbing in the Alps and the Himalayas, as well as for domestic water ice.

Chouinard's catalog—the best mail-order catalog we've ever seen —is required reading for every climber. It explains in very simple language the proper use of his equipment and, of greater importance, the discussion of the cumulative effect of man on the mountain environment.

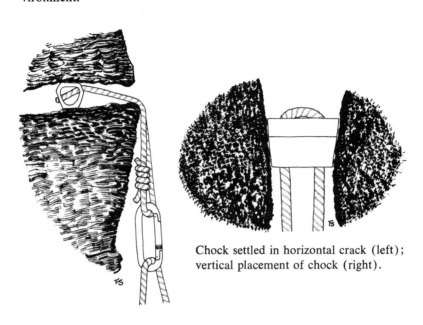

Chock settled in horizontal crack (left); vertical placement of chock (right).

New improvements in free-climbing protection—for example, the Stopper (small wire- and rope-strung nuts that virtually replace the piton as a safety protection device) and the Chouinard Hexcentric (a six-sided aluminum chock with incomparable taper bite action)— can slow or stop the destructiveness of mass climbing. Every climber owes a debt of gratitude to Chouinard for his distinctive (and profitable) role as a leader in the development of the American climbing industry.

Gross Industries, Inc.   ORDER DIRECT
Box 1785
Poughkeepsie, New York 12601
914-462-1631

If you're a woman mountaineer who's had the all too invigorating experience of having to pull down your knickers or down pants during winter conditions in order to urinate, Gross' Feminine Hygiene Device (FHD) may seem a gift from heaven. It's a strange white plastic gismo that's extremely easy to use and clean—and it permits women to stand up (that is, just unbutton the fly of your climbing pants) while urinating. No dripping—and no toilet paper needed. It's really an amazing device and ought to be of great use to female backpackers, travelers, and those who have inconvenient attacks of modesty during Big Wall climbs. At the present time, all FHD orders are being handled through mail order. The cost of $3.00 (including $.50 mailing and handling) covers two FHDs in sealed plastic wrapping, a sealable carrying case, and very clear instructions for use.

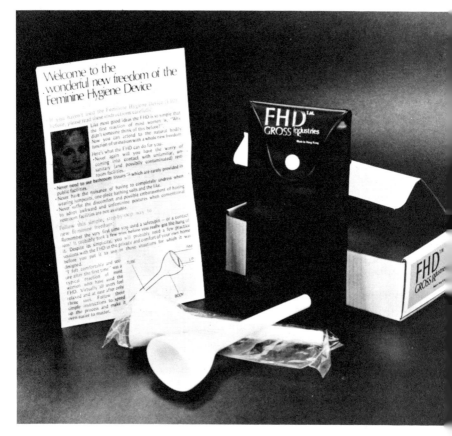

Feminine Hygiene Device. *Photo courtesy of Gross Industries, Inc.*

Hans Klepper Corporation   ORDER DIRECT
35 Union Square West
New York, New York 10003
212-CH3-3428

Hans Klepper produces a variety of backpacking tents not well suited for mountaineering. They do have a top selection of canoes, racing kayaks, and folding boats.

Hexcel Sports, Inc.   ORDER SPORTS
Wilton, Maine

Imports and distributes ski and mountaineering equipment featuring bindings that adapt to mountaineering boots.

High and Light   ORDER DIRECT
139½ East 16th Street
Costa Mesa, California 92627
714-642-1970

High and Light is another manufacturer using the innovative sleeping-bag design incorporating a built-in foam pad on the bottom. Covered with a thick V-baffled down quilt, the "Numero Uno" is as fine as its name implies. If you are short (height, not cash—the "Uno" is expensive), there is an "Uno Poco" for people under five-foot-four. They also produce a fine line of down jackets, vests, booties, and other down equipment.

Himalayan Porters Stick   ORDER DIRECT
T. Dion Warren
P. O. Box 4775
Santa Barbara, California 93103

The Porter stick is a walking cane (a derivative of the Alpenstock) with a T-shaped carved handle. A 35mm camera can be mounted to the top of the shaft.

Himalayan (System) Industries, Inc.
P. O. Box 5668
Pine Bluff, Arkansas 71601

These products can be found in many discount stores such as Sears and Montgomery Ward. They should remain in such stores. Their tent might make an interesting doghouse.

Hine/Snowbridge
Box 1459
Boulder, Colorado 80302

Hine/Snowbridge produces a fine range of soft backpacks for day hiking and climbing. Their Serex Pack is suited for expedition carries when large and bulky loads need to be transported to higher camps. The load suspension system enables adjustment in the shoulders, the carry straps, the hip belt, and the load height, as well as being fitted with tightening straps that reduce unwanted bulk of the pack during technical climbing situations. Because of the multi-adjustment system, the pack can be used by many differently built climbers during the course of an expedition. The materials, construction, and their

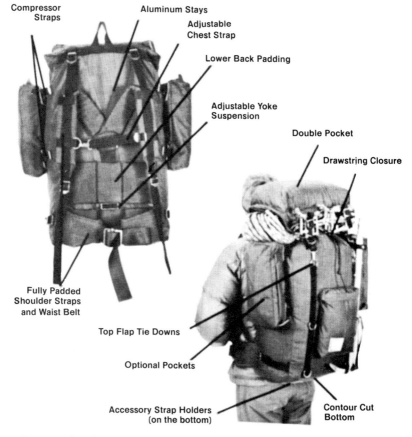

Serex Pack. *Photo courtesy of Hine/Snowbridge.*

unique suspension system combine to produce the finest internal frame rucksack-type pack now available on the American market. We heartily recommend the Serex as an alternative to the bulky and clumsy external frame system packs commonly used in most expedition climbing.

Hirsch Weiss (White Stag)
5203 Southeast Johnson Creek Boulevard
Portland, Oregon 97206

Manufacturers of a line of sleeping bags filled with either duck or goose down, as well as Fiberfill II. The only bags we could recommend are the Alpine, The Hiker, and the Hiker Twin. All these models are duck down bags, and compare favorably for warmth with goose down bags of similar design, with the extra benefit of a considerable cash savings; they are also quite durable. Hirsch Weiss also has a complete range of pack bags and frames that are of a quality more suitable for the very occasional backpacker than the serious mountaineer. The latter would undoubtedly prefer a different frame system. Their tents are well known on the National Campground circuit, where they belong—not on wilderness back trails.

Holubar Mountaineering, Ltd.   ORDER DIRECT
1875 30th Street
Boulder, Colorado 80302

Holubar Mountaineering has been a favorite of climbers for over thirty years. Their Royalight and Expedition sleeping bags are excellent. If you need the warmest possible down parka, their Paragon Incalescent has been designed to keep its wearers warm even at a temperature of −80° F. They also manufacture Carikits.

Chouinards in vertical placement.

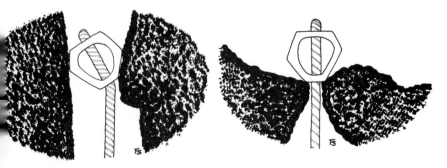

Hy-Score
200 Tillary Street
Brooklyn, New York 11201
212-624-5251

Has a complete line of equipment from Stubai (Austria); aluminum ware from Sigg (Switzerland), Markill (Germany), and Haderware Aluminum (England); Bonaiti and Salewa Carabiners. Also the Brixia-Cassin Rock and Ice Climbing boot.

JanSport   ORDER DIRECT
Paine Field Industrial Park
Everett, Washington 98208
206-353-0200

JanSport is run by Lou Whittaker, and the JanSport line was chosen for use on K-2. Their catalog is really quite lovely, with a nice taste of the spirit of last century's mountaineers. JanSport's domed

Rover dome tent. *Photo courtesy of JanSport.*

tents are famous for their ease of erection and stability in high winds. The tent prices compare favorably with other tents on the market, but the rest of the JanSport line—all very good-quality material and workmanship—seem a bit expensive.

Kalmar Trading Corporation   INQUIRIES INVITED
P. O. Box 77343—Department CSB
San Francisco, California 94107
415-647-6474

Kalmar is the importer and distributor of one of the most comprehensive lines of European technical mountaineering equipment available in this country. From Italy, they import Interalp nylon chest harnesses, nylon seat harnesses, four-step étriers, hardware slings,

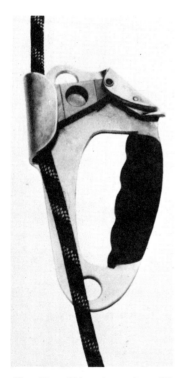

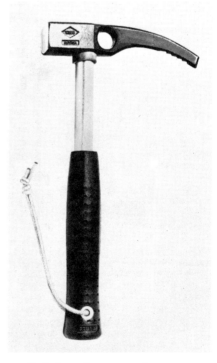

Clog Expedition Ascenders. *Photo courtesy of Kalmar Trading Corporation.*

Stubai nut hammer. *Photo courtesy of Kalmar Trading Corporation.*

MOUNTAINEERING EQUIPMENT

STUBAI
AUSTRIA

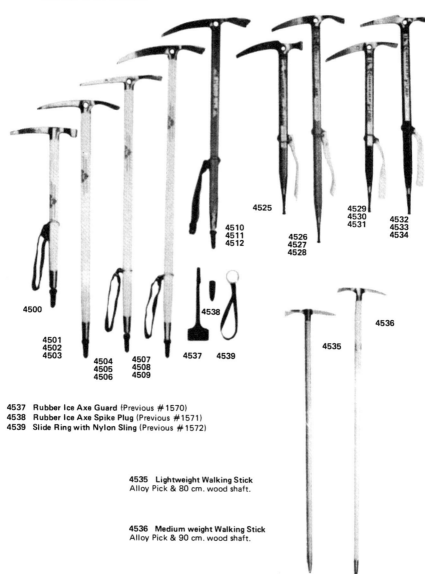

4500

4501
4502
4503

4504
4505
4506

4507
4508
4509

4510
4511
4512

4525

4526
4527
4528

4529
4530
4531

4532
4533
4534

4538

4537   4539

4535

4536

4537   Rubber Ice Axe Guard (Previous #1570)
4538   Rubber Ice Axe Spike Plug (Previous #1571)
4539   Slide Ring with Nylon Sling (Previous #1572)

4535   Lightweight Walking Stick
Alloy Pick & 80 cm. wood shaft.

4536   Medium weight Walking Stick
Alloy Pick & 90 cm. wood shaft.

ICE AXES

New No.	Previous No.	Manufacturer	Model	Type of Shaft	Shaft length in centimeters	Wt. in grams
4500	1578	Stubai	Ice Hammer	Ash	55	800
4501	1583	Stubai	Stubai	Ash	75	840
4502	1584	Stubai	Stubai	Ash	85	880
4503	1585	Stubai	Stubai	Ash	97	920
4504	1586	Stubai	Aschenbrenner	Ash	75	800
4505	1587	Stubai	Aschenbrenner	Ash	85	840
4506	1588	Stubai	Aschenbrenner	Ash	97	920
4507	1589	Stubai	Nanga Parbat	Ash	75	800
4508	1590	Stubai	Nanga Parbat	Ash	85	840
4509	1591	Stubai	Nanga Parbat	Ash	97	920
4510		Stubai	Nanga Parbat	Fiberglass	55	770
4511		Stubai	Nanga Parbat	Fiberglass	70	850
4512		Stubai	Nanga Parbat	Fiberglass	80	910
4525	1592	Interalp	Fitz Roy	Steel	55	820
4526	1593	Interalp	Cerro Torre	Steel	50	800
4527	1594	Interalp	Cerro Torre	Steel	60	850
4528	1595	Interalp	Cerro Torre	Steel	70	900
4529	1596	Interalp	Alpamayo	Steel	50	800
4530	1597	Interalp	Alpamayo	Steel	60	850
4531	1598	Interalp	Alpamayo	Steel	70	900
4532	1599	Interalp	Devouassoux	Steel	50	800
4533	1600	Interalp	Devouassoux	Steel	60	850
4534	1601	Interalp	Devouassoux	Steel	70	900

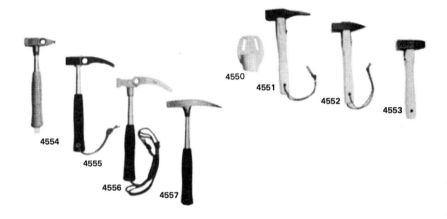

HAMMERS

NEW NO.	Previous NO.	Brand NAME	DESCRIPTION
4551	1576	Stubai	Universal Climbing Hammer with Sling
4552	1577	Stubai	Wood Shaft Climbing Hammer with Sling
4553	1573	Salewa	Wood Shaft Rock Hammer
4554	1574	Salewa	Metal Shaft Rock Hammer
4555		Stubai	Metal Shaft "Nut Hammer" with Sling
4556	1602	Interalp	Baltoral "Nut Hammer" with Sling
4557		Stubai	Metal Shaft Geologist Pick
4550	1603	Interalp	Nylon Hammer Holster

rock hammers, the Fitz Roy, Cerro Torre, Alpamayo, and Devouas-soux ice axes. The Interalp company produces the finest crafted imported ice axes for serious climbing available on the American market.

Kalmar's line of Austrian equipment features Stubai hardware, including a complete range of pitons, carabiners, and ice climbing screws, piton hammers, ice hammers, and ice axes—the best of which is the Nanga Parbat model with fiberglass shaft. Aso available from Stubai is the Tirol twelve-point adjustable crampon, an excellent adjustable crampon that maintains its sharp points longer than others we have tried.

From Wales, Kalmar carries a comprehensive line of Clog hardware and carabiners (UIAA approved), including the recently introduced Clog Expedition Ascenders. These high-strength aluminum alloy ascenders work on a principle similar to Jumars. They have an improved handle grip that is large enough to accommodate a mittened hand, as well as having a molded rubber gripping device for easier use on long summer wall climbs. The Clog twelve-point crampon, an exclusive Kalmar import, has been successfully tested on the Southwest Ridge of Everest by Dougal Haston. Other Clog imports include the Clog Deadman and Clog caving ladders.

Kelty Mountaineering   ORDER DIRECT
1801 Victory Boulevard
Glendale, California 91201

Kelty packs and frames are the best products for the dedicated hiker and mountaineer. Upon returning from a winter traverse of the Presidential Range, during which one of us carried seventy-five pounds of equipment, including full climbing rack and two ice axes, we were completely satisfied with the comfort of the Kelty frame. Their two best models are the Tioga Packbag and the Serac, both of which fit on the Massif frame.

Kenyon Industries
Kenyon, Rhode Island 02836

Kenyon Industries manufactures flameproof and downproof material for the construction of tents, sleeping bags, and parkas. A good source for those interested in purchasing bulk lots of nylon material.

Leeper Equipment   ORDER DIRECT
Wall Street, Colorado 80302
303-442-3773

Ed Leeper puts out very little equipment, but whatever he produces is invariably dynamite. The famed hooks used in Yosemite
were Leeper Cliff Hanger Skyhooks. This is an indispensable tool for
extreme artificial aid climbing. Chouinard tried to modify Leeper's
designs, as is his habit, but the Chouinard Cliff Hanger doesn't equal
Leeper's. The Leeper Z-section piton is the strongest-channeled pin
of the ¼-inch-to-⅝-inch size range. Leeper Bolt Hangers constructed of aircraft-quality 4130 chromium molybdenum alloy steel
(the steel with which Chouinard revolutionized the piton), hardened
and drawn to R/C 40, are the most commonly used hangers in
stances where normal protection will not suffice.

Leeper has also been working on two new products, which ought
to be on the market as this book appears. The descriptions are his
own:

The *Antipiton* is simply a piton with reversed taper (big at the tip,
small at the eye). It is designed to be stacked with a regular piton at
right angles to it, and *does not require a hammer* for placement.
Downward force on the eye of the Antipiton (to which the rope is
clipped) causes the pair to tighten in the crack as the Antipiton
moves. The action is like that of a well-placed nut, except that the
Antipiton works best in smooth, straight cracks (and it will work in
somewhat flared cracks).

Antipiton placement requires skill and care, just as does any clean
climbing. Anchors should be doubled and tripled for safety. The
main point of technique is that the intersection of the piton and Antipiton should not be too close to the tip of the Antipiton, because
the Antipiton may move as much as two inches or more when a fall
is caught. With a large force, it will move more than you expect.
That movement can be reduced if the piton is hammered into place;
this is dirty climbing, of course, but gives better holding power than
a standard piton placement. A compromise is to tap the piton with
whatever is handy on a hammerless ascent. This is "slightly smutty
climbing" and is the kind of thing somebody would do who taps on
his nuts. The Slightly Smutty Hooker is made for this purpose.

A long hero loop of ½-inch webbing should join the eye of the
stacked piton to the carabiner clipped into the Antipiton (to avoid

losing the piton). It should be long enough not to pull the piton out of position when the Antipiton moves in a fall.

When stacking an angle piton with the Antipiton, the angle piton should be placed with the edges against the rock and the rounded side against the Antipiton. Otherwise the anchor can be dragged out of place in a fall. With luck and skill, Antipiton placements will sometimes hold several thousand pounds. (Any statement about strength of clean-climbing equipment should be qualified in that way.) Leeper Antipitons are made in standard (½-inch tip) and thin (¼-inch tip) sizes. The standard size should be used if it will fit, as it tapers faster and therefore moves less when catching a fall.

The *Hooker* is a long, flat steel hook for wiggling nuts in and out of place. It comes in two versions: The Clean Hooker is a light-

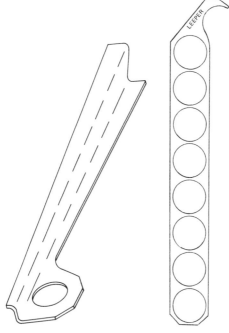

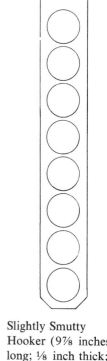

Leeper Antipiton (length: 6 inches).

Clean Hooker (6⅞ inches long; $\frac{1}{10}$ inch thick; 2 ounces).

Slightly Smutty Hooker (9⅞ inches long; ⅛ inch thick; 4½ ounces).

weight version with lightening holes. The Slightly Smutty Hooker is of heavier stock and has an unperforated head for tapping on things. However, there is no way that a Slightly Smutty Hooker can safely drive a standard piton. Both hookers are helpful for levering loose an Antipiton placement that has caught a light fall. (A heavy fall may require leaving the Antipiton and piton for the next party with a hammer.)

Lowe Alpine Systems   ORDER DIRECT
1752 N. 55th St.
Boulder, Colorado 80301
303-442-4791

If your local retail store carries Lowe products, it's a good indication that the shop carries the best climbing materials on the market.

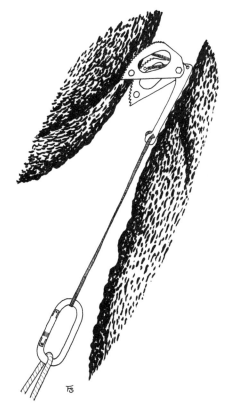

Lowe Cam Nut in
flaring crack.

While not aesthetically pleasing, Lowe Alpine System's products are extremely versatile and functional. In difficult nut placements in flared and parallel cracks, the Split Cam Nut many times will provide the only stable anchor point. The nut consists of two orientation bars and two constant angle cams connected by a bolt. A small spring makes it self-adjusting and keeps it stationary. When a force is applied to the orientation bar, the cam is pressed against the crack wall. The harder the force, the greater the cam pressure and thus the greater the holding power. Tests in parallel cracks in granite, sandstone, and quartzite have demonstrated that the connecting carabiner or sling invariably breaks before the cam slips. This eminently useful cam nut ought to be a regular part of your rack.

Lowe also produces an inexpensive belay device and a fine-quality, soft, large-capacity technical climbing pack.

Mammut Ropes
The North Face
1234 5th Street
Berkeley, California 94710
415-524-8432

The North Face is the distributor of Mammut ropes. Mammut is a well-worked design whose handling characteristics are fine even when iced up. Mammut also has a waterproof Super Dry model that resists freezing and the usual doubling of weight of a wet rope. Mammut also produces one-piece rope slings (one continual fiber—no knot) and tape harnesses. Yvon Chouinard's ropes, marketed under his own name, are Mammut ropes. (Note the difference in price and see if the difference in color is worth that much to you.)

Maran Packs   ORDER DIRECT
P. O. Box 931
Kent, Washington 98031

Maran produces a pack more appropriate for hikers than for climbers. Quality materials are used throughout the construction of this pack.

Mountain Paraphernalia
906 Durant Street
Modesto, California 95352
209-529-6913

Mountain Paraphernalia is Royal Robbins' importing and distributing company. They're the sole distributor of Galibier boots. They also handle Edelrid ropes (consistently trustworthy), and Selewa products, including tubular ice screws, the Sticht belay plate, adjustable crampons, ice axes, and the Robbins Selewa carabiner. In addition, Robbins and Mountain Paraphernalia distribute Karrimor

The Yosemite boot
by Royal Robbins.

Selewa tubular ice
screws.

The Robbins
carabiner.

packs, gaiters, haulsacks and bivouac bags, all excellent products, for which Dougal Haston functions as technical adviser. They also wholesale a great deal of mountain literature, including *Mountain* magazine.

Mountain Products Corporation
123 South Wenatchee Avenue
Wenatchee, Washington 98801

Mountain Products Corporation is another distributor whose excellent line includes sleeping bags, parkas, and vests of Fiberfill II. They distribute the French Jet gas stoves and lanterns, whose simplicity of use is famous, as well as the Kastinger mountaineering boots. The new model, Pala, is a fine rock and ice boot. All prices are competitive, with very great quality control. Lute Jerstad, one of the first Americans on the Everest summit, is one of their advisers for product development.

Mountain Safety Research, Inc.   ORDER DIRECT
631 South 96th Street
Seattle, Washington 98108

People who go into the manufacturing and importing/distributing of climbing equipment are almost invariably themselves climbers, and no more anxious to experience equipment failure than you or we. But sometimes a hunger for profit begins to interfere with otherwise fine climbing sense, and a store or distributor may continue to carry, for example, a safety helmet that's known to be markedly less safe than others on the market. As yet, no climbing organization has seen fit to institute a complete, ongoing study of the safety of both climbing equipment and methods used in this country. Occasionally, each of the climbing magazines features comparative statistics on a certain piece of equipment or technique, and these are always worth reading. Also, the American Alpine Club publishes annually *Accidents in American Mountaineering,* by implication a kind of how-not-to-climb. But until Larry Penberthy of Mountain Safety Research appointed himself (to the chagrin of many) the watchdog of mountaineering equipment safety, only a handful of diligent climber/manufacturers and retailers, including some of the most prominent, overly concerned themselves with the relative safety of the equipment they featured. Penberthy's impact on mountaineering has been considerable. While it was in fact Colorado Mountain

Industries who first introduced the metal-shafted axe, it was Penberthy and MSR who emphasized its superiority over even the finest-grained wooden-shafted ice axes, popularized its use in this country, and created the impetus that led to European production of ice tools of similar construction. MSR's metal-shafted ice axes and hammers continue to be among the best available.

For some reason, climbing safety helmets continue to be a source of controversy. As has been proven innumerable times, a good safety helmet drastically reduces the incidence of head and scalp injuries from falling rock and ice, and during falls may provide the critical difference between surviving or a fatal head injury. In the past, climbing helmets were heavy, miserably hot, and at times ineffective. While the Joe Brown helmet still has its partisans, the MSR safety helmet is light, well ventilated, and probably the best available on the American market—if less than pretty.

MSR also produces and distributes its own climbing rope—the least expensive rope available on the American market. It is, however, mushy and limp and lacks the preferred handling characteristics of other ropes.

The Mountain Safety Research *Newsletter* is published sporadically, usually twice a year, and is well worth the $3.00 donation. Included are MSR's latest test findings, as well as their mail-order catalog. Reprints of earlier issues are available.

Nestor Designs
Ed Nestor
7 Fieldston Road
Princeton, New Jersey 08540

Ed Nestor designed and produces a drive-in ice-climbing piton (a fancy lag bolt) called the "Super Screw." On rare occasions adequate placement can be obtained; it makes a great little can opener.

The North Face   ORDER DIRECT
1234 5th Street
Berkeley, California 94710
415-524-8432

A well-established firm that produces superior down garments. For years, The North Face expedition-grade sleeping bag was the warmest available. Construction features of this bag have been copied by numerous companies whose products come close but never quite achieve the same caché as the company's own "North Face." Their St. Elias expeditionary mountain tent was, for years, the standard two-man tent used by Americans in the Himalayas and the northern ranges of Alaska. Its popularity has decreased somewhat in recent years, but it's still considered one of the top two-man expedition-grade tents.

 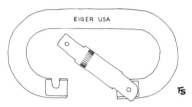

Locking-gate and oval carabiners.

Optimus International
A. B. Optimus, Inc.
P. O. Box 4147
Fullerton, California 92634

The best stove produced by Optimus is their 111-B. It is one of the most efficient and frequently used base-camp and high-altitude stoves. The smaller version, the Optimus 8-R, has become increasingly popular with backpackers because of its ease of use and stability. Both stoves burn white gas, are easily maintained, and parts are available at most climbing retailers.

8-R stove with new mini-pump. *Photo courtesy of Optimus International.*

Optimus 99. *Photo courtesy of Optimus International.*

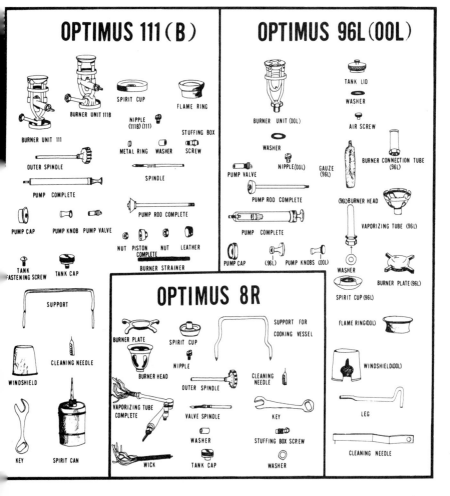

The Outdoorsman
P. O. Box 268
Boston, Massachusetts 02134
617-277-4054

Distributors of Edelweiss rope, Bonaiti and Stubai hardware. Their retail outlet, Backcountry, in the Boston area, is one of the few firms to still carry the famed Dolt Blueboot (the first EB-type boot imported into this country).

Paul Petzoldt Wilderness Equipment   ORDER DIRECT
Box 78
North Lander, Wyoming 82520

Paul Petzoldt Wilderness Equipment was the first manufacturer to use only Fiberfill II in all of its sleeping bags, jackets, booties, and gloves. His equipment has been used on Mount McKinley, the first winter ascents of the Grand Teton, and in severe and hostile weather conditions in the Wyoming area. Boy Scout troops, church groups, educational institutions (prep schools, colleges, and universities), and special-assistance programs funded partially or wholly by government funds (federal, state, or local) can purchase equipment direct at a special institutional price reflecting a considerable savings over the normal retail cost.

Pinpackers, Inc.   ORDER DIRECT
P. O. Box 693
Smithtown, New York 11787

This innovative pack system is the most versatile on the market. The frame can be converted to a stretcher or a ladder for crossing crevasses or for climbing a sheer wall—the only frame marketed for this use. The frame disassembles for use also as tent poles, and with their optional canvas back functions as a seat. The ultimate is that it also converts to a toilet seat. The price of this system with all options is excessive and, realistically, is not needed by climbers.

Precise/A Leisure Division of Esquire, Inc.

3 Chestnut Street
Suffern, New York 10901
914-EL7-6200

Precise is the U.S. distributor of Wenger Swiss Army knives,
K & R pedometers, SUUNTO compasses, and the famed Austrian

KB-14 SUUNTO
compass. *Photo courtesy
of Precise Imports Corp.*

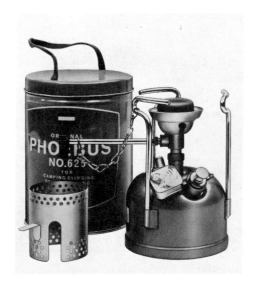

Phoebus 625 camp stove.
*Photo courtesy of Precise
Imports Corp.*

Phoebus stoves. Phoebus stoves perform particularly well at high altitude. The self-priming and cleaning features make the stove hassle free. It can be ignited with mittened hands in high winds. The tank will last from 2½ to 4 hours of constant use before needing a white gas refill. The steady heat produced by the Phoebus prevents scorching while melting snow. The Phoebus 6-25 is their best mountaineering stove. Their Model 7-25, a miniaturized version of the mountain stove, will serve the backpacker and hiker quite adequately.

Precise imports the SUUNTO KB-14, which is the most accurate pocket transit and optical reading compass available in the United States—an indispensable tool for gaining bearings in difficult mountainous terrain and for cave mapping. The KB-20 has all the advantages of the KB-14, but at a considerable savings. Precise Imports' Wilkie M-107F, a West German copy of the bearing compass, proved to have a six-degree incorrect reading during our own tests.

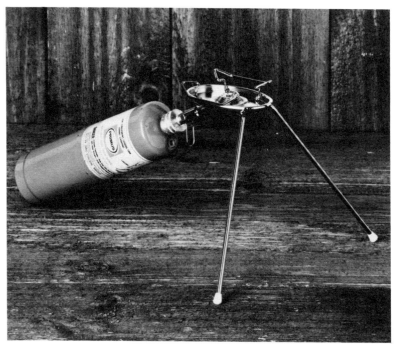

The Grasshopper stove. *Photo courtesy of Primus-Sievert.*

Primus-Sievert
354 Sackett Point Road
New Haven, Connecticut 06473
203-239-2554

The distributor of Primus lanterns, stoves, and heaters. They carry propane cylinders and compact backpacking stoves. Most of their products are more appropriate for use at a base camp than as assault equipment. Their Grasshopper stove is an easy-to-use propane cylinder stove of value chiefly to the recreational camper.

Ptarmigan Designs
P. O. Box 431
Silverton, Colorado 81433

Distributors of Rocca Ropes and Clog climbing gear. Rocca Ropes of West Germany have just recently become available in the United States. They meet UIAA testing standards.

Recreational Equipment, Inc., Co-op   ORDER DIRECT
1525 11th Avenue
Seattle, Washington 98122
206-323-8333

Founded in 1938, REI is the largest outdoor equipment co-op in the United States. Membership is currently in excess of 400,000. They produce their own line of equipment, all of it fully tested on Mount Rainier, Mount St. Elias, as well as the summit of Everest. Jim Whittaker, first American to reach the summit of Everest, is general manager. Their equipment includes parkas, pants, down underwear, mitts, booties, rainwear, boots, tents, and rock and ice hardware, as well as skis. Membership is $2.00. If you buy their equipment, there is a credit rebate at the end of the year that is good toward further purchases. Possibly the best prices anywhere. A selection from their catalog appears on pages 196–99.

HOW STRONG
IS YOUR ICE AXE?

The ice axe is the most useful piece of equipment for a snow and ice climber. Even a beginning climber will need an ice axe for the most basic snow climbs. The most common use for an ice axe is as a walking stick to help maintain balance when cilmbing on steep snow. Other functions that an ice axe may be called upon to perform are: self arrest, boot axe belay, step chopping, probing for crevasses, hand hold for aid climbing, anchor for belay crevasse rescue, digging holes for human waste, anchor or prop for shelter, and possibly others.

How strong must the ice axe be to perform these functions satisfactorily?

The shaft is the most critical part of the ice axe if used as an anchor or for belaying. With a properly set up boot axe belay, the load on the ice axe should be well within the strength limits of an ash shaft. For those climbers desiring a stronger or more uniform shaft, several models are available. The laminated Rexilon and bamboo shafts are no stronger than the average ash. but are more uniform in strength. Aluminum and fiberglass shafts are the strongest. The strengths of the various ice axe shafts are shown in Table I.

The attachment of the head to the shaft is another very important feature of an ice axe. While the loads exerted on the attachment in a self arrest are relatively low. a good joint between the head and shaft will increase the reliability of the ice axe in a self arrest.

The adz is sometimes bent when the ice axe is used for prying out chunks of hard snow or ice while chopping steps. Such use is not recommended; however, the adz should be strong enough to withstand some abuse. The spike is not normally loaded to any great extent, but several axes have had the spike broken off or badly bent when the spike becomes caught between bridge planks or rocks while the axe is used as a walking stick.

Table I gives the strengths of the various parts of the ice axes, and figures 1-4 show how the ice axes were set up for the tests.

All ice axes at REI with natural wood shafts are proof tested before going into stock. The shaft is loaded to 400 pounds with the load applied as in Figure 1. The head to shaft attachment is also proof tested to 100 pounds at a point 500mm from the top of the head as shown in Figure 2.

Tests have shown that the proof testing of the ice axe shafts does not weaken the shafts of those ice axes that pass the test.

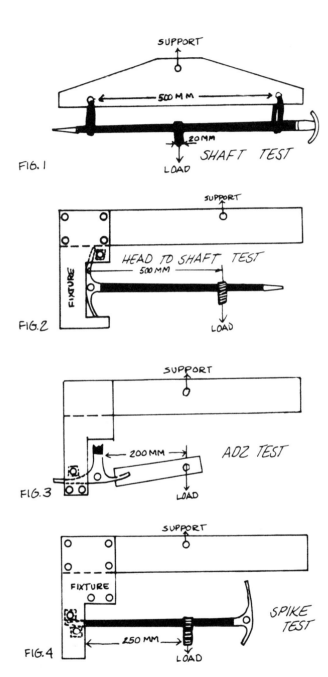

SUPPORT

500 MM

20 MM

SHAFT TEST

FIG. 1

LOAD

SUPPORT

FIXTURE

HEAD TO SHAFT TEST

500 MM

FIG. 2

LOAD

SUPPORT

ADZ TEST

200 MM

FIG. 3

LOAD

SUPPORT

FIXTURE

SPIKE TEST

250 MM

FIG. 4

LOAD

TABLE I

FAILURE LOAD IN POUNDS

MODEL	SHAFT MATERIAL	Shaft (See Fig. 1)	Head to Shaft (See Fig. 2)	ADZ Neck (See Fig. 3)	Spike (See Fig. 4)	Weight of 85cm ounces
REI METAL	ALUMINUM	945	512	590	595	40
INTERALP CERRO TORRE	ALUMINUM	1100	250	380	175	31
SIMOND METALLIC	ALUMINUM	1140	320	235	120	26
MSR THUNDERBIRD	ALUMINUM	1035	495	264	270	32
STUBAI GFX	FIBERGLASS	1505	340	170	220	33
REI McKINLEY	ASH	690	235	620	205	34
STUBAI MOD WALLNER	ASH	585	298	425	170	33
STUBAI NANGA PARBAT	ASH	585	298	405	170	31
STUBAI ASCHENBRENNER	ASH	585	298	410	170	37
RALLING HIMALAYA	ASH	730	205	255	110	33
RALLING EVEREST	ASH	730	205	220	110	31
INTERALP SENTINELLE ROUGE	REXILON	570	248	825	170	35
CHOUINARD-FROST	LAMINATED BAMBOO	550	208	530	190	32

Testing Ice Pitons

Technical ice climbing is becoming more popular throughout the year as climbers challenge glaciers the year around and frozen waterfalls in the winter. Several different types of ice pitons are available to the ice climber, and a knowledge of the capabilities of the various models will aid the climber in selecting the best pitons for a particular use.

A series of tests were conducted on the lower Nisqually Glacier on Mount Rainier to determine the holding power of the pitons in hard glacier ice at various temperatures.

The test pitons were driven into the ice and then connected to a hydraulic pulling cylinder by a chain connected to the piton with a carabiner. The opposite end of the cylinder was anchored to the ice by means of two pitons and a length of chain to divide the load between the anchors. Pressure was applied to the cylinder by a hand pump until failure occurred.

Tests were run with the load applied approximately 90° to the axis of the piton (side load) and also with the load directly in line with the axis of the piton (end load). An ice axe was placed through the carabiner to prevent the screw pitons from winding out.

The table shows the average load developed before failure. Unless otherwise indicated, the failure was due to the piton pulling out of the ice.

Some conclusions drawn from the tests are: The strength of the ice increases as the temperature is lowered. The ice becomes more brittle at low temperatures and is more easily shattered by driving the pitons. The hammer-in type of pitons shatter the ice more readily than screw-in type. At low temperatures, the ice is stronger if the piton is allowed to stand for a time after driving before a load is applied.

At temperatures above freezing, pitons will melt the ice in contact with the piton and thus reduce the strength of the anchor.

The loads obtained in these tests may not be reached in other types of ice, however these tests do give a good idea of the load capacity of the ice pitons in hard glacier ice, and the relative holding power of the pitons.

TABLE II

DESCRIPTION OF PITON	ICE TEMPERATURE					Suitability for Ease of Driving				Ease of Removal	Weight Ozs.
	8°-10°F	20°-30°F	32°F	10°-18°F	32°F	Aid	Lead or Anchor	Cold	Warm		
	Side Load lbs.			End Load lbs.							
STUBAI 3¼"	1292	753	790	1184[4]	725	E	P	G	E	E	1.5
STUBAI 5"	3446[1]	___	1265	1939[4]	860[5]	E	F	F[6]	E	E	3.0
STUBAI 7"	2908	1831	1245	2154	1160	E	F	F[6]	E	E	3.5
CHARLET MOSER	3877	2262	1750	2800[3]	1400	E	G	F[6]	E	E	3.5
SALEWA TUBULAR 6½"	5170	3770	2260[3]	3662	2450[4]	E	E	E[7]	E	G	4.0
SALEWA TUBULAR 8"	5385+[2]	3446	3230	3795	1990[4]	G	E	E[7]	E	G	4.5
SALEWA TUBULAR 12"	5385+[2]	5062	___	4577	___	G	E	E[7]	E	G	6.25
SALEWA WART HOG	2908	1938	1340	1400	485	G	F	p[6,8]	G[8]	F	5.25

NOTES:

(1) In overnight at 5°-8°

(2) Beyond limit of test gauge

(3) Piton broke

(4) Ice fractured

(5) Wound out

(6) Ice fractures easily

(7) Ice core must be removed from tube before redriving

(8) Hammer required

E=Excellent G=Good F=Fair P=Poor

Reproduced from REI's Winter 1974–75 catalog by permission of Recreational Equipment, Inc. © Recreational Equipment, Inc., 1974.

Rivendell Mountain Works   ORDER DIRECT
P. O. Box 198
Victor, Idaho 83455
208-787-2746

Rivendell's Jensen pack is the original and still the most comfortable of the frameless packs. It is possibly the most imitated pack of the 1970s. Versions of its wrap-around support system and closely fitted profile are now appearing in England and Europe. The pack is unparalleled for its technical climbing stability on the most severe rock pitches. The Jensen pack is available in two size capacities, one

The Jensen Pack by Rivendell Mountain Works. *Photos by Verne McCullough, courtesy of Rivendell Mountain Works.*

being suitable for multiday climbs, the other for expedition lengths and loads.

Rivendell's Bombshelter tent may be the strongest two-man A-frame tent available. The Bombshelter combines all the advantages of the St. Elias tent by North Face, the Sierra Designs' Glacier, and the Gerry Expedition Mountaineering tent, and is the best A-frame mountaineering tent available anyplace.

The Bombshelter tent by Rivendell Mountain Works. *Photos courtesy of Rivendell Mountain Works.*

Seattle Manufacturing Corporation
12880 Northrup Way
Bellevue, Washington 98005
206-833-0334

SMC is one of the leading manufacturers of American-produced mountaineering hardware. Their line includes pitons, climbing chocks, carabiners, metal-shafted ice axes, and the new rigid 12-point vertical ice-climbing crampon—the latter providing the only alternative to the foreign-made Chouinard rigid crampon. All their equipment is of high quality and design, and each carries a replacement guarantee against failure during climbing situations. We used the SMC oval carabiners during four months of steady climbing, and on two occasions the rivet that holds the carabiner gate closed has popped out. If the SMC crampon is used with a boot other than a stiff, rigid-soled model, it will result in crampon breakage. By using ¼-inch plywood cut to the shape of your boot sole, the rigid crampon can be used with excellent results with semiflexible boots.

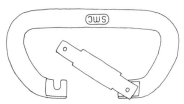

SMC D—carabiners, not UIAA approved.

Sherpa Designs, Inc.   ORDER DIRECT
3109 Brookdale Road E.
Tacoma, Washington 98446
206-531-4114

Sherpa Designs' snowshoes come in four models: Featherweight, Lightfoot, Tracker, and Bigfoot. The Featherweights and Lightfoots have been used on numerous expeditions, most recently in the Pamirs, by the group led by Pete Schoening. Sherpa Designs' snow-

Sherpa Designs'
snowshoe with
binding and traction
cleat. *Photos
courtesy of Sherpa
Designs, Inc.*

shoes were also chosen by the 1975 K-2 Expedition. All of their snow shoes give greater maneuverability and efficiency of movement than any other snowshoe currently available. They are the best of their type on the American market, and we recommend them to all serious mountaineers.

Sierra Designs   ORDER DIRECT
4th and Addison
Berkeley, California 94710

The originators of the now much-copied 60/40 mountain parka. The 60/40 has since become a generic term, but the original product has never been duplicated in either quality or design. Sierra Designs' traditional A-frame Glacier tent, very light in weight at seven pounds, eleven ounces, complete with poles and pegs, is a good buy and will stand up to rigorous winter mountain conditions. This company also produces a full range of down sleeping bags and garments.

Silva, Inc.
2466 North State Road 39
Laporte, Indiana 46350
219-362-9586

Silva, Inc., a division of Johnson Diversfield, is an importer-distributor of the complete line of Silva compasses, which are the most readily available in the United States. The Silva compasses are generally accurate and inexpensive, making them the standard compass for the general climber and mountaineer.

The Ranger compass by Silva, Inc. *Photo courtesy of Silva, Inc.*

Snow Creek Pack Factory   ORDER DIRECT
Der Sportsmann
837 Front Street
Leavenworth, Washington 98826
509-548-5623

The Snow Creek Pack Factory produces a wrap-around large capacity framcless rucksack, the Baby Huey, designed for climbing and ski mountaineering. The pack is a result of combining the best features of the Chouinard Ultima Thule, the Jensen Pack, and the Hine/Snowbridge top pocketing system. At present this pack is available only in size large through the Snow Creek Pack Factory at a little over $50.

Snowlion Corporation
1330 9th Street
Berkeley, California 94710
415-525-4010

Snowlion Corp. makes extremely well-designed sleeping bags, the best of which is the Limited Edition, filled with thirty-two ounces of down. They also produce bags and comforters constructed of Polarguard, another fine man-made insulating material that recovers loft and consequent protection against cold immediately after being wetted. Snowlion products are invariably carried by the best American mountaineering and camping stores.

Sportsman Products
P. O. Box 1082
Boulder, Colorado 80302

Makers of plastic American snowshoes best suited for emergency use by snowmobilers.

Stephenson's Warmlite   ORDER DIRECT
RFD ♯4/Box 398
Winnipesqukee Highlands
Gilford, New Hampshire 03246

Stephenson's Warmlite has distinguished itself in recent years by producing the most sexist ads and catalogs in their field. Climbers being a notoriously butch group, the Warmlite advertising approach has been very well received. All their sleeping bags are custom constructed—of particular interest to unusually short or tall people who

Custom expedition sleeping bag by Stephenson's Warmlite. *Photo courtesy of Stephenson's Warmlite.*

Custom mountaineering tent by Stephenson's Warmlite. *Photo courtesy of Stephenson's Warmlite.*

might ordinarily have a difficult time fitting a standard bag. The bag has a built-in foam pad and features two V-baffled covers that can be used separately or combined, depending upon exterior temperature, making this an excellent year-round bag.

Survival Research Laboratories
17 Marland Road
Colorado Springs, Colorado 80906
303-633-4423

Manufacturers of survival kits for the military and for camping concerns. This year they will introduce a line of survival kits under their own label.

Susie Gaiter Works   ORDER DIRECT
Galiseao, New Mexico
505-982-1589

Susie makes the best canvas gaiters in the United States. They're available in limited quantities by writing to the above address or through the Pathfinder of West Virginia (see climbing equipment retail stores' listings in Part III). More expensive than the Karrimor gaiter, but worth it.

Tempco
414 First Street
South Seattle, Washington 98104
206-623-4194

Manufacturers of down sleeping bags and down jackets. They produce equipment for other companies who market them under their own label. They are generally acceptable products, but a friend of ours has noted that the stitching on his Tempco-made bag has pulled out.

Trail Head Outdoor Equipment Company
653 Fillmore Street
Denver, Colorado 80206
303-322-7129

Importer of Fairy Down bags by Arthur Ellis & Co. of New Zealand. They are less expensive than American sleeping bags of the same construction and quality.

Trail Tech   ORDER DIRECT
254 36th Street
Brooklyn, New York 11232
212-965-6640

Trail Tech produces a complete line of Polarguard sleeping bags, jackets, parkas, bicycle capes, and foul-weather gear. Trail Tech is a newcomer to the outdoor sports clothing market and seems like a very dynamic young company with a quality line.

Trailwise—The Ski Hut   ORDER DIRECT
1615 University Avenue
Berkeley, California 94703

Trailwise makes packs and frames of convenient design, with heavy use intended. They make very fine down bags, with a double sleeping bag for couples who like to cuddle. They also make jackets and a full line of outdoor items. Their rope and iron prices are cheaper than almost anyone else.

Tubbs Products   ORDER DIRECT
Vermont Tubbs, Inc.
Wallingford, Vermont 05773
802-446-3581

The foremost snowshoe maker in the United States produces snowshoes in a variety of models, the most aesthetically pleasing of which is their all-gut snowshoe in their traditional Green Mountain Bearpaw shape. Both their Trail Shoe and Modified Michigan models incorporate all-gut or neoprene nylon construction laced about New England white ash frames. With proper maintenance, a gut snowshoe will last years. Neoprene snowshoes seem to sell to outdoor enthusiasts who would rather not put time into maintenance.

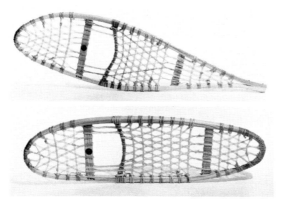

Modified Michigan snowshoe. *Photo by Sanders H. Milens, courtesy of Tubbs Products.*

Green Mountain Bearpaw by Tubbs. *Photo by Sanders H. Milens, courtesy of Tubbs Products.*

Visi-Therm Products, Inc.   ORDER DIRECT
247 Madison Avenue
Bridgeport, Connecticut 06604

Makers of electrically heated socks, tents, vests, mittens, and sleeping bags—very convenient if you happen to carry a generator on your climb.

Wilderness Experience   ORDER DIRECT
9421 Winnetka Avenue, Suite M
Chatsworth, California 91311
213-999-1191

Wilderness Experience is a company manufacturing high-quality packs for the discerning climber. They'll make custom packs, one of their latest having been a sound equipment bag for Clint Eastwood's *Eiger Sanction* film. Another cheesecake catalog.

Wonder Corporation of America
24 Harborview Avenue
Stamford, Connecticut 06902
203-357-1850

Distributors of Bluet stoves and fuel cartridges successfully used on the '63 Everest Expedition (and in innumerable National Parks). They work well under extremely cold conditions, and at high altitudes. Require no priming and start immediately upon the application of a lit match. The cartridges, however, are pretty heavy to carry in any quantity and can't be changed when they're partly used up.

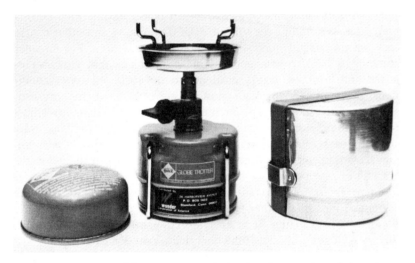

Globe Trotter stove. *Photo courtesy of Wonder Corporation of America.*

Woolrich
Woolrich, Inc.
Woolrich, Pennsylvania 17779

A clothing company that's recently broadened their line to include down jackets and sleeping bags. They're famous for their wool shirts and knickers. A Woolrich shirt—with a designer label—was recently featured in *Vogue.*

CHAPTER 2

Hiking and Mountaineering Boot Distributors

Different climbing circumstances require the use of a variety of footwear. On soft sandstone outcrops, an extremely flexible rock boot is preferable to a midweight Vibram boot. On granite and other coarse rocks, a more rigid boot will allow edging technique. For summer climbing, a tight or near comfortable fit with one thin sock is preferred and heightens one's sensitivity to the rock. In winter conditions, a mountaineering boot must be perfectly fitted, for any constriction of the foot restricts circulation and invites possible frostbite. Fit all winter mountaineering boots while wearing two thick wool socks on each foot—the same socks you will be wearing in a mountain environment. An overboot will in many cases increase the warmth of a properly fitted boot.

There are styles and fads in mountaineering boots as there are styles and fads in all other types of equipment purchase. Improperly fitted boots, no matter how "in," are enough to seriously handicap anyone's climbing ability. If the boot doesn't fit, don't buy it.

Brixia Cassin Boots
Hy-Score
Quality Leisure Sports Products
200 Tillary Street
Brooklyn, New York 11201
212-624-5251

Brixia produces a heavy-duty rock-and-ice-climbing boot that is endorsed and tested by Cassin, the well-known Italian Alpinist. These boots have been gaining great popularity in the New England area.

Montagna Cassin boot. *Photo courtesy of Hy-Score.*

Montebelluna boot. *Photo courtesy of Hy-Score.*

Chippewa Shoe Company
2895 River Street
Chippewa Falls, Wisconsin 54729

Produces boots suitable for hiking and backpacking. Their boots are comfortable and easily broken in. They do not carry a line of boots suitable for any serious mountaineering.

Danner Shoe Manufacturing Company   ORDER DIRECT
110 Southeast 82nd Street
Portland, Oregon 97216

Backpack magazine considers Danner hiking boots their top choice in the hiking line. Danner produces only one boot that is suit-

Model 7509 light mountaineering boot. *Photo courtesy of Danner Shoe Mfg. Co.*

Danner hiking boots for light, moderate, and rough terrain. *Photos courtesy of Danner Shoe Mfg. Co.*

able for technical mountaineering. The boot, Model 7509, is constructed of imported German leather. It will retain its shape and rigidity during moderate ice and snow climbs. The "Yellow Label" Vibram Montagna Brevetta sole is attached to twenty-one irons of midsole. The middle soles are hand-stitched to the uppers and the insoles. The boot is available in sizes 4 to 14, widths AA to EEEE. These boots are constructed as ordered. This is the widest-width moderate mountaineering boot available in the United States.

Dexter Shoe Company
31 St. James Avenue
Boston, Massachusetts 02116
617-542-9026

Dexter has recently introduced an excellent heavyweight hiking boot, called the Dexter Boot. The boot is good for rough terrain and long-distance walking and hiking and heavy loads. Suitable for only very light mountaineering situations.

Donner Mountain Corporation
2110 5th Street
Berkeley, California 94710

Donner Mountain Corp. is the distributor of Pivetta's complete line of technical mountaineering boots and hiking footwear. Their best rock shoe is the "Red Spider," an excellent and inexpensive rock-climbing boot. The La Cima model is their best mountaineering boot. DMC also distributes the EB—the ballet shoe of vertical rock walls.

Dunham's
Brattleboro, Vermont 05301

At the present time, Dunham is developing a line of technical mountaineering boots that will be on the market in late 1975. Their boots available now are best suited for use around college campuses or for street hiking, having uppers that resist the strongest waterproofing, and Vibrams of soft, poor-quality rubber and little ankle or arch support.

Fabiano Shoe Company, Inc.
850 Summer Street
South Boston, Massachusetts 02127
617-268-5625

Fabiano makes boots for cross-country skiing, general hiking, and rock and ice climbing. Their best ice and winter mountaineering boot is the Fabiano Cragsman. When purchasing the Cragsman, an inner bootie can be fitted, turning this good single boot into an adequate double boot. The Fabiano Company, aware of the fact that many Americans have large feet, carries sizes up to 16 length and EE width. For sizes 14 or over, there is an additional charge.

Galibier
Mountain Paraphernalia
906 Durant Street
Modesto, California 95350

Galibier boots are among the finest-crafted boots in the world, used on numerous expeditions to Nepal, hundreds of thousands of Alpine ascents, and innumerable rock climbs. Their rock boots, the PA, RD, and RR, still set the trends in climbing today. The Terray and Super RD are fantastic on rock and ice, respectively. Their mountaineering double boot, the Hivernale, is the best-designed double boot on the market, equally at home on vertical ice walls as for delicate 5.8–5.9 rock work.

The RD rigid friction boot by Galibier. *Photo courtesy of Mountain Paraphernalia.*

The Pierre Allain rock-climbing shoe. *Photo courtesy of Mountain Paraphernalia.*

G. H. Bass & Company
Main Street
Wilton, Maine 04294
207-645-2556

At present, G. H. Bass manufactures a limited selection of general-purpose hiking boots. They have no technical mountaineering boots.

Lowa
Snowlion Corporation
1330 9th Street
Berkeley, California 94710

Snowlion is the importer and distributor of Lowa boots. The Lowa boot has a well-established reputation as a proficient mountaineering boot. The materials are high-quality leather, and the construction is superb throughout their entire line. The Civetta model is a superior technical rock and ice boot and has a wide last.

Mountain Products Corporation
123 Wenatchee Avenue
Wenatchee, Washington 98801

MPC is the distributor of high-quality Kastinger boots. The Atlas and Everest models, both available in sizes 5–13, medium width, are their best winter mountaineering boots. While not as popular in the United States as other brands, these boots are well made.

Norstar Ski Corporation Ltd.
Londonderry, New Hampshire 03053

Norstar is a distributor of Munari boots. This exceptional line includes some of the most impressive new boots on the American market. The Ranger is a ski mountaineering boot that handles exceptionally well on ice and rock, as well as being a nicely designed ski boot. Munari's Cervino model ought to give the French Terray a run for its money.

Peter Limmer and Sons   ORDER DIRECT
Intervale, New Hampshire 03845
603-FL6-5378

The Limmer family has been custom crafting hiking and mountaineering boots for three generations. Their handmade hiking boot, available in both summer and winter models, is the most sought-after footwear of its type in the United States. At present, there is a six-teen-month waiting list for a pair of Limmer boots. In the White Mountains, it is not that unusual to encounter hikers who have been enjoying the same pair of Limmer boots for twenty years. In addition to making their own boot, they carry in-stock sizes of Rummel Everest Model single-weight ice-climbing boots and the Nepal Model Rummel double boot; both of these shoes, while inexpensive, break down in a few seasons and are not recommended as long-term investments.

Raichle
200 Saw Mill River Road
Hawthorne, New York 10532

Raichle made the climbing and hiking boots used on the 1973 American Dhaulagiri Expedition, and the American Pamir Expedition of 1974. These boots are finely crafted and are of excellent quality. A free booklet on the care and use of mountain boots is available upon request.

The Raichle Annapurna technical climbing boot. *Photo by Marc Cohen, courtesy of Raichle.*

Summit Boots   INQUIRIES INVITED
Kalmar Trading Corporation
P. O. Box 77343—Dept. CSB
San Francisco, California 94107

The Summit boot line includes light hiking boots, heavyweight hiking boots, cross-country ski boots, and a technical climbing shoe. Their most popular lightweight hiking boot, the High Noon, is available in women's as well as men's sizes. It is suitable for light trail walking and beginning rock climbing. Their heavyweight hiking boot, the Tenaya, is a good all around heavy hiking, tromping, and light winter mountaineering boot.

Summit Tenaya boot. *Photo courtesy of Kalmar Trading Corporation.*

Summit High Noon boot. *Photo courtesy of Kalmar Trading Corporation.*

Sport-Obermeyer, Ltd.
P. O. Box 130
Aspen, Colorado 81611
303-925-3037

They carry Garmish climbing boots for mountaineering and rock climbing. Garmish is a good name for ski boots, but not for mountaineering.

Todds   ORDER DIRECT
5 South Wabash Avenue
Chicago, Illinois 66603

They carry a good selection of hiking boots only.

Vasque Voyageur
Red Wing Shoe Company
113 Main Street
Red Wing, Minnesota 55066

They produce a fine line of hiking and mountaineering boots. Their heavy-duty mountaineering boot, the Rainier, is excellent on snow and moderate ice. Its built-in steel shank prevents the breaking down of the welt that used to undermine its prototype. The Sequoia I is a very popular and comfortable trail shoe. The Vasque Shoenard, a summer climbing boot designed under the technical advice of Yvon Chouinard and Tom Frost, is moving ahead in acceptance and popularity on rock crags across the United States. The new Ascender II Rock Boot is the newest version of the Vasque Shoenard.

CHAPTER 3

Boot Reconditioning and Repair

When well treated and cared for, hiking and climbing boots will last many seasons. Eventually, it becomes necessary to have any pair of boots resoled. Some of the following people will work only on particular types of boots. Write first, describing what kind of boot you have, its condition, and what work you suspect you need done. Each cobbler listed will then estimate the approximate cost.

The Cobbler
1702½ West Colorado Avenue
Colorado Springs, Colorado 80904
303-475-7626

   Will work on all mountaineering boots.

Colorado Shoe Company
3103 East Colfax Avenue
Denver, Colorado 80206

   Will work on all mountaineering boots.

Leroy Gonzales
Telemark Ski and Mountain Sports
416 East 7th Avenue
Denver, Colorado 80205

   Will repair all mountaineering boots.

Steve Komito
Davis Hill
Box 2106
Estes Park, Colorado 80517

Steve Komito is the best known of the boot resolers. He has had articles on boot repair published in *Summit* and *Off Belay*. He also sells a complete line of climbing equipment at his store. We can highly recommend his work.

Mountain Boot Repair
P. O. Box 94
Ketchum, Idaho 83340
208-726-9935

Niall McGinnis has resoled several pair of boots for us and for many of our climbing friends. He does a great job on Robbins boots, PA's, and all other Vibram mountaineering boots. The pair of RD's that we had resoled by him, though, lacked the flexibility of a new boot. (In order to repair the RD, an extra ¼ -inch insole of rubber is added to bind the new sole in place; to the best of our knowledge, this is the same procedure followed by all boot repairers.) McGinnis is one of the best and least expensive of the climbing cobblers.

Mountain Traders
1711 Grove Street
Berkeley, California 94709

Neptune Mountaineering
1750 30th
Boulder, Colorado 80301

Neptune Mountaineering has the most interesting approach to resoling RD's and PA's. By substituting EB replacement soles for the normal RD and PA soles, the finished product improves the quality of the original rock shoe. The result is a boot with EB smearing power and the desirable RD edging qualities.

Dave Page Cobbler
346 Northeast 56th Street
Seattle, Washington 98105
206-523-8020

Will work on all mountaineering boots.

Ritz Shoe Rebuilders
1869 Solano Avenue
Berkeley, California 94707

Will resole all mountaineering boots.

Starlight & Storm—Mountain Boot Repair
3288 South 13th East
Salt Lake City, Utah 84106
801-466-6714

Will resole all mountaineering boots.

Table Mesa Shoe Repair
665 South Broadway
Boulder, Colorado 80303
303-494-5401

Will repair all mountaineering boots.

USM—United Shoe Machinery
719 School Street
North Brookfield, Massachusetts 01535

Vibram sale company of Quabang Rubber Company. Main distributor for all Vibram replacement soles. No individual boot repairs.

CHAPTER 4

Kits

Kits reflect a substantial savings over preassembled products, in some cases up to 50 per cent. Since there are so few companies manufacturing kits, it's relatively easy to check out the design characteristics of each to be sure you will be getting the features you need. All are fairly easy to assemble and cover a wide range of camping and mountaineering needs, including tents, sleeping bags, down parkas, and vests in sizes for children and adults.

Altra, Inc.
3645 Pearl Street
Boulder, Colorado 80301
303-449-2401

A newcomer to the industry, this small firm features mountain parka kits, day packs, vests, and jackets. Their jacket has a Velcro-sealed flap over the zipper, making this a warmer garment than, for example, the exposed-zipper Frostline down sweater.

Carikit Outdoor Equipment Kits   ORDER DIRECT
1975 30th Street
Boulder, Colorado 80302

Carikit features patented "Packetts"—premeasured down sealed in a plastic pouch that is sewn right into each compartment of the garment and which dissolves upon washing the completed garment. Their Inchworm is a sleeping bag designed for a child; it can be easily added to as your child grows, and eventually will yield a full-sized bag. All Carikit products reflect the fine design characteristics and materials for which Holubar, their parent company, is renowned.

Country Ways, Inc.   ORDER DIRECT
3500 D Highway 101
Minnetonka, Minnesota 55343
612-473-4334

One of the first companies producing kits exclusively of Polar-guard material—reputedly the most difficult filling material for a manufacturer to handle. Their kits include sleeping bags, vests, jackets, and booties.

Eastern Mountain Sport Kits   ORDER DIRECT
1041 Commonwealth Avenue
Boston, Massachusetts 02215

These kits are available at all Eastern Mountain retail outlets. One of their most recent kits is a Fiberfill II parka, the most inexpensive Fiberfill II expedition-grade parka on the market. Their 60/40 kits do not compare favorably with those of Carikit or Frostline.

Frostline Kits   ORDER DIRECT
452 Burbank
Broomfield, Colorado 80020

Frostline was the originator of the outdoor equipment kit idea, and to date has the largest and most diversified selection of kits. They're a bit stingy with material in their parka and down sweater kits, not taking into consideration the fact that some people have longer arms and torsos than others.

Mountain Adventure Kits
P. O. Box 571
Whittier, California 90608
213-698-7311

Kits of sleeping bags, parkas, jackets, vests, and mitts using Polar-guard and Fiberfill insulating materials.

Sherpa Designs, Inc.   ORDER DIRECT
3109 Brookdale Road East
Tacoma, Washington 98446
206-531-4114

Sherpa Designs offers two self-assembly snowshoe kits, featuring tubular frames, neoprene lacing material, bindings, and easy-to-follow instructions. Both kits include the flawlessly-designed Sherpa snowshoe binding with built-in snow cleat. Savings is more than $14 over preassembled snowshoes. These are the best snowshoe kits available on the American market.

Tubbs   ORDER DIRECT
Wallingford, Vermont 05773

A snowshoe kit, including preconstructed frame and neoprene nylon webbing material and disassembled snowshoe binding, is handled by Tubbs. The only kit of its type available on the market today, it reflects a 35 per cent savings over preassembled snowshoes. It is available in a variety of models.

CHAPTER 5

Custom Equipment

The Alpine Guild
300 Queen Anne Avenue, North
North Seattle, Washington 98109
206-283-6030

The Alpine Guild is a collective of individuals who personally design and construct custom camping equipment. The exceptionally well-priced Alpine Guild down sleeping bags are perfect for anyone needing a particularly short or long bag. One of their specialties is a bag roomy enough even for the most substantial defensive lineman.

Arcata Transit Authority
650-A 10th Street
Arcata, California 95521

Makers of "Blue Puma" brand custom down vests, sleeping bags, and jackets. Prices upon request.

Bugaboo Mountaineering
170 Central and Pacific Grove
Monterey, California

Produces a limited number of individually constructed sleeping bags and down jackets for the hard-to-fit. There is a considerable boost in price over their preassembled line.

Carla's Custom Packs
1554 Northeast 95th Street
Seattle, Washington 98115

Another member of the Alpine Craft Guild, Carla constructs custom haulpacks and rucksacks of excellent quality.

Crescent Quilting
Anne Crippen at the Alpine Crafts Guild
300 Queen Anne Avenue, North
North Seattle, Washington 98109

Very reasonable prices for down clothing for the hard-to-fit.

Early Winters Ltd.
300 Queen Anne Avenue, North
North Seattle, Washington 98109

Their Omnipotent is a superbly designed rounded profile tent that offers substantially more usable internal space than any traditional A-frame two-man expedition-quality tent. It weighs a pound less than the North Face and Glacier tents, and is slightly more expensive than either. It is definitely one of the top five two-man expedition tents.

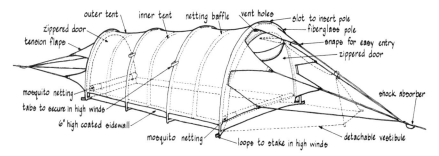

The Omnipotent Tent. *Courtesy of Early Winters Ltd.*

Fir Country Equipment—Patty Renner
1360 South 2nd
Springfield, Oregon 97477
503-747-8416

Fir Country will add additional down to existing sleeping bags and will restuff and repair other equipment.

Peter Limmer and Sons
Intervale, New Hampshire 03845
603-FL6-5378

Custom construction of the famous Limmer boot. See listing under

Part II, Chapter 2 in this book, "Hiking and Mountaineering Boot Distributors."

Stephenson's Warmlite
23206 Hatteras Street
Woodland Hills, California 91364

Custom sleeping bags and tents. The tents follow three distinctive patterns. The sleeping bag is the only bag that features a custom foam padding. See listing under Part II, Chapter 1 in this book, "Manufacturers, Importers, and Distributors of Technical Climbing Equipment."

Wilderness Experience
9408 Irondale
Chatsworth, California 91311

Custom construction of haulbags and backpacks for special purposes (will design around your special requirements). Also repairs zippers, tents, and sleeping bags. Write for prices of custom items.

CHAPTER 6

Climbers with Special Needs

Alaska Glacier Flights
Wilson Air Service
Gulkana Airfield, Box 114
Glenallen, Alaska 99588
907-TA2-3368
Jack E. Wilson

Arrangements for equipment drops and personnel delivery in the Alaskan ranges.

Greg Betts
Box 251
Jackson, New Hampshire 03846

Betts offers mountain- and woods-oriented first-aid and rescue courses in the White Mountains area. The instructor's background includes four years' teaching experience for the American Red Cross, the New Hampshire Emergency Medical Technician's Ambulance Course, and two years teaching experience at the American Academy of Orthopedic Surgeon's Annual Emergency Care course held at Harvard University. He has also worked with the Appalachian Mountain Club, and is the author of *A Guide to Patient Care and Evacuation in the White Mountains.*

Grade VI Mountain Works
406 South Beaver
Flagstaff, Arizona 86001

Ice axe pick droop modifications and repairs. They will do droop modifications on the pick, including new or increased serrations to your ice-climbing requirements. Will also flatten the adze of your axe, or do reshafting of your broken ice axe. Excellent workmanship, inexpensive. Lee Dexter also produces a bolt extractor for the Rawl Drive Studs, which should be removed in many climbing areas.

Hudson Air Service
Talkeetna, Alaska 99676
907-733-2121

Reasonable glacier and bush flying to Mount McKinley, Mount Hunter, Mount Foraker, etc.

Jackson Hole Mountain Guides
Teton Village, Wyoming 83025
307-733-4979

Mountain Photography Course—Camp IV—Five-day camp spent with a professional photographer and guide. Travel at comfortable pace, exploring and photographing Alpine surroundings. Careful attention placed upon improving photography skills, with specific regard to problems of high-altitude photography. All food and technical climbing equipment provided. Limited to four people. Moderately priced. Camps held June through August.

Mountain Valley Products
Food Preservation Research Center
P. O. Box 878
Mesa, Arizona 85201

Markets an electrically powered food dehydration machine for picky eaters planning long expeditions. Electric drying requires only four to thirty-six hours for most fruits, vegetables, meats, poultry, and herbs, as compared with one to three weeks for sun drying.

North Country Mountaineering, Inc.
P. O. Box 951
Hanover, New Hampshire 03755

North Country Mountaineering, Inc., will write, design, and produce direct mail catalogs, brochures, advertisements, and other promotional materials for any outdoor or climbing-related business or organization.

Northern Lights Alpine Recreation
Box 399
Invermere, British Columbia, V0A 1K0
Canada

Alpine Photography Course—Very fairly priced one-week sessions offered early July to mid-October. The prettiest items in this area are usually found in mid-August and late September. Most peaks are "walk-up," but technical climbs can be included. Instruction offered in the problems and tricks of high Alpine photography.

Scott Surgical Supply
724 East 17th Avenue
Denver, Colorado 80203
303-832-9074

They make climbing boots for amputees and physically handicapped individuals. They do not make custom boots for people with overlarge or long feet.

Silva
2466 North Street
R.D. 39
Laporte, Indiana 46350

The Silva Type 16-B compass is a unique invention designed in co-operation with organizations for the blind in the United States, Canada, and Sweden to help blind people locate directions. All significant parts are raised for touch orientation. Size is two inches by three inches.

Lightweight Climbing Foods

Climbers planning expeditions of more than a couple of weeks' duration should always consult well beforehand with a trained nutritionist or doctor, preferably one with a sustained interest in the complicated problems of mountaineering medicine and nutrition. Total reliance upon prepackaged backpacker-oriented foods is at best expensive, boring, and nutritionally suspect. A good source of information about foods for mountaineering are the appendices to recent expedition accounts published in book form, and related articles published in magazines for climbers. Mountaineers who find themselves unusually weary after ingesting foods high in carbohydrates (for example, the climber who falls asleep after two beers) ought to have themselves tested for hypoglycemia before embarking on even a few days away from their easy chairs. Keep in mind that conditions of stress, prolonged exertion, and altitude can deplete any climber's reserves of fluid and minerals (a question of more than just salt), and that mountaineering nutrition and medicine are still growing bodies of knowledge.

The weekend climber, or the climber who makes one- or two-week forays into wilderness areas, faces on the whole less potentially debilitating nutritional situations; a well-fed, well-exercised body can stand a remarkable amount of abuse. Excessive reliance upon starch-based, preservative-, and additive-loaded prepackaged foods, however, can help wear down even the most well-conditioned climber.

The consensus seems to be that an active day's climbing requires about four thousand calories of food intake per day, that figure varying by up to five hundred calories with body weight, build, and technical conditions encountered. A common mistake made by many climbers while in the field is underconsumption of protein—meats, cheese, soy beans, peanut butter, and nuts—foods that may take longer to digest, but that provide a constant source of energy while staving off feelings of hunger. Salami, we might add, the classic Big Wall food, is frighteningly rich in sodium nitrite—a chemical suspected of being a major cause of cancer of the colon in this country.

Climbing diets seem to be as subject to an occasional fad as any other aspect of climbing. Our own feeling is that a well-balanced, protein-rich diet, supplemented by quick-energy munchies ("gorp"), is essential for proper body functioning—whether one is spending a weekend camping and climbing on Mohonk Trust land, or carrying loads up Mount McKinley.

At least one manufacturer of lightweight foods produces a line high in protein and free from emulsifiers, artificial flavorings, and defoaming agents found in most commercially available trail foods. In time, perhaps other manufacturers will recognize that chemical-laced, carbohydrate-loaded, dehydrated and freeze-dried food are not where it's at.

Many climbers prepare their own lightweight trail foods from commonly available supermarket ingredients. For suggestions about make-your-own trail foods at considerable savings, see recipes featured regularly in such publications as *Backpack* magazine and the newsletters of clubs such as the Knickerbocker Chapter of the Adirondack Mountain Club.

Eventually, manufacturers of freeze-dried foods should have to specify carbohydrate and protein grams as well as other nutritional information on their packaging. It's time, in fact, that outdoor clubs and related publications start encouraging/pressuring manufacturers to state such information on their packaging as soon as possible.

Chuck Wagon Foods
Micro Drive
Woburn, Massachusetts 01801
617-729-7450

A good variety of meal plans; generously sized, filling servings for two, four, or six people. The cooking time is short (averaging about twenty minutes to prepare a full meal). Their food doesn't have a heavy, starchy taste. We can recommend their food products for the hiker and backpacker, but feel that their products should be used only as a supplement to expedition meal planning.

Chuck Wagon does offer several survival food packages. The Woodsman Packet, which is conveniently sized to fit into any rucksack, comes complete with fire starter, plastic water bag, emergency compass, water purification tablets, pemmican, tropical chocolate (nonmelting), candy-coated gum, a razor blade, and individually packaged toilet paper (good in helping to stop blood flow from smaller wounds). This minisurvival kit could well turn out to be a life saver. Their Pocket-Size Emergency Food Kit, with a total weight of only eight ounces, is completely waterproof and will float. It contains a basic survival instruction sheet, a single-edged razor blade, salt packets, chocolate bars, compressed cereal bar, fish hooks and fishing line, toilet tissue, a sheet of aluminum foil, waxed wood matches, and a jelly bar. The kit is guaranteed to last two years from date of purchase.

If you would like to try the Chuck Wagon line for under $10 for two people for one day, they have a sampler, containing breakfast, lunch, and dinner.

What they do have of real use to the climber is canned pemmican (a tasty, high-energy food) in 3½-ounce tins.

Freeze-Dry Foods Ltd.
579 Speers Road
Oakville, Ontario L6K 2G4
Canada
416-844-1471

Manufacturers of HarDee brand freeze-dried foods. All of Har-Dee's packaging materials are completely burnable—leaving infinitely less trash to pack out. Two of HarDee's freeze-dried meats—the Beef Steaks and Boneless Pork Chops are among the very best freeze-dried foods we've yet tasted. They're both excellent. HarDee's whole strawberries are also excellent—a welcome and rare treat. Their main meal packages, Beef Stew Mix and Chili Con Carne, went over very well, their Chicken Stew somewhat less so. HarDee's instant desserts, particularly the Peaches and their Applesauce, made no one happy.

Mountain House Freeze Dried Foods
Oregon Freeze Dry Foods, Inc.
770 West 29th Avenue
P. O. Box 1048
Albany, Oregon 97321
503-926-6001

One of the best of the commercially prepackaged outdoor foods. Main courses are packaged in clearly labeled vacuum-sealed aluminum pouches. Within each is a disposable preparation bowl, which saves on clean-up time. No long-term cooking required. All preparation consists of mixing boiling water with these precooked and freeze-dried foods. Two of the main courses we tried, the Beef Stew and their Noodles and Chicken, were tasty and filling. We did notice that a slight additional amount of boiling water should be added to negate the cardboard consistency from which almost all freeze-dried meats (with the exception of the aforementioned HarDee steaks and pork chops) suffer. One of the problems of using Mountain House main meals during cold weather is that the boiling water cools very quickly after being added to the food product, making for tepid meals.

The Mountain House Sausage Patties are excellent—one of the best freeze-dried meat products we've tried. Their scrambled eggs are the best of the freeze-dried eggs on the market—but are, of course, rubbery.

We would recommend Mountain House foods for climbing and extended outings, especially in cases where there is limited time available for the preparation of meals. We feel that the best combination, if you are going to depend upon prepackaged, lightweight foods, would be to use the Mountain House Freeze Dried Foods as a quick hot meal before the day's climb, and Natural Food Backpack Dinners for a warming, relaxing evening meal (requiring more preparation time) before turning in. HarDee's freeze-dried beefsteaks would go gloriously with either. Speedy Chef's unbelievably delicious Green Beans with Mushrooms in Wine-Flavored Sauce would also be nice at any time.

The drawback to Mountain House foods is their expense; if you are preparing meals for two hungry eaters, the daily cost can be a bankrupting proposition.

Mountain House has recently begun to market a line of compressed freeze-dried foods. The compressed rice-based dishes are a problem as the rice grains break easily as you break the disc for cooking. Their Shrimp Creole, in the new line, is quite good—but short on shrimp. Their Green Bean discs make good low-calorie snacks uncooked.

Photos courtesy of Oregon Freeze Dry Foods, Inc.

National Packaged Trail Foods
18607 St. Clair Avenue
Cleveland, Ohio 44119
216-481-1963

This company is the marketing agency for dealer and retail sales of Ad Seidel's Trail Packets and Wilson's Campsite Freeze Dry meats.

We found the products we tested very heavy, very starchy, and quite unpalatable. In controlled cooking over a variety of available camp stoves under the best possible cooking conditions, the food stuck to the bottom of the pan and burned. The dinners we tried— Ham and Potatoes, Beef Stew, and Chicken à la King—rate as the worst prepackaged outdoor foods we have tried. Fitzroy, the dog, ordinarily no gourmet, wouldn't eat these either.

Natural Food Backpack Dinners   ORDER DIRECT
P. O. Box 532
Corvallis, Oregon 97330

Natural Food Backpack Dinners are a fairly new and welcome addition to the range of available lightweight foods. They're not full of preservatives or devitaminized belly fillers. They taste quite good, they're not expensive, and they are easy to prepare, with a usual cooking time for main dishes of twenty minutes. Their Mexican Style Dinner Mix is our favorite. Its aroma seems to attract even compulsively picky eater/climbers. Ingredients for this one are ground kidney beans, corn meal, parmesan cheese, soy grits, dehydrated onions, chili powder, salt, garlic powder, herbs, and spices. They also produce a "Middle Eastern Style" dinner mix of cracked wheat, soy grits, pumpkin seeds, currants, dehydrated onions, sea salt, herbs, and spices—a filling, very tasty dish, though we didn't find it particularly "Middle Eastern." The company has a relatively limited line at present, including Lentil Soup Mix and Mountain Macaroni (whole wheat macaroni base). Write to them for current price list (they take mail orders), or check your local health food store. An extremely refreshing change from the usual prepackaged food.

Prices are extremely good, from $.85 to $1.25 for a two-serving dinner. These are unusually low local co-op-type prices.

Rich-Moor

P. O. Box 2728

Van Nuys, California 91401

Two- and four-person-sized packages. Easy-to-prepare foods with easy-to-read directions. Their trail snack, "gorp," consists of nuts, chocolate, and fruit, and is convenient and nourishing to munch on during a climb. Definitely one of the better food-packaging companies. Other top-line items are freeze-dried meat bars such as steaks, chicken, hamburgers, jerky, and meat balls. Rich-Moor also produces a portable gas-operated backpacking stove that works on readily available butane containers. It is one of the lightest collapsible portable gas stoves available and can be purchased directly from them.

Speedy Chef Foods, Inc.

2395 Middlegreen Court

Lancaster, Pennsylvania 17601

717-299-5656

Speedy Chef is the company packaging trail foods for Eastern Mountain Sports. Their food is packaged in foil envelopes into which boiling water can be poured, eliminating pot cleaning, a definite plus as far as we're concerned. Carrying out the soiled foil envelopes, however, can be messy. One of the most delicious freeze-dried foods we've tasted is their Green Beans with Mushrooms in Wine-Flavored Sauce; it's good enough for us also to want to keep some in the house as a superb convenience food—something we couldn't say about more than one or two other freeze-dried foods. Unfortunately, the dish contains MSG, a chemical we would ordinarily avoid ingesting. Speedy Chef's Candied Squash Blend with Nut Flake Topping isn't quite as fine as the Green Beans with Mushrooms, but it's darn good—a great trail food for squash enthusiasts. One of our ideal meals for rather luxe winter evenings in the mountains is Speedy Chef Green Beans with Mushrooms, Speedy Chef Candied Squash, and HarDee Beef Steaks. Even more gluttonous would be to prepare first one of the delicious Japanese instant chicken or leek soups with rice noodles sold in Japanese specialty food shops for between 30 to 45 cents a package (also sold in some Chinese neighborhoods).

Not quite in the same flavor league, but good enough, is Speedy Chef's Chicken Stew. Their Beef Chop Suey is very beefy in flavor, but too salty. Speedy Chef's Green Beans and Potatoes with Textured Vegetable Protein (hamlike chunks) was warm and filling; the ham-flavored vegetable protein was pretty good, but the green beans here were tough and the potatoes mushy. Speedy Chef's Chickenlike Textured Vegetable Protein is a handy addition to trail stew made from, for example, instant gravy mix, noodles, and freeze-dried peas. Generally quite a good line of food.

Stow-A-Way Sports Industries
166 Cushing Highway (Route 3A)
Cohasset, Massachusetts 02025
617-383-9116

Stow-A-Way food is the only freeze-dried and lightweight food supplier that offers custom food preparation for camp, school, and expedition menu requirements adjusted to group meal-size needs. They will mail food packages along the entire length of the Appalachia Trail, from Georgia to Maine, using selected post office points as delivery centers. This service is exceptional for hiking and traveling camps or those planning long hikes. They offer a 20 per cent discount on purchases over $300.

They have a sampler packet for $10 that includes a full day's meal for two.

All packaging used on their foods is burnable, and their prices are reasonable. The food is palatable and not all starch-based.

Western Globe Products, Inc.
8985 Venice Boulevard
Los Angeles, California 90034

Western Globe Products has introduced a new "Dinner Pot" line that promises to be a boon to climbers. Four varieties are available: Hobo Stew, Ranch Chili, Farm Style Chicken, and Country Style Cheese. They need only water and simmering for about fifteen minutes. The protein content is rated at 18 per cent.

PART III

Climbing Equipment Retail Stores

Climbing Equipment Retail Stores

Climbing equipment retailers have become almost as important a resource as the rock itself. They're more than just purveyors of goods. The stores in the following state-by-state guide are invariably staffed by resident climbers with an excellent knowledge of the areas in which you'll be climbing. They can clue you in to peculiarities of weather, and changes in guidebook routes caused by rockfall. They know the best of the campsites and climbers' pubs. Usually, there's someone at the store who either teaches climbing or knows of someone else who does. They're also an excellent source of information about local cliff mores and politics.

KEY TO SYMBOLS

 A store carrying a complete line of technical rock-climbing equipment.

 A store carrying a complete line of technical climbing equipment, including ice-climbing gear.

 A store with guidebooks to local crags and news of most recent routes.

 Store offering rock-climbing instruction.

 Store carrying downhill ski equipment.

 Store carrying cross-country ski equipment.

 Store handling bicycle sales.

 Store selling canoes and kayaks.

ALABAMA

Huntsville

Outdoor Omnibus
Huntsville Shopping Center
Huntsville, Alabama 35801
205-533-4131

ALASKA

Anchorage

Barneys Sport Chalet
906 West Northern Lights Boulevard
Anchorage, Alaska 99504

Eberhards Sport Shop
307 East Northern Lights Boulevard
Anchorage, Alaska 99503

Muskeg Outfitters
10197 Klatt Station
Anchorage, Alaska 99502
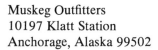

ARIZONA

Flagstaff

The Alpineer
406 South Beaver Street
Flagstaff, Arizona 86001
602-774-7809

Village Sports Den
116 South Beaver Street
Flagstaff, Arizona 86001
602-774-2271

Phoenix

Desert Mountain Sports
4506 North 16th Street
Phoenix, Arizona 85016
602-265-4401

High Adventure Headquarters
3925 East Indian School Road
Phoenix, Arizona 85018
602-955-3391

Prescott

The Benchmark
208 West Gurley
Prescott, Arizona 86301
602-445-8310

Tempe

High Adventure Headquarters
1039 East Lemon
Tempe, Arizona 05281
602-968-2712

Tucson

Summit Hut
3254 East Speedway
Tucson, Arizona 85716
602-327-8002

CALIFORNIA

Arcata

Arcata Transit Authority
650A 10th Street
Arcata, California 95521
707-822-2204

Berkeley

Co-op Wilderness Supply
1432 University Avenue
Berkeley, California 94702
415-843-9300

Mountain Traders
1702 Grove Street
Berkeley, California 94709
415-845-8600

North Face
2804 Telegraph Avenue
Berkeley, California 94705
415-548-1371

Recreational Equipment, Inc.
Corner Gilman and San Pablo
Berkeley, California 94706
415-527-4140

Sierra Designs
4th and Addison Street
Berkeley, California 94710
415-843-2010

Ski Hut, Inc.
1615 University Avenue
Berkeley, California 94703
415-843-6505

Bishop

Bike Shoppe
772 North Main Street
Bishop, California 93514
714-873-5070

Campbell

Mountain Life
Campbell Plaza
2513 Winchester
Campbell, California 95008
408-374-7777

Castro Valley

Co-op Wilderness Supply
3667 Castro Valley Boulevard
Castro Valley, California 94546
408-886-4550

Chico

Mountain Man Sports
217 Main Street
Chico, California 95926
916-345-4542

Claremont

Backpacker Shop
743 East Foothill
Claremont, California 91711
714-624-0618

Corte Madera

Co-op Wilderness Supply
47 Tamal Vista Boulevard
Corte Madera, California 94925
415-924-7780

Skip Sports
41 Corte Madera Drive
Corte Madera, California 94525
415-924-2892

Cupertino

Antelope Camping Equipment
21740 Granada Avenue
Cupertino, California 95014
408-253-1913

Any Mountain, Ltd.
20630 Valley Green Drive
Cupertino, California 95014
408-255-6162

El Cajon

Adventure 16, Inc.
656 Front Street
El Cajon, California 92020
714-444-2161

Fresno

Robbins Mountain Shop
7180 North Abbey Road
Fresno, California 93650
219-439-0745

Glendale

Kelty Cyclery
1756 Victory Boulevard
Glendale, California 91201
213-247-6170

Kelty Mountaineering
1801 Victory Boulevard
Glendale, California 91201
213-247-3110

Glendora

Pack and Piton
1000 East Alosa Avenue
Glendora, California 91740
213-335-0414

Goleta

Granite Stairway Mountaineering
330 South Kellogg
Goleta, California 93017
805-964-5417

Upper Limits
133 North Fairview Avenue
Fairview Shopping Center
Goleta, California 93017
805-967-0476

Kentfield

Alpine House
1028 Sir Francis Drake
Kentfield, California 94904
415-454-8543

LaCanada

Sport Chalet
P. O. Box 626
951 Foothill Boulevard
LaCanada, California 91011
213-790-2717

Lafayette

Colliers
3543 Mount Diablo Boulevard
Lafayette, California 94549
415-283-0410

La Habra

Sport and Trails
1491 West Whittier Boulevard
La Habra, California 90631
213-694-2164

La Jolla

San Diego Ski Chalet
7522 La Jolla Boulevard
La Jolla, California 92057
714-459-2691

Los Angeles

West Ridge
11930 West Olympic Boulevard
West Los Angeles, California 90034
213-477-5250

Mammoth Lakes

Kittredge Sport Shop
P. O. Box 598—State Highway 203
Mammoth Lakes, California 93546
714-934-2423

Merced

Downhill Ski Sports
422 West 17th Street
Merced, California 95340
209-722-0281

Mill Valley

Tetons West
87 East Blithedale Avenue
Mill Valley, California 94941
415-383-4050

Modesto

Robbins Mountain Shop
1508 10th Street
Modesto, California 95354
209-529-6913

Napa

Skip Sports
Grapeyard Shopping Center
Napa, California 94558
707-252-6055

Nevada City

Wilderness Grubstake
309 Commercial Avenue
Box 1414
Nevada City, California 95959
916-265-5851

Northridge

Kelty Pack
9020 Tampa Avenue
Northridge, California 91324
213-993-0887

Palo Alto

Sierra Designs
217 Alma Street
Palo Alto, California 94301
415-325-3231

Pasadena

The Backpacker Shop
2084 East Foothill Boulevard
Pasadena, California 91107
213-796-3749

Redding

Alpine Outfitters
1538 Market Street
Redding, California 96001
916-243-7333

Riverside

Highland Outfitters
6410 Magnolia
Riverside, California 92502
714-683-7414

Ski and Sport
6744 Brockton
Riverside, California 92506
714-784-0205

Sacramento

Alpenhaus
2760 Fulton Avenue
Sacramento, California 95821
916-483-9528

Antelope Camping Equipment
1621 Fulton Avenue
Sacramento, California 95825
916-489-9591

Sierra Outfitters
2903 Fulton Avenue
Sacramento, California 95821
916-481-2480

San Bruno

Skip Sports
Bay Hill Shopping Center
San Bruno, California 94066
415-588-5416

San Diego

Adventure 16, Inc.
3679 Sports Arena Boulevard
San Diego, California 92110
714-224-4216

Adventure 16, Inc.
Aztec Center
San Diego SU
San Diego, California 92115
714-287-2166

San Diego Ski Chalet and Mountain Shop
4004 Sports Arena Boulevard
San Diego, California 93401
714-224-3439

San Francisco

Eddie Bauer, Inc.
120 Kearny Street
San Francisco, California 94108
415-986-7600

Sierra Equipment
747 Polk Street
San Francisco, California 94109
415-771-8636

Swiss Ski Sports
559 Clay Street
San Francisco, California 94105
415-434-0322

The Mountain Shop
228 Grant Avenue
San Francisco, California 94108
415-362-8477

The Smiley Company
575 Howard Street
San Francisco, California 94105
415-421-2459

San Jose

Freemans'
840 Town and Country Village
San Jose, California 95128
408-244-7300

San Luis Obispo

Granite Stairway Mountaineering
871 Santa Rosa
San Luis Obispo, California 93401
805-541-1533

Mountain Sports
858 Higuera Street
San Luis Obispo, California 93401
805-544-7141

Santa Ana

The Backpacker Shop
1318 North Grand Avenue
Santa Ana, California 92701
714-836-6474

Santa Barbara

Granite Stairway Mountaineering
3040 State Street
Santa Barbara, California 93105
805-682-1083

Santa Maria

Mountain Sports
223 South Broadway
Santa Maria, California 93454
805-922-8271

Santa Rosa

Skip Sports
733 4th Street
Santa Rosa, California 95404
707-527-7050

The Backpackers Tent
533 5th Street
Santa Rosa, California 95401
707-544-2040

Backpacking

Sonora

Hide and Sole
171 North Washington Street
Sonora, California 95370
209-532-5621

South Lake Tahoe

The Outdoorsman
P. O. Box 8877
South Lake Tahoe, California 95731
916-541-1660

Sunnyvale

Freemans'
711 Town and Country Village
Sunnyvale, California 94086
408-732-3300

Tarzana

The Mountain Store
5425 Reseda Boulevard
Tarzana, California 91356
213-881-5111

Torrance

The Ski Racquet
20611 Hawthorne Boulevard
Torrance, California 90503
213-371-3533

Upland

Pack and Piton
1252 West Foothill Boulevard
Upland, California 91786
714-982-7408

Ventura

Great Pacific Iron Works
235 West Santa Clara
Ventura, California 93001
805-643-6074

Volcano

The Basecamp
P. O. Box 271
Volcano, California 95689

Walnut Creek

Co-op Wilderness Supply
1295 South Main Street
Walnut Creek, California 94596
415-935-6150

West Covina

Alpine Country
1629 West Garvey Avenue
West Covina, California 91790
213-962-4311

Yosemite

Mountain Shop
Yosemite Park and Curry Co.
Yosemite, California 95389
209-372-4611

COLORADO

Aspen

Aspen Mountaineering, Ltd.
203 South Galena—Box 3259
Aspen, Colorado 81611
303-925-1166

Boulder

The Boulder Mountaineer
1329 Broadway
Boulder, Colorado 80302
303-442-8355

Holubar Shops
1975 30th Street
Boulder, Colorado 80302
303-449-1731

Mountain Sports
821 Pearl
Boulder, Colorado 80302
303-443-6770

Neptune Mountaineering
1750 30th Street
Boulder, Colorado 80302
303-442-3551

Colorado Springs

Holubar Shops
131 South Tejon Street
Colorado Springs, Colorado 80903
303-634-5279

Denver

Eastern Mountain Sports
1428 15th Street—Corner Blake Street
Denver, Colorado 80202
303-571-1160

Eddie Bauer, Inc.
1616 Welton Street
Denver, Colorado 80202
303-534-3050

Forrest Mountaineering, Ltd.
1517 Platte Street
Denver, Colorado 80202
303-433-3373

Holubar Shops
2490 South Colorado Boulevard
Denver, Colorado 80222
303-758-7366

Ptarmigan Mountain Shop
938 South Monaco Parkway
Denver, Colorado 80222
303-377-2783

Durango

Colorado Alpine Sports
7th and Main Street
Durango, Colorado 81301
303-247-1935

Estes Park

Colorado Mountain Sports
237 West Elkhorn
Estes Park, Colorado 80517
303-586-2829

Steve Komito
Davis Hill—Box 2106
Estes Park, Colorado 80517
303-586-5791

Fort Collins

Alpine Distributors
328 Link Lane—No. 5 J.C.
Fort Collins, Colorado 80521
303-482-0311

Alpine Haus
328 Link Avenue
Fort Collins, Colorado 80521
303-482-2043

Holubar Shops
2715 South College Avenue
Fort Collins, Colorado 80521
303-484-2872

The Mountain Shop
128 West Laurel
Fort Collins, Colorado 80521
303-493-5720

Frisco

Christy Sports
P. O. Box 6
Frisco, Colorado 80443
303-668-6250

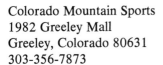

Greeley

Alpine Haus
1600 8th Avenue
Greeley, Colorado 80631
303-352-2563

Colorado Mountain Sports
1982 Greeley Mall
Greeley, Colorado 80631
303-356-7873

Gunnison

Carrol's, Ltd.
125 Main Street
Gunnison, Colorado 81230
303-641-1127

Lakewood

Christy Sports
9885 West Colfax Avenue
Lakewood, Colorado 80227
303-273-0475

Ptarmigan Mountain Shop
1949 South Wadsworth Boulevard
Lakewood, Colorado 80227
303-986-5541

Louisville

Lowe Alpine Systems, Inc.
931 Main Street (Box 151)
Louisville, Colorado 80027
303-666-6650

Steamboat Springs

Mountaincraft
Box 359
Steamboat Springs, Colorado 80477
303-879-2368

Vail

Christy Sports
Box 937
307 East Bridge
Vail, Colorado 81657
303-476-2244

CONNECTICUT

Essex

Outdoor Traders, Inc.
Main Street
Essex, Connecticut 06426
203-869-7950

Greenwich

Outdoor Traders Mountain Shop
79 East Putnam Avenue
Greenwich, Connecticut 06830
203-869-7950

Hartford

Eastern Mountain Sports, Inc.
1 Civic Center Plaza
Hartford, Connecticut 06103
203-278-7105

Veterans Sport Shop
281 Asylum Street
Hartford, Connecticut 06103
203-247-7504

Litchfield

Outdoor Traders, Inc.
West Street
Litchfield, Connecticut 06759
203-567-8010

New Haven

The Ski Hut, Inc.
15 Whitney Avenue
New Haven, Connecticut 06510
203-865-1659

West Hartford

Clapp and Treat
672 Farmington Avenue
West Hartford, Connecticut 06119
203-236-0878

West Simsbury

Great World, Inc.
250 Farms Village Road
P. O. Box 250
West Simsbury, Connecticut 06092
203-658-4461

Wilton

Ski Hut, Inc.
Keeler Building
Wilton, Connecticut 06897
203-762-8324

DELAWARE

Newark

Wicks Ski Shops
Chestnut and Marrows
Newark, Delaware 19711
302-737-2521

Wilmington

Wicks Ski Shops
1201 Philadelphia Pike
Wilmington, Delaware 19809
302-798-1818

FLORIDA

Cocoa

The Wilderness Shop
1426 Lake Drive
Cocoa, Florida 32922
305-632-3070

Jacksonville

Jesse Browns' Backpacking
6720 Arlington Expressway
Jacksonville, Florida 32211
904-725-3633

GEORGIA

Athens

Charbon Outfitters
229 East Broad
Athens, Georgia 30030
404-548-7225

Atlanta

American Adventures
6300 Powers Ferry Road Northwest
Atlanta, Georgia 30327
404-993-9644

Deans, Inc.
1240 West Paces Ferry Road Northwest
Atlanta, Georgia 30327
404-262-2911

Decatur

Georgia Outdoors
1945 South Candler Road
Decatur, Georgia 30032
404-289-9717

To the best of our knowledge, this is the only retail store offering *free* climbing instruction.

HAWAII

Honolulu

Camper Town
1336 Bingham Boulevard
Honolulu, Hawaii 96814
808-847-4467

IDAHO

Boise

Sawtooth Mountaineering
5200 Fairview Mini Mall
Boise, Idaho 83704
208-376-3731

Idaho Falls

Solitude Sports
170 Elm
Idaho Falls, Idaho 83401
208-523-7000

Ketchum

Snug Mountaineering
Ketchum, Idaho 83340
208-726-4593

Moscow

Northwestern Mountain Sports
410 West 3rd Street
Moscow, Idaho 83843
208-882-0133

Sun Valley

Mountain Shop of Sun Valley
P. O. Box 87
Sun Valley, Idaho 83353
208-622-9305

ILLINOIS

Champaign

Bushwacker, Ltd.
702 South Neil
Champaign, Illinois 61820
217-359-3353

Chicago

Eddie Bauer, Inc.
123 North Wabash Avenue
Chicago, Illinois 60602
312-263-6005

Erewhon Mountain Supply
1252 West Devon
Chicago, Illinois 60626
312-262-3832

Traveler's Abbey
2934 North Broadway
Chicago, Illinois 60657
312-549-3270

Win Sum Mountain Shop
455 West Armitage
Chicago, Illinois 60614
312-751-1776

Elmhurst

Campfitters Limited
210 North York Road
Elmhurst, Illinois 60126
312-834-5410

Evanston

Campfitters Limited
924 Davis Street
Evanston, Illinois 60201
312-864-1940

Maywood

Easy Camping
510 South Wood
Maywood, Illinois 60153
312-744-4454

INDIANA

Indianapolis

Sitzmark
819 East Westfield
Indianapolis, Indiana 46220

KANSAS

Lawrence

Gran Sport
Seventh and Arkansas
Lawrence, Kansas 66044 ·
913-843-3328

Leavenworth

Gran Sport
905 South 4th
Leavenworth, Kansas 66048
913-682-2233

Topeka

Gran Sport
527 Topeka Avenue
Topeka, Kansas 66603
913-354-1656

Wichita

Mountain High, Inc.
2936 East Douglas
Wichita, Kansas 67214
316-684-4121

LOUISIANA

New Orleans

The Canoe and Trail Shop
624 Moss Street
New Orleans, Louisiana 70119
504-488-8528

MAINE

Brewer

Hanson's
395 South Main Street
Brewer, Maine 04412
207-989-7250

Freeport

L. L. Bean
305 Main Street
Freeport, Maine 04032
207-865-3111

Kingfield

Sugarloaf Ski Specialists
Main Street
Kingfield, Maine 04947
207-265-2621

MARYLAND

Baltimore

H & H Camper's Haven
424 North Eutaw Street
Baltimore, Maryland 21201
301-752-2580

Ellicott City

Appalachian Outfitters
Baltimore National Pike
Ellicott City, Maryland 21043
301-465-7227

Gaithersburg

Hudson Bay Outfitters
315 East Diamond Avenue
Gaithersburg, Maryland 20760
301-948-2474

Kensington

Hudson Bay Outfitters
10560 Metropolitan Avenue
Kensington, Maryland 20795
301-949-2515 and 949-9669

Silver Spring

Wilderness Outfitter   To open soon
2706 Scarfield Avenue
Silver Spring, Maryland 20910
301-589-3050

MASSACHUSETTS

Amherst

Eastern Mountain Sports
Route 9
Amherst, Massachusetts 01002
413-253-9504

Boston

Eastern Mountain Sports
Bargain Basement
1041 Commonwealth Avenue
Boston, Massachusetts 02215
617-254-4250

Eastern Mountain Sports
Mail Order Dept.—P. O. Box 27
1047 Commonwealth Avenue
Boston, Massachusetts 02215
617-787-2626

Wilderness House
117 Brighton Avenue
Boston, Massachusetts 02134
617-277-5858

Chelmsford

Moor and Mountain
Chelmsford, Massachusetts 01824
617-256-6538

Northampton

Don Gleasons Camper Supply
9 Pearl Street
Northampton, Massachusetts 01060
413-584-4895

Wellesley

Eastern Mountain Sports
189 Linden Street
Wellesley, Massachusetts 02181
617-237-2645

MICHIGAN

Ann Arbor

Raupp Campfitters
637 South Main
Ann Arbor, Michigan 48103
313-769-5574

Birmingham

The Sportsman
184 Pierce Street
Birmingham, Michigan 48011
313-646-1225

Detroit

Eddie Bauer, Inc.
21110 Greenfield Road
Oak Park, Michigan 48237
313-399-8484

Raupp Campfitters
3539 Concord
Detroit, Michigan 48207
313-571-7251

East Lansing

The Weathervane
4887 Down Avenue
East Lansing, Michigan 48823

Limited

Farmington Hills

The Benchmark
29450 West Ten Mile at Middlebelt
Farmington Hills, Michigan 48024
313-477-8116

Kalamazoo

Raupp Campfitters
1801 West Main Street
Kalamazoo, Michigan 49001
616-344-1337

Lansing

Raupp Campfitters
2208 East Michigan Avenue
Lansing, Michigan 48914
517-484-9401

Mount Pleasant

The Weathervane
207 East Bellows
Mount Pleasant, Michigan 48858
517-772-0303

Royal Oak

Raupp Campfitters
421 South Washington
Royal Oak, Michigan 48103
313-547-6969

MINNESOTA

Duluth

Continental Ski Shop
1305 East 1st Street
Duluth, Minnesota 55805

Minneapolis

Burger Brothers
2828 Southeast University Avenue
Minneapolis, Minnesota 55101
612-331-1561

Backpacking

Eddie Bauer, Inc.
821 Marquette
Minneapolis, Minnesota 55402
612-339-9477

Hoigaards, Inc.
3550 South Highway 100
Minneapolis, Minnesota 55416
612-929-1351

Midwest Mountaineering
1408 Hennepin Avenue
Minneapolis, Minnesota 55403
612-336-3884

St. Paul

Eastern Mountain Sports Lob Pine
1627 West Country Road "B"
St. Paul, Minnesota 55113
612-631-2900

Gokey Company
West 5th Street
St. Paul, Minnesota 55101
612-222-2581

MISSOURI

Kansas City

Campfitters, Limited
3936 Broadway
Kansas City, Missouri 64111
816-531-0200

MONTANA

Great Falls

Great Falls Sporting Goods
820 Central
Great Falls, Montana 59401
406-453-1241

Kalispell

Sportsman's Ski Haus
40 East Idaho
Kalispell, Montana 59901
406-756-2106

Red Lodge

Sir Michaels Sport Shoppe
P. O. Box 1150
Red Lodge, Montana 59068
406-446-1613

NEVADA

Las Vegas

Highland Outfitting Company
600 South Highland Drive
Las Vegas, Nevada 89106
702-382-5093

NEW HAMPSHIRE

Durham

Wilderness Trails
12 Pettee Brook Lane
Durham, New Hampshire 03824
603-868-5584

Hanover

Dartmouth Co-op
Hanover, New Hampshire 03755
603-643-3100

Backpacking shop

Littleton

Stod Nichols, Inc.
Theatre Building
Littleton, New Hampshire 03561
603-444-5597

Limited

Limited technical climbing gear, including some ice gear. Bill Nichols
is chairman for AMC Trails in New Hampshire and offers free trail
information to hikers not familiar with the area.

North Conway

Eastern Mountain Sports
Main Street
North Conway, New Hampshire 03860
603-356-5433

International Mountain Equipment
Box 494—Main Street
North Conway, New Hampshire 03860
603-356-5287

North Woodstock

Skimeister Sport Shop
Main Street
North Woodstock, New Hampshire 03262
603-745-2767

Peterboro

Hancock Village Outfitters, Inc.
Peterboro, New Hampshire 03449
603-924-7211

NEW JERSEY

Paramus

Morsan
810 Route 17
Paramus, New Jersey 07652
201-445-5000

Princeton

Wooden Nickel
354 Nassau Street
Princeton, New Jersey 08540
609-924-3001

Flemington

Wooden Nickel
150 Main Street
Flemington, New Jersey 08822
201-782-1600

NEW MEXICO

Albuquerque

Mountain Chalet
1406 Eubank Northeast
Albuquerque, New Mexico 87112
505-298-4296

Santa Fe

Alpine Sports
121 Sandoval
Santa Fe, New Mexico 87501
505-983-5155

Peak and Plain Outfitters
P. O. Box 2538
Santa Fe, New Mexico 87501
505-982-8948

NEW YORK

Ardsley

Eastern Mountain Sports
725 Saw Mill River Road
Ardsley, New York 10502
914-693-6160

Armonk

Kreeger & Son
130 Bedford Road
Armonk, New York 10504
914-273-8520

Binghamton

Eureka Camping Center
625 Conklin Road
Binghamton, New York 13902
607-723-4179

Buffalo

Nord Alp, Inc.
3260 Main Street
Buffalo, New York 14215
716-837-3300

Canton

Camping Specialties
15 East Main Street
Canton, New York 13617
315-386-8360

Ithaca

Nippenose Equipment
DeWitt Mall
Cayuga and Seneca Street
Ithaca, New York 14850
607-272-6868

Lake Placid

Eastern Mountain Sports
Main Street
Lake Placid, New York 12946
518-523-2505

Liverpool

Liverpool Sports Center
125 1st Street
Liverpool, New York 13088
315-457-2290

New Paltz

Rock and Snow
44 Main Street
New Paltz, New York 12561
914-255-1311

New York City

American Youth Hostels, Inc.
132 Spring Street
New York, New York 10012
212-431-7100

Kreeger & Sons Ltd.
30 West 46th Street
New York, New York 10036
212-541-9704

Paragon Sporting Goods
867 Broadway
New York, New York 10010
212-255-8036

Tent and Trail
21 Park Place
New York, New York 10007
212-227-1760

Camping store with some rock
equipment

Syracuse

Nippenose Equipment
3006 Erie Boulevard
Syracuse, New York 13274
315-446-3838

Tarrytown

Campers Center
635 White Plains Road
Tarrytown, New York 10591
914-631-0409

Tonawanda

Eastern Mountain Sports
1270 Niagara Falls Boulevard
Tonawanda, New York 14150
716-838-4200

Troy-Schenectady

Hanson's Trail North
960-A Troy-Schenectady Road
Latham, New York 12110
518-785-0340

NORTH CAROLINA

Asheville

Mountaineering South
344 Tunnel Road
Asheville, North Carolina 28805
704-298-4532

Boone

Footslogger
204 Blowing Rock Road
Boone, North Carolina 28607
704-264-5565

Charlotte

Jesse Brown's Backpacking Mountaineering
2843 Eastway Drive
Charlotte, North Carolina 28205
704-568-2152

Greensboro

Blue Ridge Mountain Sports
1507 Spring Garden
Greensboro, North Carolina 27403
919-275-8115

Carolina Outdoor Sports
844 West Lee Street
Greensboro, North Carolina 27403

Raleigh

Carolina Outdoor Sports
1520 Dixie Trail
Raleigh, North Carolina 27607

Winston-Salem

Pack 'n' Paddle
P. O. Box 4856
4240 Kernersville Road
Winston-Salem, North Carolina 27107
919-784-7402

OHIO

Akron

European Connection and Trail Hutte
469 East Exchange Street
Akron, Ohio 44304

Chagrin

Ski Haus, Inc.
49 West Orange
Chagrin Falls, Ohio 44022
216-247-4901

Cincinnati

Speleo Alpine Show
947 Hatch Street
Cincinnati, Ohio 45202

Cleveland

Adler's Camping, Inc.
728 Prospect Avenue
Cleveland, Ohio 44115
216-696-5222

Cleveland Heights

The Ski Haus
12413 Cedar Road
Cleveland Heights, Ohio 44106
216-462-2420

Columbus

Outdoor Store, Inc.
1025 Dublin Road
Columbus, Ohio 43215
614-488-9701

Sheffield Lake

Ohio Canoe Adventures
5128 Colorado Avenue
Sheffield Lake, Ohio 44054
216-934-5345

South Euclid

Adler's Camping, Inc.
4505 Mayfield Road
South Euclid, Ohio 44124
216-382-7282

OKLAHOMA

Tulsa

P. & S. Sales
P. O. Box 155
Tulsa, Oklahoma 74102

Wilderness Adventurer
6508 East 51st Street
Tulsa, Oklahoma 74145
918-628-1161

OREGON

Ashland

Sun Cycle
337 Main Street
Ashland, Oregon 97520
503-482-5761

Corvallis

Sporthaus
137 Southwest 3rd
Corvallis, Oregon 97330
503-752-7200

Eugene

Berg's Nordic Ski Shop
11th and Mill
Eugene, Oregon 97401
503-343-0013

Oregon City

Larry's Sport Center
Oregon City Shopping Center
Oregon City, Oregon 97045
503-656-0321

Limited climbing equipment

Portland

Alpine Hut
1250 Lloyd Center
Portland, Oregon 97232
503-284-1164

Cloud Cap Chalet
625 Southwest 12th Avenue
Portland, Oregon 97232
503-277-0579

Mountain Shop
628 Northeast Broadway
Portland, Oregon 97232
503-288-6768

Salem

Anderson Sporting Goods
141 Commercial Northeast
Salem, Oregon 97301
503-363-5934

PENNSYLVANIA

Bryn Mawr

James Cox Sportshop
931 Lancaster Avenue
Bryn Mawr, Pennsylvania 19010
215-LA5-3163

Camp Hill

The Pathfinder
1104 Carlisle
Camp Hill, Pennsylvania 17011
717-761-3906

Easton

Forks Valley Sportsworld
P. O. Box 805
Easton, Pennsylvania 18042
215-253-1111

Exton

Wicks Ski Shops
403 Pottstown Pike
Exton, Pennsylvania 19341
215-363-1893

Harrisburg

The Pathfinder
Cedar Cliff Mall
Harrisburg, Pennsylvania 17101
717-761-3906

Ohiopyle

Wilderness Voyagers Outfitters
P. O. Box 97
Ohiopyle, Pennsylvania 15470
412-329-8336

Paoli

James Cox Sportshop
23 State Road
Paoli, Pennsylvania 19301
215-644-9325

Philadelphia

Base Camp
121 North Mole Street
Philadelphia, Pennsylvania 19102
215-567-1876

Pittsburgh

The Mountain Trail Shop
5435 Walnut Street
Pittsburgh, Pennsylvania 15232
412-687-1700

Springfield

Wicks Ski Shops
321 Woodland Avenue
Springfield, Pennsylvania 19064
215-543-5445

State College

The Pathfinder
137 East Beaver Street
State College, Pennsylvania 16801
814-237-8086

Williamsport

Nippenose Equipment Company
133 West 4th Street
Williamsport, Pennsylvania 17701
717-323-6496

Yardley

J. D. Sachs and Company
Wilderness Outfitters
Afton Avenue
Yardley, Pennsylvania 19067
215-493-4536

RHODE ISLAND

Cranston

The Outdoorsman, Inc.
753 Oaklawn Avenue
Cranston, Rhode Island 02920
401-783-8519

Providence

The Summit Shop
185 Wayland Avenue
Providence, Rhode Island 02906
401-751-5052

Wakefield

The Outdoorsman, Inc.
415 Kingstown Road
Wakefield, Rhode Island 02879
401-783-8519

SOUTH CAROLINA

Greer

Jesse Brown's Backpacking Mountaineering
100 East Poinsettia Street
Greer, South Carolina 29651
803-877-8405

SOUTH DAKOTA

Mitchell

Herter's, Inc.   Backpacking only
R. R. No. 2—Interstate 90
Mitchell, South Dakota 57301
605-996-6621

Rapid City

Mountain Goat
4328 Jackson Boulevard
Rapid City, South Dakota 57701
605-342-4165

TENNESSEE

Johnson City

Footslogger
2220 North Roan Street
P. O. Box 3865
Johnson City, Tennessee 37601
615-926-0781

Memphis

Camp & Hike Shop
4674 Knight Arnold Road
Memphis, Tennessee 38118
901-365-4511

Camper's Corner
2050 Elvis Presley Boulevard
Memphis, Tennessee 38106
901-946-2566

Nashville

The Packrat, Inc.
4004 Hillsboro Road
Nashville, Tennessee 37215
615-297-0569

TEXAS

Austin

Whole Earth Provision Company
2410 San Antonio Street
Austin, Texas 78705
512-478-1577

Dallas

Mountain Chalet—Suite 502
5500 Greenville Avenue
Dallas, Texas 75206
214-363-0372

Houston

J. Rich Sports, Ltd.
2367 Rice Boulevard
Houston, Texas 77005
713-529-8767

Wilderness Equipment
624 Town and Country Village
Houston, Texas 77024
713-461-3550

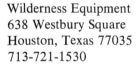

Wilderness Equipment
638 Westbury Square
Houston, Texas 77035
713-721-1530

Lubbock

Sport Haus
2309 Broadway
Lubbock, Texas 79401
806-762-2923

UTAH

Salt Lake City

Timberline Sports
3155 Highland Drive
Salt Lake City, Utah 84106
801-466-2101

VERMONT

Ferrisburg

Dakin's Mountain Shop
Route 7
Ferrisburg, Vermont 05456
802-877-2936

Middlebury

Ski Haus
Mountain Sports
Middlebury, Vermont 05753
802-388-2823

South Burlington

Eastern Mountain Sports
City Center-Dorset Street
South Burlington, Vermont 05401
802-864-0473

VIRGINIA

Charlottesville

Blue Ridge Mountain Sports
1417 Emmet Street
Charlottesville, Virginia 22901
804-977-4400

Norfolk

Blue Ridge Mountain Sports
1104 West Little Creek Road
Norfolk, Virginia 23505
804-423-7395

Oakton

Appalachian Outfitters
2930 Chain Bridge Road
Oakton, Virginia 22124
703-281-4324

Richmond

Alpine Outfitters
818 West Grace Street
Richmond, Virginia 23220
804-358-2101

Alpine Outfitters
11010 Midlothian Turnpike
Richmond, Virginia 23235
804-794-4172

Salem

Appalachian Outfitters
Route 3, Box 7A
Salem, Virginia 24152
703-389-1086

WASHINGTON

Leavenworth

Der Sportsmann
837 Front Street
Leavenworth, Washington 98826
509-548-5623

Seattle

Alpine Hut, Inc.
2650 University Village
Seattle, Washington 98105
206-LA2-4480

Alpine Hut Magnolia
2215 15th West
Seattle, Washington 98105
206-AT4-3575

Eddie Bauer, Inc.
1926 3rd Avenue
Seattle, Washington 98101
206-622-2766

Recreational Equipment, Inc.
1525 11th Avenue
Seattle, Washington 98122
206-323-8333

Swallow's Nest
909 East Boat Street
Seattle, Washington 98105
206-633-0408

Spokane

Selkirk Bergsport
West 30 International Way
Spokane, Washington 99220
509-328-5020

Western Outdoor Sports
N. 111 Vista
Spokane, Washington 99206
509-926-1543

WEST VIRGINIA

Morgantown

The Pathfinder
499 High Street
Morgantown, West Virginia 26505
304-292-5223

Mouth of Seneca

The Gendarme
Mouth of Seneca, West Virginia 26884

WISCONSIN

Madison

Erewhon Mountain Supply
State and Gorham
Madison, Wisconsin 53703
608-251-9059

Petries in Madison
44 East Towne Wall
Madison, Wisconsin 53705
608-241-3448

Petries in Madison
1406 Emil Street
Madison, Wisconsin 53705
608-257-7811

Petries in Madison
644 State Street
Madison, Wisconsin 53705
608-256-1343

Petries in Madison
Hilldale Shopping Center
702 North Midvale Boulevard
Madison, Wisconsin 53705
608-231-2447

Milwaukee

Laacke & Joys Company
1433 North Water Street
Milwaukee, Wisconsin 53202
414-271-7878

WYOMING

Cheyenne

Alpine Haus
111 West 17th Street
Cheyenne, Wyoming 82001
307-635-2446

Jackson

Peter Carmans
Highline
Box 700
Jackson, Wyoming 83001
307-733-4684

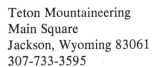

Teton Mountaineering
Main Square
Jackson, Wyoming 83061
307-733-3595

Teton Mountaineering
P. O. Box 1533—Crabtree Corners
Jackson, Wyoming 83061
307-733-3595

Jackson Hole

Wyoming Outfitters
Box 1659-B
Jackson Hole, Wyoming 83001
307-733-3877

Lander

Paul Petzoldt
Wilderness Equipment
Lander, Wyoming 82520

Laramie

Alpine Haus
303 South 17th Street
Laramie, Wyoming 82070
307-745-7373

Rocky Mountaineering
211 2nd Street
Laramie, Wyoming 82070
307-742-3191

PART IV

Technical Rock- and Ice-climbing Areas and Local Guidebooks

Technical Rock- and Ice-climbing Areas and Local Guidebooks

The following is a general listing of some of the most commonly used technical rock- and ice-climbing areas in the United States. In cases where a guidebook to a specific area or range is available, we have indicated that fact. The best source of information about climbing areas, conditions, and local customs is invariably the climbing equipment retailer in the area where you intend to climb. Where no separate guidebook address is indicated, the guidebooks are usually available through the local retail store. A comprehensive listing of retailers appears in Part III.

It is usually lack of common courtesy that can lead to restriction of rock climbing. If a cliff or rock outcrop is on private property, request permission from the landowner before using the area. Do not leave any trash or worn sling material around any climbing area. Do not destroy or pull out small trees from any climbing wall. Wood fires for cooking and warmth may be a great joy and a traditional part of evening camp life, but refrain from using them; conditions, obviously, are changing, and you should try to limit yourself to drinks or food warmed over the portable stove you carry as part of your gear.

Unwanted expansion of trails leading to the cliff base are another source of possible tension, causing destruction of cliff base flora. The key at all times, whether on public or private land, must be to walk light and climb clean.

ALABAMA

Great Smoky Mountains.
Dick Murlless and Constance Stallings, *Hiker's Guide to Smokies* (San Francisco: Sierra Club, 1974), $7.95.

ALASKA

Byron Glacier, Matanwsra Glacier: Both offer ice work near Anchorage.

Porter Rock: for technical rock work near Anchorage.
Mountaineering Club of Alaska, *55 Ways to the Wilderness in South Central Alaska* (Seattle, Wash.: The Mountaineers), $7.95.
Richard W. Montague, *Exploring Mount McKinley National Park* (Anchorage: Alaska Travel Publication, 1972).

ARIZONA

Pinnacle Peak: 25 miles from Tempe. Information available at High Adventure (retail store) in Tempe, Arizona.

Carefree Rocks: within 40 minutes from Tempe. Information available at High Adventure.

Camelback Mountain: 12 miles from Tempe.

Camel's Head: located on the west end of Camelback Mountain within Phoenix city limits.

Superstition Mountains: within commuting distance from Phoenix.

Granite Mountain: near Prescott, Arizona.
David Lovejoy, *Granite Mountain Guide*. Write to him c/o Outdoor Action, Prescott College, Prescott, Arizona 86301.

MacDonald and Tatum Rocks: near central Arizona.
Larry Treiber and Bruce Grubbs, *Central Arizona Climbing Guide*. Guidebook can be purchased at Desert Mountain Sports in Phoenix.

CALIFORNIA

Castle Rock: bouldering area, Castle Rock State Park, Skyline Boulevard.

High Sierra.
> Hervey Voge and Andrew J. Smatko, *Mountaineer's Guide to the High Sierra* (Sierra Club), $7.95.

Hinterlands: just north of Bass Lake.
> Royal Robbins, *A Guide to the Hinterlands.*

Stoney Point: bouldering area near Chatsworth.

Patrick Point State Park: approximately 20 miles north of Eureka on State 101.

Tollhouse Rock: 45 miles northeast of Fresno.
> Fresno Big Wall Society, *Climber's Guide to Tollhouse Rock.* Available at Robbins Mountain Shop, Fresno, $.50.

Mission Gorge: Idyllwild, California.
> Werner Lantry, *Climber's Guide to Mission Gorge,* $2.50.

Snow Creek: north face of Mount San Jacinto. An ice-climbing area.

Mount Shasta.
> Allen Steck, *Guide to Mount Shasta* (Sierra Club), $1.00.

Donner Summit and Sierra Buttes: in northern Sierra.
> Erick Beck, Tahoe City Department of Parks and Recreation, *Climber's Guide to Lake Tahoe and Donner Summit,* $2.00.

Joshua Tree National Monument: at the Palisades Glacier.
> *Climber's Guide to Joshua Tree* (San Jacinto, Calif.: Arrow Printing Company), $3.50.

Gibraltar Rock: in Sesspe, Santa Barbara.

Santa Clara Valley.
> *Day Climber's Guide to Santa Clara Valley* (Starr Craig Publishers), $2.00.

Grissley Dome: on Highway 70.

Tahquitz and Suicide Rocks.
> Charles Wilts, *Climber's Guide to Tahquitz and Suicide Rocks* (American Alpine Club), $5.00.

Pinnacles: in the Santa Cruz Mountain Range.
> *Guide to Pinnacles* (Sierra Club), $4.95.

Lover's Leap: at Strawberry, California, at Highway 50.
> Gene Drake, *Guide to Lover's Leap,* $1.50.

Thompson Peak: ice climbing in the Trinity Alp Wilderness.

Yosemite.
> Steve Roper, *Climber's Guide to Yosemite Valley* (Sierra Club of California, 1971), $6.95.

Yosemite: for ice climbing, Mount Dana, Mount Conness, near
    Tioga Pass.
    Wheelock, *Southern California Peaks,* $1.50.
    John W. Robinson, *Camping and Climbing in Baja,* Third Edi-
    tion (Glendale, Calif.: La Siesta Press, 1972).

COLORADO

Boulder Canyon: west of Boulder. Rock and ice climbing.
    Pat Ament and Jim Erikson, *5.10,* an upgraded supplement to
    High over Boulder.

X's Rock: 2 miles north of Durango city limits.

Eldorado Springs Canyon.
    Pat Ament and McCarthy, *High over Boulder* (Boulder, Colo.:
    Pruett Press), $5.50.

Rocky Mountain National Park: near Estes.
    Walter W. Fricke, Jr., *Climber's Guide to the Rocky Mountain
    National Park Area,* $6.00.

Longs Peak, Notch Top, Loch Vale: for ice climbing.
    Nesbit, *Longs Peak: Its Story and Climbing Guide,* 72 pp., 50
    photographs, $2.00.

Ten Mile Canyon: 3 miles from Fresno, Colorado.

Wampama Rock: at Hetch Hetchy Reservoir, 40 miles from
    Yosemite Valley.

Black Canyon: 17 miles from Montrose. The Black Canyon of the
    Gunnison offers many routes if you can get by the rangers.

Mount Harris: 25 miles west of Steamboat Springs.

Glenwood Canyon: Marble Canyons; 50-to-500-foot ice climbs.

Taylor Canyon.

Spring Creek.
    Robert Ormes with the Colorado Mountain Club, *Guide to the
    Colorado Mountains,* 6th Revised Edition (Chicago: The Swal-
    low Press, 1974), $6.00.

CONNECTICUT

Race Brook: on the Connecticut/Massachusetts border. Good prac-
    tice ice area. Information available at Sitzmark (retail store) in
    New Haven.

Lime Rock: near Lakeville.
> Guide available through the Outing Club, The Hotchkiss School, Lakeville, Connecticut.

Ragged Mountain: in Southington.
> Yale Mountaineering Club, *Climber's Guide to Ragged Mountain,* $2.00; Ken Nichols, *Ragged Mountain Supplement,* $.85.

DISTRICT OF COLUMBIA

Carderock: at Carderock State Park. An outcrop on the Potomac.

GEORGIA

Mount Yonah: 3 miles north of Cleveland, Georgia.

Tallulah Gorge: information available at Georgia Outdoors (retail store) in Decatur.

IDAHO

Table Rock: a sandstone quarry 20 minutes from Boise.

Chimney Rock: 250 feet of excellent climbing on the west face, with an interesting approach, especially during winter; northern Idaho.

The Sawtooths: Central Idaho. Excellent ice climbing.

ILLINOIS

Mississippi Palisades: in Savanna.
> James Kolocotronis, *Guide to Mississippi Palisades.* Available directly from J. Kolocotronis, South Ohioville, New Paltz, New York 12561.

INDIANA

Portland Arch: north of Covington.
> Pete Zvengrowski, *Portland Arch Guide.* Write to Simian Outing Society, University of Illinois, Urbana, Illinois; $1.00.

Shades State Park: west-central Indiana. Ice-climbing area.

KANSAS

Wichita: There is a short, rotten practice area near Wichita. If you find yourself here and desperate for a place to climb, contact Sally Ottaway or Christine Nickel at Mountain High (retail store) in Wichita.

The Rock Quarries: 15 minutes from Topeka. Information at Gran Sport (retail store) in Topeka.

MAINE

Clifton Rock.
> Leslie Ellison, *Clifton Rock Climbs* (Orno, Me.: Maine Outing Club), $2.00.

Bucks Ledge: near Locke Mills. A 250-foot granite cliff.
> Dwight Bradley and Tad Pfeffer, *The Obscure Crags Guide to Cliffs in Maine, Vermont, and New Hampshire,* $1.00. Write to them directly in Randolph, New Hampshire.

Mount Katahdin: in Millinocket. The best ice climbing in the eastern United States. This area has never been completely worked. Unlike Mount Washington in New Hampshire, Katahdin has no state-maintained highway offering easy access. In order to climb here, you must have a backup rescue crew. Very difficult winter conditions, sometimes brutal.

Mount Kineo: a 600-foot local outcrop near Moosehead Lake.

Mount Desert Island: Many cliffs of modest height located near the ocean. Cliffs include St. Sauveur Mountain (400 feet of granite), Beech Cliff, and Otter Cliffs. For information, see *The Obscure Crags Guide.*

Tumbledown Mountain: near Weld, Maine. A 700-foot cliff of metamorphic rock, similar to a schist-gneiss—very solid.
> Jean Stephenson, editor, *Katahdin Section of Guide to the Appalachian Trail in Maine,* 7th Edition (Kents Hill, Me.: The Maine Appalachian Trail Club, 1969).

MARYLAND

Carderock: near Potomac, Maryland.

MASSACHUSETTS

Black Rock: near Sheffield.

A students' *Guide to Black Rock* is available through the Outing Club, the Berkshire School, Sheffield, Massachusetts.

Crow Hill: in Leominster. A well-used area.

Steve Hendricks and Sam Striebert, *Climbing in Eastern Massachusetts* (Milgamex Co., 1975), $3.95.

Reppy and Striebert, *A Guide to Crow Hill.* A new guide is currently in preparation by Sam Striebert and Ed Webster.

Barn Ledge: also called Rattlesnake Gutter. Near Leverett, Massachusetts. Very hard and good routes, mostly crack climbing, on rock composed of gneiss. Situated on privately owned land.

Quincy Quarries: in Quincy.

William R. Crowther and Anthony W. Thompson, *A Climber's Guide to the Quincy Quarries* (Cambridge, Mass.: MIT Outing Club), $1.00.

The Waban Arches: in Wellesley. On a viaduct, the Arches provide a long, vertical, artificial climbing wall capped by an ominous overhang. Excellent vertical climbing on 5.9 and 5.10 levels. This is an excellent place to develop superb balance and fingertip strength. A large percentage of the routes here were pioneered by "Hot Henry" Barber, and the Arches have contributed greatly to the development of other Massachusetts climbers. Until this past year, the Arches were one of many "secret" climbing areas covetously protected by locals—until it was unexpectedly featured in *Mountain.*

MICHIGAN

Grand Ledge.

Bruce Bright, *Climber's Guide to Grand Ledge, Michigan,* $.30. Write direct: 14261 Spartan Village, East Lansing, Michigan 48823.

MINNESOTA

Mississippi River Banks: ice climbing near Saint Paul.

Taylor's Falls.
   Climber's Guide to Taylor's Falls, Midwest Mountaineering,
   Minneapolis, Minnesota, $.45.

MONTANA

Beartooths: South of Red Lodge at Twin Lakes Headwall.
   An interesting account of early climbs in this area can be found
   in Miriam Underhill, *Give Me the Hills* (London: Methuen &
   Co., Ltd., 1956), pp. 225–38.
Lost Lark: at Highwood Mountain.
The Mission Range: excellent description of area in *Give Me the
   Hills,* pp. 187–210.
Sunset Crags.
   Montana Rock Climbs in the Mission Range.
Swan Range: There is hard hiking to reach these mountains and
   Swan Peak.

NEBRASKA

Chimney Rock: a National Historic Site on the famed Oregon Trail.
   Climbing here is restricted.
Scotts Bluff National Monument: a massive bluff along the North
   Platte Valley. This is also a National Landmark, and climbing
   here is discouraged.

NEW HAMPSHIRE

White Horse and Cathedral Ledges: in North Conway. Webster
   Cliff, Mount Washington, Huntington Ravine. These and
   other crags and outcroppings are described in: Joseph Cote's
   A Climber's Guide to Mount Washington Valley (Topsfield,
   Mass.: Fox Run Press, 1972).
Cannon Cliff: in Franconia.
   John Porter, David Tibbetts, and Howard Peterson, *A Guide
   for Climbers Cannon* (South Lancaster, Mass.: Three Owls
   Productions), $1.50.
   Howard Peterson, *Cannon: A Climber's Guide,* (South Lan-
   caster, Mass.: Three Owls Productions, 1975).

Holts Ledge: in Lyme, New Hampshire, near Dartmouth Skiway. *Climber's Guide to Holts Ledge,* in preparation by Chris Ellms, Canaan, New Hampshire.

NEW JERSEY

Cranberry Ledge: information available at the Wooden Nickel (retail store) in Flemington.

City of Newark Watershed: near Newfoundland, New Jersey. Nice practice area for top-roped climbs.

NEW MEXICO

Sandia Mountains: east of Albuquerque. Limited ice work.
Bob Kyrlach, *Guide to the Sandia Mountains,* $1.75.

The Tooth of Time: Cimarron. Several difficult rock climbs on property of Philmont Scout Ranch.

NEW YORK

Cattaraugus Gorge: good ice climbing in Cattaraugus County.

Chapel Pond: good rock and ice climbing.
Trudy Healy, *A Climber's Guide to the Adirondacks: Rock and Slide Climbs* (Adirondack Mountain Club), 2nd edition, revised, 1972.

Rogers Rock: on Lake George. One gets to this wall via boat.

Shawangunks: New Paltz, New York. The most heavily populated climbing area in the eastern United States. Daily land use passes sold: six-month and one-year passes available from the Mohonk Trust.
Richard C. Williams, *Climber's Guide to the Shawangunks* (American Alpine Club), $7.00.

Bronx River, New York Botanical Gardens: Bronx. Several conveniently located boulders and rock gorges about 20 feet high, just under and beside the footbridge over this narrow, dirty river. Routes are generally 5.7 and 5.8. The local police know that a few people boulder here and may or may not restrict the area.

Central Park: Every climber in New York eventually finds himself or herself literally climbing the walls. To avoid being pinched as a second-story man, one can boulder here. Prominent Central Park boulderers have included Lionel Terray, Jim McCarthy, and Chris Bonington.

World Trade Center: first ascent awaiting new technical developments.

Niagara Gorge: Nord Alp (retail store) uses the gorge for its climbing instruction.

Storm King Mountain.
A Student's Guide to Storm King Mountain supposedly available through the Storm King School.

NORTH CAROLINA

Linville Gorge: one hour from Asheville. Information available at Mountaineering South (retail store) in Asheville.

Table Rock: north of Morganton, North Carolina.
Art Williams, *Climber's Guide to the Carolinas* (Greenville, S.C.).

Stone Mountain: North Wilkesboro.
Alex Holden, *The Carolina Crags*.

Crowders Mount: at Kings Mountain.

Devil's Courthouse: Looking Glass Area, near Brevard, North Carolina.

White Face Mountain.

Moor's Wall.

Hanging Rock.

OHIO

Clifton Gorge: John Brian State Park. Climbing recently banned in what was the best and only multipitch climbing area in the state.

OKLAHOMA

Chandler Park: A very easy practice area within Tulsa city limits.

Oklahoma Narrows: information available from Mountain Chalet (retail store) in Dallas, Texas.

OREGON

Three-finger Jack Area: Bend, Oregon.

Elliot Glacier: Mount Hood.
Oregon Climber's Guide—out of print.

Smith Rocks: Terrehonne.

Baughton's Bluff: Trout Dale.

Mount Jefferson, Mount Hood, the Three Sisters Peaks: three of many notable Oregon mountains requiring rock, snow, and ice techniques.

PENNSYLVANIA

Ralph Stover State Park: Upper Bucks County. Guide appeared in John F. Gyer, "The Climbing Cliffs of Stover," *Appalachia,* Vol. XXXV, No. 4 (Dec. 15, 1965), pp. 741–55. There is also a guide available for $2.00 from Alp Trail Outfitters, Easton, Pennsylvania.

Tillbery Terrace: on Route 11.
A guide to Tillbery Terrace to be published by American Alpine Club.

Ricketts Glen State Park: limited ice climbing located about 40 miles from Williamsport. Information available at Nippenose Equipment in Williamsport.

Coburn Rock: for information, check at the Pathfinder Shop in State College, Pennsylvania.
Ivan Jirak, *Pittsburgh Area Climber's Guide* (Pittsburgh, Pa.: 1971).

SOUTH DAKOTA

The Needles: in the Black Hills of South Dakota.
Bob Kamps, *A Climber's Guide to the Needles in the Black Hills of South Dakota* (New York: American Alpine Club, 1971).

TENNESSEE

Bee Rock: Monterey.

TEXAS

Enchanted Rock: Fredericksburg.

UTAH

Dolomite Spire: a 300-foot pinnacle north of Moab.

Little Cottonwood Canyon: 10 miles from Salt Lake City. Guide-book available at Timberline Sports in Salt Lake City.

Salt Lake Crags.
> David R. Smith, *Climber's Guide to the Salt Lake Granite* (Wastch Publishers). Available at Starlight and Storm, Salt Lake City.

Wildcat Canyon: Sandstone climbing in the back country of Zion National Park.

VERMONT

Bolton Rock: near Burlington, Vermont. Offers outstanding granite multipitch climbing, with good winter rock climbing.

Connecticut Palisades: Fairlee, Vermont. A Dartmouth College hangout with good ice in winter.

Smugglers Notch: Stowe, Vermont. Very good ice climbs and a selection of good rock work. Situated on the Mountain Road at Mount Mansfield.

Eagle Rock: Follow the Interstate into Thetford.

Eagle Ledge: Vershire, Vermont. From the junction of Vt. 113 and U.S. 5 in Fairlee, drive west on 113 for 11.6 miles. Turn right, drive 1.3 miles.

Willoughby Lake: near West Burke. A 25-mile drive from St. Johnsbury. Interesting climbing at a variety of standards.

WASHINGTON

Index Town Wall: within 45 minutes of Seattle. Information available at Swallow's Nest (retail store), Seattle.

Leavenworth.
> Fred Beckey and Eric Bjornstad, *Climber's Guide to Leavenworth,* $2.50.

Finch's Market Ice Wall: Pullman, Washington.

Granite Point: on the Snake River, 22 miles south of Pullman.
Washington State University Alpine Club, *Granite Point Guide.*

Mount Rainier: 1½ hours from Seattle.

Mount Hood.

Mount Baker: 2½ hours from Seattle.

Spire Rock: Spanaway, Washington. An artificial climbing wall built by Explorer Post 634 of Spanaway; 27 feet high, 40 feet long.

Schurman Rock: at Camp Long. An artificial climbing wall built in 1939 with WPA funds. West Seattle.

Miscellaneous boulders and cliffs.
Climber's Guide to Lowland Rock in Skagit and Whatcome Counties (Signpost Publications), $2.50.

Area north of the Columbia River:
Fred Beckey, *Cascade Alpine Guide* (Seattle, Wash.: The Mountaineers), $9.50. A detailed, thorough, complete guide.
Tom Miller, *The North Cascades* (Seattle, Wash.: The Mountaineers), $12.50.
Fred Beckey, *Challenge of the North Cascades* (Seattle, Wash.: The Mountaineers), $7.95.

The Painted Rocks: 150-foot crag within the State Park on Highway 12, Yakima. It has many 5.10 and 5.11 climbs.

Minnehaha Rocks: just outside Spokane. Mostly boulder problems, but with a few 5.7 climbs.

WEST VIRGINIA

Cooper Rocks: a very nice sandstone practice area about 20 miles from Morgantown with many 5.9 and 5.10 routes.
A. Clark, *Climbing Guide to Cooper's Rocks,* $.50, available at The Pathfinder of West Virginia, Morgantown.

Champe Rocks: north of Seneca. Private land. A clean 350-foot wall. Information available at The Pathfinder of West Virginia, Morgantown.

Seneca Rock: Mouth of Seneca.
Potomac Appalachian Trail Club, *Climber's Guide to Seneca,* now out of print. New guide currently in preparation.

Nelson Rocks: at Spruce Knob. Just down the road from Seneca, with both hard climbing and moderate routes.

Greenland Gap.

Other areas yet to be developed include Maysville Gap, Kline Gap, Hopville Canyon, and the Smoke Hole Gorge. Many new routes yet to be done in this area. Inquire at The Pathfinder, Morgantown.

WISCONSIN

Gibraltar Rock: sandstone, located near Lodi.

Baraboo Bluffs: 30 miles north of Madison.

Devil's Lake State Park: 30 miles north of Madison.

> D. Smith and R. Zimmerman, *Climber's and Hiker's Guide to Devil's Lake,* $1.75. Write to D. Smith, Wisconsin Hoofer Mountaineers Memorial Union, University of Wisconsin, Madison, Wisconsin 55706.

WYOMING

Tetons and Wind River Range.

> Lee Ortenberger, *Climber's Guide to the Tetons* (San Francisco: Sierra Club, 1965).
>
> Paul Lawrence, *Hiking the Teton Backcountry* (Sierra Club), $4.95.

Snowy Range: 40 miles from Laramie.

> Ray Jacquot, *Snowy Range.*
>
> Jim Halfpenny, *Guide to South East Wyoming.*

Vedavoo area: 25 miles from Cheyenne on Interstate 80.

> Jerry Sublet, J. Garson, and R. Zimmerman, *Vedavoo Climbs,* $2.50.

PART V

Mountain Media

CHAPTER 1

Periodicals

What follows is a list of interesting English-language publications re-
porting mountain news, activities, expedition details, personality pro-
files, equipment testing and development—and, in some cases, equipment failure. Because of the rapidly changing technology of mountaineering, it is important (as well as pleasant) to keep up with all
the advances and developments. These magazines provide stimulus
for future exploits as well as providing one with enough name-drop-
ping expertise to hold one's own in any pub.

Back issues of almost all the magazines listed are hard to find outside the major mountaineering libraries. A rapidly growing coterie of
mountaineering magazine buffs have made complete collections of almost any of the magazines mentioned a complement to their private
stashes of antiquated mountaineering iron.

The American Alpine Journal
American Alpine Club
113 East 90th Street
New York, New York 10028
Annual $8.00 (soft cover)

The publication of the American mountaineering Establishment
covers international climbing productivity of sanctioned AAC climbs
and climbers. Feature articles have included reports on the American
Everest climb, American Himalayan climbing, Alaskan climbing,
South American climbing in the Patagonian Mountain Gap, etc. The
articles, while generally rather dry and devoid of personal feeling,
are accurate, technical, and informative. Usually very fine photography. Back issues of the *AAC Journal* become more valuable with
age.

Appalachia
Appalachian Mountain Club
5 Joy Street
Boston, Massachusetts 02108
Biannual   Members' price, $2.50 per issue
                                            Nonmembers', $3.50 per issue

Appalachia covers climbs made by members of the AMC throughout the United States and all major foreign climbing areas. There are
articles of local news, reports on equipment development, reports on
accidents, and book reviews (some of which are among the best
being published). Back issues are of historic importance, reflecting
the development and growth of climbing in the eastern United States.
Primarily of interest to eastern climbers.

Ascent The Sierra Club Mountaineering Journal
Sierra Club
1050 Mills Tower
San Francisco, California 94104
Annual $6.00
Edited by Steve Roper, Allen Steck, Jim Stuart, and Lito Tejada-
Flores

The finest climbing publication from the western United States.
The articles cover the California scene, Alaska, Nepal, and all areas
where Americans are climbing (for example, a recent issue covered
climbing in Dresden). Excellent photography and articles. Each issue
becomes a collector's item. Mandatory reading.

Canadian Alpine Journal
P. O. Box 1026
Banff, Alberta
Canada
Annual $4.25
Editor: Moira Irvine
Published by the Alpine Club of Canada

We include the *Canadian Alpine Journal* on our list as an information resource and text for American climbers who will be traveling in
the Canadian mountain ranges and would like to keep up with
mountaineering advancement there. The *Journal* usually includes

some fine photography, articles of about 5.6 interest, and features a change of diet from the usual Lito Tejada-Flores contingent.

Climbing
Box E
Aspen, Colorado 81611
Six issues per year $4.50 annually
Edited by Michael Kennedy

Readership tends to be more youthful and less established in the national climbing scene than readers of *Summit*. *Climbing*'s articles are slanted toward coverage of local crags and their development rather than the international pro circuit. Frequently interesting reading, especially when providing the only magazine forum for discussions of issues such as the AAC Guide Certification program.

The Eastern Trade
P. O. Box 312
Tillson, New York 12486
Published irregularly $2.50 annually
Edited by John Stannard

This newsletter, dedicated to the improvement and preservation of climbing in the Shawangunk area of New York State, the most popular climbing area in the East, features articles covering conservation, equipment testing, local developments, the changing climbing scene, and route and rock improvements. Interesting reading. A must for all eastern climbers.

Mountain
Mountain Magazine, Ltd.
56 Sylvester Road
London N. 2, England
Ten issues yearly $10.00 annually
Edited by Ken Wilson

Informative articles on British mountaineering, Australian climbing, American mountaineering, and accurate and up-to-date news of the international mountain community. Has published some fine, sophisticated satire. A highly important magazine because of its equipment updates and climbing news section. This is the slickest climbing magazine now being published—with the occasional lapses of taste one expects to find in the slicks (for example, Issue No. 40's, "first coloured man to make a major first ascent" "People" entry). Nevertheless, this is a magazine well worth reading and saving.

Mountain Gazette
Rite on Publishing House, Inc.
2025 York Street
Denver, Colorado 80205
Monthly $6.00 annually
Edited by Mike Moore and Nan Babb

Contributing editors include such well-known climbing figures as Galen Rowell, Barry Corbet, Doug Robinson, Lito Tejada-Flores, and Harvey Manning. This is the above-ground underground magazine. Its oversized format includes articles covering everything from pollution to climbing mores to motocross mountain racing. A consistently interesting magazine that sometimes includes quality fiction. A really good, dynamic magazine.

Mountain Life
British Mountaineering Council
26 Park Crescent
London W1N 4EE, England
Six issues yearly $10.00 annually
Editor: Bruce L. Bedford

Features news of British climbing, primarily climbs done by members of the British Mountaineering Council. Back issues have become collectors' items. Recently, the rights to *Mountain* magazine have been acquired by *Mountain Life*. We expect to see some format changes in *Mountain* similar to that of *Mountain Life*.

North American Climber
P. O. Box 9131
Providence, Rhode Island 02940
6 issues yearly $7.50 annually

An eastern-based publication, *North American Climber* is the newest climbing magazine. Some of its correspondents are excellent. They're attempting a *Mountain* magazine-type format, but so far they haven't equalled *Mountain*'s quality, especially in prose style. An up and coming magazine.

Off Belay
12416 169th Avenue S.E.
Renton, Washington 98055
Six issues per year $6.00 annually
Edited by Ray Smutek

Off Belay has a following centered in the northwestern United States. It's an extremely sedate magazine with little visual impact. Nevertheless, it does include reports on, for example, the findings of the UIAA Belaying Methods Committee, and enthusiastic if not superbly crafted pieces on such topics as glacier response and rock glaciers. Interesting reading for the dedicated mountaineer. Occasionally features excellent articles on equipment innovation and testing, and climbing history.

Summit
P. O. Box 1889
Big Bear Lake, California 92315
Ten issues yearly $7.50 annually
Edited by Jene M. Crenshaw and H. V. J. Kilness

The most established climbing magazine in the United States with the exception of *The American Alpine Journal*. Publishes articles of international scope. Regularly covers the internal American climbing scene and equipment testing and updates. Announcements of defective or recalled equipment appear here first. Essential reading.

CHAPTER 2

Some Recommended Mountaineering Books

Beginning climbers seem to read every mountaineering book they can possibly get their hands on, so there may be many books on the following list with which you're intimately familiar. Our list includes just a few of the contemporary classics, and we've made no attempt to cover some of the earlier great books (almost all published abroad) such as Mummery's *My Climbs in the Alps and Caucasus* (a new edition of which was recently published here) and Leslie Stephen's *The Playground of Europe.* A few of the most recently published books may not be on our list; for these, our readers need look at the review pages of any of the periodicals mentioned in Part V, Chapter 1.

If you're in the process of assembling even a small home mountaineering library, you might want to watch for first or early editions of the books you'll be collecting. Four of the booksellers listed in Chapter 3 carry old mountaineering books and will be pleased to try to fill requests for early editions. Used-book stores often have just a few mountaineering books (sometimes shelved in the travel book section), but you might be able to find early editions there at extremely reasonable prices. Keep in mind that intact dust jackets increase the value of modern first editions.

A few of the mountaineering pamphlets we've listed have become increasingly difficult to find in the original edition. A copy of Bradford Washburn's *Frostbite,* in the Museum of Science first printing, for example, is a rather prestigious item. (If one were a particularly zealous mountaineering literature collector, *The American Alpine Journal,* June 1962, and *The New England Journal of Medicine,* May 10, 1962, would be necessary adjuncts to the 1963 Museum of Science pamphlet.)

Older mountaineering books, particularly, are a joy to own. Cold, rainy afternoons spent with one such as Smythe's *A Camera in the Hills* can be as pleasurable, in their way, as a day on good granite.

INSTRUCTIONAL MATERIALS AND MANUALS

Harvey Manning, ed., *Freedom of the Hills,* 3rd ed. (Seattle, Wash.: The Mountaineers, 1975). $9.95.

Since the publication of the first edition in 1960, this hardcover text has become the accepted mountaineering reference work. It covers all phases of mountaineering, from weather to avalanche dangers. Ice climbing and rock climbing are treated in separate chapters. Snow climbing illustrations used in previous editions had shown incorrect procedures, but this has been corrected in the third edition. A must for climbers.

MIT Outing Club, Massachusetts Institute of Technology, *Fundamentals of Rock Climbing,* 1973 ed. Soft-covered pamphlet. $1.25.

The first edition of this informative instructional pamphlet was published by the MIT Outing Club in 1956. Interesting sketches on crack and chimney technique are complemented by the step-by-step coverage of pin placement, nut placement, runner use, rappel rigging, free and aid climbing, and prusiking, as well as a most important chapter, "Accidents and Associated Problems," covering important leadership errors. Also included are belaying errors, equipment problems, and what to do if the leader falls. Required reading at a modest price. A nice gift for a climbing friend or acquaintance.

Royal Robbins, *Basic Rockcraft* (Glendale, Calif.: La Siesta Press, 1970). Paperback original. $1.95.

This text and advice manual by one of American climbing's most solid citizens is the first climbing how-to any aspiring climber should read. With explanations and interesting sketches, the author covers basic techniques of balance and movement, pin and nut craft, belaying, and rappelling, as well as knots and equipment. The most important section to read and reread is "Ethics and Style"—the part of climbing most beginners find hard to grasp.

Royal Robbins, *Advanced Rockcraft* (Glendale, Calif.: La Siesta
    Press, 1973). Paperback. $2.95.

Designed and written for the advanced climber, this important text
clears up many questions about Big Wall technique. Chockcraft for
extreme aid and all-nut ascents are thoroughly discussed, and illustrations of placements are clearly shown. Also covered: Jumar uses
—and potentially dangerous misuses—in hauling and seconding;
solo climbing for the long or short route; advanced gadgetry, such as
the use of hammocks and belay seats. This is the best book published
within the past few years on advanced rockcraft.

R. C. Aleith, *Bergsteigen: Basic Rock Climbing* (New York: Charles
    Scribner's Sons, 1975). Paperback. $5.95.

This superb manual, originally published as a text for the Arizona
Mountaineering Club's basic and intermediate schools, has been revised, republished, and placed on the open market in climbing equipment retail stores throughout the United States. Although it was intended for use in the Southwest, it was the best intermediate and
advanced text available before the publication of Robbins' *Advanced
Rockcraft*. Both books are "chock" full of useful information and
should be thoroughly studied.

Gaston Rebuffat, *On Snow and Rock,* trans. Eleanor Brockett (New
    York: Oxford University Press, 1963). Hardcover.

An outstanding discussion of mountaineering techniques, written
by one of France's foremost Alpinists. Gorgeously illustrated, with
step-by-step photographs of advanced and direct techniques. This is
truly a mountaineering classic that will not become antiquated.

C. W. Casewit and Dick Pownall, *The Mountaineering Handbook*
    (Philadelphia: J. B. Lippincott Company, 1968). Hardcover.
    $7.25.

As you read this book, keep in mind that mountaineering techniques change at a very fast pace. Many technical rock jocks will find
little of value in this book—but it's full of enough important climbing tips to make it a part of our permanent library.

BOOKS ON EMERGENCY SITUATIONS AND ACCIDENTS

Hamish MacInnes, *International Mountain Rescue Handbook*. Paperback available, $3.95.

An easy-to-understand treatment of mountain rescue methods, with a very comprehensive section on various types of emergency equipment. Nearly everything you might want to know about the paraphernalia of mountain rescue.

W. G. May, *Mountain Search and Rescue Techniques* (Boulder, Colo.: Rocky Mountain Rescue Group, Inc., 1974). $4.95.

The most comprehensive rescue techniques and emergency equipment guide published in this country, covering almost every conceivable emergency situation that can develop in the mountain environment. Topics include ropes, knots, steel cable use, communications, dogs and aircraft in search operations, rescue during avalanche conditions, both high- and low-angle technical rock evacuations, anchors, and hauling systems. Every organization sponsoring mountaineering programs ought to include this book in their curriculum.

James A. Wilkerson, M.D., ed., *Medicine for Mountaineering* (Seattle, Wash.: The Mountaineers, 1967). $7.50.

Although first-aid treatment for the more common emergencies such as sprained ankles or sun and heat stroke are discussed, *Medicine for Mountaineering* focuses on emergency treatment in the field in cases where it will be days or weeks until the injured can be transported to a hospital. The "Traumatic Injuries" section covers abdominal injuries, chest injuries, and injuries to the head and neck. "Environmental Injuries" discusses problems of altitude, frostbite, exposure, and injuries ranging from solar radiation to animal bites. The "Nontraumatic Diseases" section includes respiratory problems, diseases of the heart and blood vessels, and gastrointestinal and urinary tract disorders. This comprehensive and eminently useful text requires several readings for purposes of familiarization and ought to be taken along for field reference during any extended climbing trip. Its small size and easy-to-read format make this possibly the most important book of its type.

Accidents in North American Mountaineering (American Alpine Club). Published annually. Paperback pamphlet. $1.25.

Includes reports on accidents in Canada and the United States. Format includes an explanation of the accident, its location, and an analysis of how it could have been prevented. Read it, and read as many back issues as you can find.

Bradford Washburn, *Frostbite: What It Is—How to Prevent It— Emergency Treatment* (Boston, Mass.: The Museum of Science). $1.50.

This inexpensive booklet, reprinted from an article published in the June 1962 *American Alpine Club Journal,* is available at almost all ski and mountaineering shops. We consider it an essential equipment purchase for all people engaging in winter mountaineering. There may be other equally or perhaps more informative sources of information today about frostbite—but the Washburn booklet has an interesting history that may induce you to carry it with you on all cold-weather mountain excursions: Within the past decade and a half, ideas about treatment of frostbite have changed radically, but you have no guarantee that you won't encounter a physician who, through lack of reading and/or experience with the affliction, wants to amputate. We've read of at least one case of a person frostbitten while climbing in Alaska who returned to her hometown for treatment, where she was told she would have to lose several toes. Fortunately, the injured climber had a copy of the Washburn pamphlet with her, and on its authority, the doctor decided not to operate and to follow the course of treatment recommended. The young woman subsequently recovered full use of the injured toes.

A FEW RECOMMENDED BIOGRAPHIES AND AUTOBIOGRAPHIES

Reinhold Messner, *The Seventh Grade: Most Extreme Climbing* (New York: Oxford University Press, 1974). Hardcover. $8.50.

Reinhold Messner began his solo climbing with the first solo ascent of the Schubert and Micheluzzi routes over the South Face of the Piz de Ciavazes and is considered by many the most outstanding mountaineer of this decade. He's certainly one of the most controversial. The book is not continually interesting, but it does give some insight into the man's personality—not exactly the sort of fellow one might wish as part of one's rope team.

James Ramsey Ullman, *Straight Up. John Harlin: The Life and Death of a Mountaineer* (Garden City, N.Y.: Doubleday & Company, Inc., 1968).

At the time of his death during the first successful winter ascent of the Eiger Directissima, John Harlin was possibly the foremost American Alpinist and mountaineer, with a vitality and charisma that assumed almost mythic proportions. James Ramsey Ullman's style is anathema to many young climbers, but if you can persist through Ullman's verbiage and flaccid attempts to charm, you'll find one of the most disturbing and engrossing life stories you've ever read.

Miriam Underhill, *Give Me the Hills* (London: Methuen & Co., Ltd., 1956). $8.95.

A charming account of the early exploits of Miriam O'Brien Underhill, a woman who was one of the pioneers of technically demanding guideless climbing both in Europe and the United States. A must for every woman with an interest in climbing and mountains.

Nea Morin, *A Woman's Reach* with a Foreword by Eric Shipton, (New York: Dodd, Mead & Company, 1968).

It's not often one comes across as guileless an autobiography as that of Nea Morin. Her love of climbing, the mountain life, and of people who climb give both her life and her book a fine grace. An appendix devoted to the first female ascents in the Alps and Himalayas adds an interesting note to mountaineering history. Madame Morin was cotranslator into English of Maurice Herzog's *Annapurna*.

HISTORIC AND EXPEDITION ACCOUNTS

Maurice Herzog, *Annapurna: First Conquest of an 8000 Meter Peak,* trans. from the French by Nea Morin and Janet Adam Smith (New York: E. P. Dutton & Co., 1953).

The classic account of the 1950 French expedition to Annapurna. One of the best accounts of a mountaineering expedition ever written, with evocations of character and setting as finely executed as the best fiction. The first American edition of this book included a map of the Dhaulagiri and Annapurna massifs on the inside of the dust jacket, as well as colored end papers of the final summit slope of Annapurna (both beautiful and omitted from later editions).

Karl M. Herrligkoffer, *Nanga Parbat,* trans. Eleanor Brochett and Anton Ehrenzweig, (New York: Alfred A. Knopf, 1953).

The account of the ascent of Nanga Parbat—one of the most formidable mountaineering problems of the early 1950s. This was the first high-altitude expedition climb in the Himalayas in which a single climber (Hermann Buhl) had the drive and stamina to successfully complete a summit attempt alone.

Sir John Hunt, *The Conquest of Everest* (New York: E. P. Dutton & Co., 1954).

The account of the expedition to Everest that successfully climbed the world's highest mountain. Extremely useful still as an example of precise expedition planning. The last chapter is an account by Sir Edmund Hillary of the final assault—some of which has been contested by his climbing partner, Tenzing Norgay.

Terris Moore, *Mount McKinley: The Pioneer Climbs* (Fairbanks: University of Alaska Press, 1967). $6.95.

An important history of early climbs of Mount McKinley. Written with great affection for the subject in the most appealing of academic styles. A must for any future McKinley climber.

Chris Bonington, *The Ultimate Challenge* (New York: Stein & Day, 1973). $10.95.

An interesting, well-written account of the planning, execution, and failure of the British 1972 South West Face of Everest Expedition.

Howard Snyder, *The Hall of the Mountain King* (New York: Charles Scribner's Sons, 1973). $8.95.

An account of a very badly planned private expedition to Mount McKinley that resulted in the deaths of seven people. Extremely valuable as a cautionary tale for young mountaineers.

Galen Rowell, ed., *The Vertical World of Yosemite: A Collection of Photographs and Writings on Rock Climbing in Yosemite* (Berkeley, Calif.: Wilderness Press, 1974). $16.95.

An excellent collection of magazine articles tracing the development of Yosemite climbing, including the classic "Reflections of a Broken-down Climber" by Warren Harding and Yvon Chouinard's "Modern Yosemite Climbing." Other notable pieces include the *Mountain* magazine "Interview with Royal Robbins" by Ken Wilson, Allan Steck, and Galen Rowell, and "Ax" Nelson's account of his and John Salathe's "Five Days and Nights on the Lost Arrow." This is a beautifully printed book, with fine photographs, lacking only an index.

MOUNTAINEERING FICTION

The Snows of Kilimanjaro is the nearest great modern fiction has been to the life of great mountains. A few works of moderately literate pulp fiction with climbing-related episodes have in recent years reached the best-seller lists, but anyone trying to compile a suggested reading list of mountaineering fiction has mighty slim pickin's.

The White Tower, James Ramsey Ullman (Philadelphia: J. B. Lippincott Company, 1945).

An adventure story set in wartime Switzerland, considered a "classic," but sometimes very badly written and laced with chauvinism and class condescension. The actual climbing sequences are extremely well done.

Lawrence Sanders, *The First Deadly Sin* (New York: G. P. Putnam's Sons, 1973).

Murder, sex, and perversion in the life of a New York City climber. Generally offensive and dull reading, but the shop the detective visits is obviously the old L. R. Greenman's on Spring Street.

Trevanian, *The Eiger Sanction* (New York: Crown Publishers, 1972).

A fast-reading adventure tale about a hit-man/professor/climber, with culminating action set at Kleine Scheidegg and on the Eiger. Probably the best recent popular climbing fiction.

René Daumal, *Mount Analogue: A Novel of Symbolically Authentic Non-Euclidean Adventures in Mountain Climbing,* trans. Roger Shattuck (Baltimore: The Penguin Metaphysical Library, 1974). $2.50.

An unfinished, difficult, very beautiful little novel by a student of G. I. Gurdjieff. Fine characterizations, some very funny spoofs of mountaineering poetry, a lost mountain higher than Everest, and marvelous weird people rappelling out of Paris windows. If you have any affection for the *nouvelle roman* or even Pynchon, you'll enjoy this droll, disquieting tale.

CHAPTER 3

Booksellers Specializing in Mountaineering and Related Literature

There are surprisingly few specialty bookshops catering to mountaineers, but most climbing equipment retail stores carry at least a few books and periodicals. Books published by clubs such as the Adirondack Mountain Club or any of the other clubs listed in Part I, Chapter 2, can usually be ordered by writing directly to the publisher. The first four retailers listed carry rare and used books in addition to new books. If you are ordering books from a dealer in your own state, be sure to add sales tax.

Dawson's Book Shop
535 North Larchmont Boulevard
Los Angeles, California 90004
213-469-2186

Dawson's publishes an excellent catalog, but unless you order fairly quickly after it comes out, you may find that you've missed, for example, a copy of *Wall and Roof Climbing,* anon., Eton College, 1905. The range of books is excellent, including new releases and such modern classics as a first edition, London, of the *Ascent of Everest,* and vintage items such as Filippo de Filippi's *La Spedizione nel Karakoram e nell' Imalaia Occidentale,* 1909.

322   MOUNTAIN MEDIA

Gaston's Alpine Books
134 Winton Road
Harrow, Middlesex HA3 8AL
England
Proprietor: Louis C. Baume

Mr. Baume issues lists of books on mountaineering once or twice a
year and every one or two years on polar exploration and caving.
Collectors are invited to send lists of requirements. He stocks
English-language and foreign books, new, out-of-print, and antique
books. Current stock includes over three thousand titles, excluding as
many or more journals. More expensive than Dawson's Book Shop
on some items. Delivery (unless books are airmailed) takes several
weeks. One antique book we ordered was apparently roughly
handled during shipping and arrived with its binding somewhat
loosened. Nevertheless, the arrival of a package from Gaston's Alpine Books is a cheering event.

Leroy D. Cross
21 Columbia Avenue
Brunswick, Maine 04011
207-729-3246 Call after 7 P.M.

Good prices for rare and scarce items, including back issues of
American and British climbing journals. Send for current list, or
send specific requests. Orders must be placed immediately after the
list arrives or the item may be sold before you get to it.

Dr. Frances A. Mullen
2901 King Drive, No. 1017
Chicago, Illinois 60616

Send for current list. The list we saw included a magnificent selection of early alpine view books. Not inexpensive.

Speleobooks
P. O. Box 12334
Albuquerque, New Mexico 87105
Proprietors: Doug and Linda Rhodes

The Rhodes publish an interesting general catalog of current backpacking, mountaineering, first-aid, survival, and conservation books.
Retail stores may order wilderness books through their wholesale

service, in the process avoiding having to meet the minimum ordering requirements from many different publishers. They offer a 10 per cent discount on orders of ten or more books, single-title or assorted, to schools, libraries, and nonprofit organizations. Unusually speedy order fulfillment.

The Mountain Shop
228 Grant Avenue
San Francisco, California 94108
415-362-8477

Mail orders can be charged to Master Charge, BankAmericard, or American Express. Postage prepaid. A good list of current mountaineering and rock-climbing books, guides to California and the Northwest, natural history, ski touring, first-aid, and rescue books. They carry the University of California's *Natural History Guides of San Francisco, Bay Region, and Northern California*. Write for free list.

Frank Ashley
Box 291
Culver City, California 90230
213-870-3508

A good list of backpacking and climbing books, including the High Sierra Hiking Guides and autographed copies of Mr. Ashley's own *Highpoints of the States*. No minimum order, no additional handling charges. California residents must add 5 per cent tax.

Outbooks
Route 4, Box 750
Evergreen, Colorado 80439
(formerly National Park Publications)
303-674-7534

A really incredible catalog. The mountaineering section has just a few important basics, but there are many books here of interest to climbers planning to camp or climb in our National Parks. They carry a few posters, too, including the famous "Face of Half Dome" by Ansel Adams. A good selection also of books from interesting, smaller presses, such as the Museum of New Mexico Press and Superior Books (for example, *Ghost Towns of Oregon*). Standard discounts for dealers, schools, and libraries. All orders postpaid.

World Publications
Box 366
Mountain View, California 94040

The World Publications catalog is garish and poorly designed, but it's a wide-ranging source of books on many different sports, including gymnastics, T'ai Chi, raquetball, etc. The rock-climbing section is extraordinarily meager, but the books offered are excellent. Postage of $.15 is charged for each book, up to $1.00 total.

Walking News, Inc.
P. O. Box 352
New York, New York 10013

An extremely useful list that includes Dick Williams' *Shawangunk Rock Climbs* and Reif Snyder's *Hut Hopping in the Austrian Alps,* as well as many Appalachian Trail Conference guidebooks, Appalachian Mountain Club guidebooks, and Adirondack Mountain Club books. Many hikers' regional maps show marked and unmarked trails of interest to cross-country skiers and hikers in the Northeast. Other publications offered include *Mines Along the Trail,* a directory of mines in the New York/New Jersey area, with short descriptions of each, and *Historic Trails of Greenwood Lake,* with map. There is a handling charge of $.20 for each book ordered. Run by the former proprietor of L. R. Greenman's in lower Manhattan.

Eastern Mountain Sports, Inc.
1041 Commonwealth Avenue
Boston, Massachusetts 02215

There is a handling charge of $1.00 on all book orders when not placing order for other EMS equipment. The EMS catalog costs $1.00. A good list of current and recent books on technical climbing, hiking, first aid, backpacking, ski touring, etc. They include quite a few technical climbers' guidebooks, Appalachian Trail guides, and AMC guides. Many maps available. We've spent a small fortune over the years at EMS for books and have no doubt you will too.

Recreational Equipment, Inc.
1525 11th Avenue
Seattle, Washington 98122
206-323-8333

A good list of mountaineering, backpacking, and regional books and guides. They carry many books slanted toward the northwestern audience, so this is an excellent catalog to check if you live, say, in the Northeast and want more information on the Cascades, Olympics, Glaciers, Rainier, etc. Maps include Canadian National Parks, the Grand Teton, Yosemite, Wenatchee, and Everest. It costs $1.00 to join the co-op.

Book Brothers, Inc.
83-95 Warwick Street
Box 145, Forest Park Station
Springfield, Massachusetts 01108
413-785-1601

A good list of standard mountaineering and backpacking books for the sporting goods trade.

CHAPTER 4

Publishers with Strong Mountaineering and Outdoor Book Lists

This is not an inclusive list. Many of the major mountaineering clubs (for example, AMC, ADK) listed in Part I, Chapter 2, publish extensively. For current publication lists, write to them at the address listed in that section. If you're not serious about ordering books, though, don't write to them; most are working on limited budgets and can put the printing and postage costs to better use.

The American Alpine Club
113 East 90th Street
New York, New York 10028
212-722-1628

Publishes outstanding guidebooks to *The Interior Ranges of British Columbia* ($7.00), *The Needles in the Black Hills of South Dakota* ($5.50), *The Rocky Mountains of Canada/North* ($8.50), *The Rocky Mountains of Canada/South* ($8.00), and *Tahquitz and Suicide Rocks* ($5.00). Their *Bibliography of American Mountain Ascents* by Joel E. Fisher ($6.00) is on extremely useful listing of ascents recorded in mountaineering journals before 1946. A few other titles available. If you're sending for a copy of their current publications list, be sure to enclose a stamped, self-addressed legal-size envelope. Postage and handling charges are $.50 for the first book or pamphlet, $.15 for each additional book, and $.05 for each additional pamphlet. Back issues of *Accidents in American Mountaineering,* published each June, are available for $1.00 each plus postage and handling: years available at the time of this writing are 1948, 1952, 1954–59, 1960–61, 1964, 1966–68, 1970, 1972, and 1974.

The Mountaineers
719 Pike Street
Seattle, Washington 98101

Publishers of *Mountaineering: The Freedom of the Hills,* 3rd ed. ($9.95 plus postage), *Guide to Leavenworth Rock Climbing Areas* ($2.50 plus postage), *Routes and Rocks in the Mount Challenger Quadrangle* ($2.95 plus postage), *Cascade Alpine Guide: Columbia River to Stevens Pass* ($9.95 plus postage), and many other fine books on climbing and hiking in the Northwest.

Pruett Publishing Company
P. O. Box 1560A
Boulder, Colorado 80302

Many interesting outdoor and climbing books. Write for current catalog.

Sierra Club
P. O. Box 7959
Rincon Annex
San Francisco, California 94120

Publishes many posters, including U8273 "Ascent" (climbers on ridge), U8279 "Glacier Bay" (icebergs), U8289 "Gentle Wilderness" (Alpine lake and mountains), and U8302 "Grand Canyon" (granite rock) at $2.50 each. The Sierra Club calendars are always beautiful, selling for less than $4.00 each. Totebooks include Steve Roper's *Climber's Guide to Yosemite Valley* ($6.95) and *Mountaineer's Guide to the High Sierra* by Smatko and Voge ($7.95). New publications include *Huts and Hikes in the Dolomites* by Rudner ($4.95). Delivery takes up to five weeks. No additional charge for postage. Many other fine books. California residents add 6 per cent tax; in Alameda, Contra Costa, and San Francisco counties in California, 6½ per cent; New Jersey, 5 per cent.

Wilderness Press
2440 Bancroft Way
Berkeley, California 94704

The publishers of *The Vertical World of Yosemite* and many other interesting books, including the *High Sierra Hiking Guides.* Dealer inquiries.

CHAPTER 5

Mountaineering Films

Leaders of college outing clubs and other climbing and mountaineering groups occasionally find themselves scurrying about trying to locate film rentals for indoor meetings. Once again, we suspect we've uncovered just the surface of possible mountaineering film rentals.

Chouinard Equipment
Box 150
Ventura, California 93001

Fitzroy: First Ascent of the South West Buttress—16 mm color film with dialogue and music. Records third ascent of Fitzroy in the Patagonian Mountain Range. Depicts Patagonian storms, technical climbing on verglas-covered rock, and monotony of ice cave living. Climbers included are Yvon Chouinard, Dick Dorworth, Chris Jones, and Doug Tompkins. Photographed by Lito Tejada-Flores; 28 minutes. Winner of the Mario Bello Prize and City of Trento Prize at the 1969 Trento Film Festival for Mountain and Exploration Films. About $110 rental plus postage.

Sentinal: the West Face—16 mm color with narration and music documenting a climb of Yosemite's Standard Grade VI route. The climbers spend two days climbing the vertical West Face, demonstrating free and aid techniques, belaying in slings, and sleeping in hammocks. Good representation of a Big Wall climb. Climbers are Yvon Chouinard and Royal Robbins. Photographers are Tom Frost and Roger Brown; 25 minutes. Approximately $85 plus postage. Won first prize, 1968 Trento Festival, and many other awards.

Les Calanques—One of two 16 mm color films rented together. Two women climbers start from sea and climb pinnacle along French Riviera; 12 minutes. Climbers are Dany Badier and Francoise Dassinville. *Tant que Nous l'Aimerons.* Black-and-white with French narration. With brief preview, audience should be able to follow film without difficulty. Two French climbers who lost fingers and toes on the South Face of Aconcagua return to the Alps to climb the South Face of the Dent du Geant. European method of artificial climbing and good technique shots of Alpine climbing. Climbers are Lucien Bernardini and Edmund Denis; 20 minutes. Rental for the two films together, approximately $85 plus postage.

Mountain Media
Box 5411
Fresno, California 93755
209-264-0564

For the Joy of It—10 minutes, sound and color. Suitable for nonclimbing and beginning climbing audiences; $25 fee.

Balance for Life—30 minutes, sound and color. Instructional aid for rock-climbing classes; ethics and philosophy; $35.

The Other Season—30 minutes, sound and color. Instructional aid for winter ski touring, snow camping, and mountaineering, $35.

Assault on Mount McKinley—30 minutes, sound and color. A group of mountaineers with no previous expedition experience encounter the highest mountain in North America; $45.

Joe—31 minutes, sound and color. Purported to relate much of the motivation of British climber Joe Brown; $75.

Cliff Hangers—53 minutes, black-and-white. Joe Brown, Ian McNaught-Davis, Tom Patey, and Royal Robbins climb the Red Wall of the South Stack; $100.

State University Rental Programs
The most interesting of the previously listed films are generally too expensive for most college outing clubs. An alternative for most is to check with the college librarian to see if the school participates in interlibrary loans of educational films through the state interschool loan system. The National Information Center for Educational

Media (University of Southern California, University Park, Los Angeles, California 90007) publishes an *Index to 16 mm Educational Films,* distributed free to colleges participating in interlibrary film rentals. Rental fees are usually $5.00 to $35. The following are just a few of the many interesting films catalogued.

Mountains of the U.S.A.—15 minutes, 16 mm; optical sound. How the Grand Tetons, Black Hills of South Dakota, Sierra Nevada, Ozarks, and Appalachians were formed by glaciers, winter, and water, and how they've influenced this country's history and natural resources. From the *Our Land, Our People, U.S.A.* series.

Outward Bound—28 minutes. Introduces ideas and activities of Outward Bound. Stresses safety precautions in rock climbing.

The Mountains of the Moon—25 minutes. Follows scientific expedition through equatorial Africa to culminating climb of the Mountain of the Moon at source of the Nile. From the *World of Lowell Thomas* series.

The Mountain—15 minutes. Describes rehabilitation of a double amputee injured during a mountaineering expedition.

Mountain Community of the Himalaya—11 minutes. Life in a Himalayan village.

High in This Cold Air—52 minutes. Physiological testing at high altitudes and the ascent of two unclimbed Himalayan peaks.

Castles in the Snow—33 minutes. Dramatization of the death of two young people during a winter snowstorm in the Oregon Cascades, demonstrating consequences of lack of basic winter survival knowledge.

High in the Himalaya—27 minutes. Sir Edmund Hillary's expedition to the Khumbu area of the Nepalese Himalayas and the self-help programs he instituted among the Sherpas there.

Alps of Wyoming—27 minutes. High and exposed climbing. Follows retreat from summit of the Grand Teton in a thunderstorm and snowstorm. Wildlife, scenery, and weather of Grand Teton National Park.

Americans on Everest—50 minutes. Lure of mountain climbing as a sport and way of life. First transverse crossing of Mount

Everest. Filmed during the 1963 American Everest Expedition lead by Norman Dhyrenfurth.

Americans on Everest—53 minutes. Documentary account of the 1963 American Everest Expedition.

Americans on Everest—Parts I, II, and III. Narrated by Orson Welles. Recounts events of successful 1963 American Everest Expedition that placed six men on the summit.

International Film Bureau, Inc.
332 South Michigan Avenue
Chicago, Illinois 60604

Invisible Force of Direction—21 minutes, color. Good film for use in learning to understand the use of the compass.

Orienteering Services
308 West Fillmore
Colorado Springs, Colorado 80907

Adventure with Map and Compass—Filmstrip and cassette tape with teacher's manual.

Makalu '77
Box 1201
Aspen, Colorado 81611

Deathzone, written and directed by Fritz Stammberger. Camerawork by Matija Malezic (high altitude), Andre Ulyrch, and Sandy Reed. Edited by Stouffer Brothers. 1975. Story of a failed 1974 expedition to Makalu during which climbers tried to reach the 27,000-foot summit without the use of oxygen. Reported to be quite well done.

BBC Mountaineering Telecasts

The BBC has run many climbing spectaculars, including the ascent of the Old Man of Hoy by Tom Patey, Rusty Baillie, Christian Bonington, Joe Brown, Dougal Haston, Peter Crew, and Ian McNaught-Davis. At the time of writing we've not yet been able to find out how tapes of these broadcasts can be rented by interested American climbers; if you know, we'd appreciate hearing from you.

CHAPTER 6

Slide Shows and Lectures

Each of the major mountaineering clubs listed in Part I, Chapter 2, has at least a few lectures or slide shows open to the general public. Mountaineering clubs or outing groups wishing to schedule lectures can contact any one of the climbing schools and guide services listed in Part I, Chapter 1: Almost without exception, they have people on staff who will speak to groups about specific areas of mountaineering for a reasonable fee. A few of many possibilities are listed below.

American Alpine Club
113 East 90th Street
New York, New York 10028

Usually schedules at least one lecture per month by prominent mountaineers. Open to the general public, reservation required.

Appalachian Mountain Club
5 Joy Street
Boston, Massachusetts 02108

Many of their slide shows, movies, and lectures are open to the general public. Frequently, no admission fee, but a donation to help their conservation work is always in order.

AMC Pinkham Notch Camp
Pinkham Notch, New Hampshire 03846

During the winter season a variety of mountaineering slide shows and movies are offered free and are open to the general public.

Frank Ashley
9957 West Regent Street
Los Angeles, California 90034

Illustrated lecture available on Mr. Ashley's renowned state summits expedition.

Bryan and Mark Delaney
82 Westwood Drive
West Springfield, Massachusetts 01089
413-739-0502

These two young AMC-affiliated climbers offer slide shows to groups at reasonable fees. Topics cover climbing in the Alps; rock climbing in the northeastern United States; and rock climbing across the United States and in British Columbia and Alberta, Canada.

Eastern Mountain Sports Climbing School
Main Street
North Conway, New Hampshire 03860

Free lectures and slide shows Saturday evenings during the winter season.

Mountain Craft
P. O. Box 622
Davis, California 95616
916-758-4315 or 753-7323

Lectures on mountain activities in general and wilderness preservation, programmed to suit any particular interest group.

Potomac Valley Climbing School
P. O. Box 5622
Washington, D.C. 20016
202-333-3398

Introductory climbing slide show available to groups.

Recreational Equipment, Inc.
1525 11th Avenue
Seattle, Washington 98122
206-323-8333

Well-planned, illustrated lectures available to groups. Ask about their "Demo Team."

International Mountain Equipment, Inc.
Main Street, Box 494
North Conway, New Hampshire 03860
603-356-5267
Att: Paul Ross, Outdoor Programs

Illustrated lectures on European and American climbing by a transplanted Britisher, Paul Ross.

Yosemite Mountaineering
Yosemite, California 95389
May 1 to June 13; September 10 to September 29: 209-372-4611, ext. 244
June 15 to September 8: 209-372-4505

Illustrated lectures to groups on mountaineering and mountain rescue.

GLOSSARY

Advanced free climbing: climbing at the limit of one's abilities without resorting to the use of artificial climbing aids. The usual range of difficulty involved would be 5.8 through 5.11.

Aid climbing: ice or rock wall climbing during which reliance for direct support is on technical climbing equipment such as pitons, nuts, étriers.

Aimed belay: a belay stance in which the legs are braced in the direction of a possible fall, and in which the belayer is cognizant of the potential forces that will be placed upon him and the belay anchor.

Alpinism: technical mountaineering in high mountain ranges requiring the use of all aspects of climbing technique. The climber must be proficient in ice, snow, and rock climbing as well as being able to climb multi-day routes in unfavorable conditions.

Aluminum chocks: assortedly shaped pieces of soft aluminum that are strung with nylon webbing. The aluminum is inserted by the climber into fissures in climbing walls. A carabiner is attached to the nylon webbing sling, and in turn the climber passes his rope through the carabiner. In the event the climber loses his footing and begins to fall, the aluminum block becomes wedged between the walls of the crack into which it was placed, limiting the distance the climber can fall. This block is referred to as a chock, a nut, or as a piece of protection.

Anchoring: anchoring is any system used in the course of climbing resulting in direct attachment to the cliff being climbed. On anchoring for a belay, more than one point of anchoring is generally used.

Arrowhead: these copper and aluminum nuts were introduced to American climbers by Bill Forrest of Forrest Mountaineering. They are attached to a wire sling and feature a wide flat shape that tapers to the bottom. They resemble an inverted arrowhead.

Avalanche: a mass of falling, tumbling ice, snow, and/or rock that has broken off a mountain's slope.

Belaying: the use of one of several possible methods of holding a falling climber in such a way as to prevent him from dropping to the end of his climbing line. A belay can be achieved by passing the climbing rope around the back, bracing and preventing the rope from slipping by locking the line in front of you or by using a belaying device.

Big Wall technique: a climbing style usually employed when the length or aid difficulty of a climbing wall requires gadgets not needed during shorter free climbs. Jumars, étriers, haul technique, siege climbing, and aid climbing are all used during a Big Wall climb. At the minimum, such a climb would require a full day, but seven- or eight-day undertakings have become less uncommon. Developed and refined in Yosemite Valley, this climbing style has been adapted to all longer climbs in other areas and countries.

Bivouac: a night spent in the mountain environment with a minimum of equipment.

Bolt: an anchor placed in a blank wall after drilling a hole with a drill. The stud placed in these holes has a plate attached; to this plate (or hanger) the climber attaches himself.

Bong: a large aluminum or steel piton formed by folding a flat piece of metal together into a channel shape. The name is derived from the unique sound these large pitons make while being driven into cracks.

Brake rappels: any number of devices that are used to slow a descending climber. The most commonly used is a metal bar that fits across the carabiner. The rope passes through the carabiner and around the brake bar, with the resultant friction slowing the descent. A safer braking mechanism is the CMI or Clog Figure-of-8 descending devices.

Carabiners: steel or aluminum snap gates used to attach ropes to slings or pitons. Also referred to as 'biners.

Clean climbing: climbing in such a way as to leave undamaged and unaltered any rock or cliff face on which one climbs. No pitons or bolts are used, with only natural or artificial chockstones serving as protection points. In some areas, the use of chalk is frowned upon as well.

Copperheads: copper swedges attached to single-line cable. These jam nuts, which can be used as bashies, were introduced to American climbers by Forrest Mountaineering.

Crag: a Middle English word of Saxon origin used by British hard men to describe any local rock outcrop. The word is popular among American climbers wishing to affect a British accent.

Crampons: metal spikes on a steel framework that are lashed to mountaineering boots to facilitate travel over ice or snow slopes. Crampons with stiff horizontal front points are largely responsible for the recent revolution in ice-climbing standards.

Dachstein mittens: pre-shrunk water-repellent natural wool mittens that are warm and remain flexible in bitter conditions. Usually preferred over any other mitten for winter mountaineering.

Direct aid: see *Aid climbing.*

Étriers: rope or webbing ladders that are used to pass over sections of climbing walls when free methods cannot be used.

Fixed pitons: pitons that are left in place permanently in populated areas that receive much use by climbers. Constant placement and removal of pitons (pins) would seriously damage well-traveled climbs.

Foothold: any crack, ledge, or rugosity that provides purchase.

Free climbing: climbing any rock or ice wall without using artificial devices except for protection and belays.

Friction climbing: also known as slab climbing. A method of traveling over slabs, relying upon the adhesive qualities of the climbing boot sole and proper balance.

Front pointing: a method of ascending ice walls, utilizing ice axe, hammer, and the vertical front points of one's crampons.

Frostbite: the injury to tissue resulting from exposure to cold. Please read pp. 117–21 of Dr. Wilkerson's *Medicine for Mountaineering* (Seattle, Wash.: The Mountaineers, 1969), and Bradford Washburn's *Frostbite.*

Gaiters: nylon or canvas spat-like anklets that keep snow and scree from entering a climber's boots.

Glacier travel: movement over terrain in which masses of snow and ice have accumulated over many years. These rivers of rock and ice present many dangers, including the possibility of falling seracs and hidden crevasses.

Grade IV climbing pack: a climbing rucksack that doubles as a haulbag during Big Wall climbs.

Guide: an experienced mountaineer familiar with ice-, rock-, and snow-climbing techniques, and specializing in instructing other people in mountaineering, or leading climbs into mountain areas with which the remainder of the party may not be familiar.

Handhold: a crack, fissure, or bulb of rock that allows sufficient grip to allow passage over a section of rock wall.

Hanging belay: when significant purchase is not readily available, the climber can connect himself directly to a nut or piton. While hanging from this anchor point, he institutes the proper belay procedure.

Hammock bivouac: when ledges are not available and benightment on a rock wall is expected, a nylon hammock can be strung between two points of protection, providing at least a few hours of rest.

Hardware: metal technical climbing equipment such as pitons, carabiners, ice screws.

Harness: any of many sling or webbing belt systems that are tied or buckled around the climber. Ideally, in the event of a fall the shock to the climber is equally distributed around the torso.

Haulbag: any bag or climbing pack in which equipment is stored and brought after the climber by hauling it after a pitch is climbed.

Hauling technique: the establishment of a mechanical pully system using Jumars or Clog ascenders to bring up men and equipment from a previous point on a cliff.

Hooks: devices used to grab onto very small rock nubbins to allow passage without resorting to bolting. Also referred to as bat hooks, ski hooks, hangers.

Ice axe: a tool with many uses, including step chopping on snow and ice, establishment of handholds during vertical ice climbs, and probing for hidden crevasses during glacier travel.

Ice screws: devices that are either driven into or screwed into ice, providing the climber with an anchor point. Lengths of ice screws vary from seven to fourteen inches.

Jumaring: a rope-ascending method which enables the climber to follow long aid climbs while conserving strength. The Jumars are also used for cleaning long aid pitches and for rigging the haulbag.

Knife blades: a type of piton with a very thin taper that fits into knife-sized cracks.

Lead climber: the climber who ascends a climb first and who places protection points. Also referred to as the first.

Multi-day climb: usually referred to as Grade V, VI, VII, or VIII, climbs. These climbs entail at least one night on the cliff.

Pendulum: a method by which a climber can move horizontally across a rock wall by anchoring a pin and, after being lowered from it, moving sideways across the wall in an arch.

Pitons: metal spikes that are driven into cracks in the rock wall and to which a 'biner can be attached, anchoring the climber. Also known as nails, pins, iron, bongs, knife blades, Lost Arrows, and rurps.

Protection: the placement or anchoring of a bolt, piton, or climbing nut in order to attach a roped party to a cliff.

Prusiking: a method of ascending a climbing rope using various methods of attaching the climber to the line. A Prusik can be achieved with ropes, Jumars, Gibbs ascenders, or Clog ascenders.

North face: usually the steepest and most forbidding of ascent routes (i.e., the north face of the Eiger, the north face of the Matterhorn).

Novice: a person with little or no knowledge of technical mountaineering.

Nuts: see *Aluminum chocks.*

Rappelling: a method of descending a steep slope or wall using the climbing line for balance and support.

Rope handling: the proper execution of all belaying, rappelling, and coiling methods.

Roping down: see *Rappelling.*

Runners: rope or webbing lines used to lengthen the attachment between the anchor and the climber. Particularly important in avoiding rope drag.

Rurps: extremely small and thin pitons designed to be used in hairline cracks. Attachment of a carabiner to these devices is achieved by the use of very thin webbing threaded through a small hole drilled into the rurp.

Self-arrest: a method of breaking a slip down an ice or snow slope by forcing the head of the ice axe into the slope.

Slings: see *Runners.* Additionally, the cord or webbing with which nuts are threaded (also known as nut runners).

Snow flukes: large flat sheets of aluminum that are placed deep into a snow slope. The large surface area of the aluminum provides an anchor to the slope that could not otherwise be achieved.

Soloing: possibly the purest form of climbing; certainly the most dangerous. Climbing without a rope, climbing partner, or placement of protection.

Step cutting: a method of creating footholds on ice- or snow-covered slopes by hacking out platforms for the feet with one's ice axe.

Step kicking: a method of forming a staircase of shelves for the feet by kicking the boot straight into a soft snow slope.

Stirrups: see *Étriers.*

Technical mountaineering: mountaineering requiring the use of specialized equipment to ensure safe travel through the Alpine environment.

Technical rock climbing: an aspect of mountaineering specializing in the ascents of rock walls. Technical rock climbing can be learned on small crags and is becoming recognized as a sport in itself.

Tension traversing: a method of moving horizontally across a rock or ice wall. Usually achieved by direct aid and contact with an anchoring point.

Titons: aluminum t-shaped climbing nuts.

Top rope climbing: a practice climbing method in which a rope is strung from the top of a small cliff, allowing new climbers to practice belaying and climbing techniques. Occasionally used by expert climbers working on extremely difficult problems.

Walker wool gloves: a five-finger glove of Dachstein-like wool that is very useful in ice climbing.